Westlessness

About the author:

Samir Puri is an author, strategy advisor and former UK civil servant. He previously worked for RAND and the Foreign Office. After government service he became a War Studies lecturer at King's College London, during which time he also advised the Commonwealth Secretariat and the Ministry of Defence's think-tank. His most recent job was at IISS-Asia in Singapore. In 2023 he became an Associate Fellow at Chatham House's 'UK in the World' programme.

He is the author of *The Great Imperial Hangover* and *Russia's Road to War with Ukraine.*

Westlessness

The Great Global Rebalancing

Samir Puri

HODDER &
STOUGHTON

First published in Great Britain in 2024 by Hodder & Stoughton Limited
An Hachette UK company

1

A CIP catalogue record for this title is available from the British Library

Hardback ISBN 9781399722636
Trade Paperback ISBN 9781399722643
ebook ISBN 9781399722667

Typeset in Celeste by Hewer Text UK Ltd, Edinburgh
Printed and bound in Great Britain by Clays Ltd, Elcograf S.p.A.

Hodder & Stoughton policy is to use papers that are natural, renewable and recyclable products and made from wood grown in sustainable forests. The logging and manufacturing processes are expected to conform to the environmental regulations of the country of origin.

Hodder & Stoughton Limited
Carmelite House
50 Victoria Embankment
London EC4Y 0DZ

www.hodder.co.uk

To the memory of my mother
Manju Dhiri (1955–2023)
Who balanced East and West

Contents

Preface

THEY CAME FROM different sides of the world and were meeting for the first time. For everybody's sakes, we hoped they were on speaking terms when they arrived at our event. Because if their countries ever truly fell out, this incongruous pair could end up taking us closer to World War Three.

The United States of America's defence secretary made his entrance. Lloyd Austin was the first African American holder of this post, a success story for the meritocratic system in which he had risen. The besuited and baritone-voiced Austin spoke in measured tones but berated his Chinese counterpart for the 'unsafe, aggressive, unprofessional behaviour' of China's warplanes and ships around Taiwan. His key message was crystal clear.

'More members of the US military are stationed here than in any other part of the world: more than 300,000 of our men and women,' he said, referring to the regions spanning the Indian and Pacific oceans, China's backyard. Austin reiterated the US's promise to defend its allies including Australia, Japan, the Philippines, South Korea and Thailand, while drawing closer to India, a fellow democracy.

China's defence minister later took the stage. Wei Fenghe was dressed in military uniform and sharply saluted the audience, a gesture that conveyed the regimented nature of China's system. On behalf of his leaders in Beijing, he delivered a litany of complaints.

Wei accused Austin of 'smearing' China's good name while pointing out the US was trying to 'hijack countries in our region and target one specific country', namely his own. 'Global affairs should be handled through consultation by all stakeholders, instead of being dictated by just one country,' he said of the US. Wei warned Austin: 'If anyone dares to split Taiwan from China, the Chinese will not hesitate to fight to crush any attempt of Taiwan's independence.'

At least they were talking to one another even if it was not always diplomatic. It was June 2022 and US–China relations had already plunged to a new low. Austin and Wei were meeting in Singapore, the Asian city-state that was now akin to Geneva in the Cold War, a neutral place to meet at a time of tension. I had moved to Singapore two years previously to join the small team that ran this big annual security summit. After a lull in face-to-face diplomacy caused by the pandemic, we were finally up and running.

There were other world leaders to hear from too, offering a snapshot of the world at a time of division and change. Japan's Prime Minister Fumio Kishida, a close Western ally, delivered the keynote speech and furrowed his brow at any hint of Chinese adventurism. No surprises here, as Japan and China had their own deep enmity. Kishida spoke with alarm about events in Europe, warning of the 'very foundations of the international order being shaken by Russia's aggression against Ukraine'.

Later on, President Volodymyr Zelensky of Ukraine beamed in live from his bunker in Kyiv. He appeared as a veritable

Ghost of Christmas Future, his presence a warning to Asians of the perils awaiting them if their resident authoritarian behemoth acted as Russia had done in his country, invading and killing without remorse. As we rose from our chairs to applaud Zelensky, we endorsed the idea that preserving Western, and most of all US, global leadership, was the best path to averting yet more chaos.

My empathy for Ukraine's struggles was deep, having lived and worked there during Russia's first invasion. Thinking more generally about the world, however, I wondered if a stage-managed tale of 'evil authoritarians' and 'virtuous democracies' camouflaged more than it elucidated. International affairs, my chosen profession, becomes more complex the closer you study it. Herein lies its true essence.

For a start, the summit's host Singapore was as wealthy and high-functioning a state as one could imagine for its size, but it had eschewed Western-style democracy ever since independence from British and then Malay rule. It has balanced simultaneous friendships with Western countries and China while never vocally picking a side between them, hence its reputation for neutrality in Asia.

I was also struck listening to Prabowo Subianto, Indonesia's defence minister and later its president-elect, describe Indonesia – South East Asia's largest economy and the sixteenth largest in the world – as a 'survivor of colonialism' from Dutch rule while praising China's historical role in Asia. Prabowo told the gathering, 'Your enemy is not necessarily my enemy,' words he borrowed from Nelson Mandela to remind us Indonesia was not recruitable into an anti-China alliance.

These were precisely the complexities I wanted to interact with by moving to Singapore. On paper, it was next in a series of jobs like it I had held since the 2000s. I started working life at RAND, the US defence think tank with a Cold War vintage, before serving in Britain's Foreign Office. Alongside many amazing colleagues, I played my own humble role responding to the big security challenges of the day, countering terrorism in the long aftermath of 9/11, and monitoring Russia's invasion of Ukraine by living in the Donbas region in 2014–15.

Although I was not overly conscious of it at the time, I enjoyed burnishing my credentials as a Brit representing my country, allied to the US as a card-carrying member of the transatlantic Western world. It was a validating way to earn my keep, and perhaps more so since my family roots were far from the West, in the colonies and commonwealths of empire and after-empire in Asia and Africa.

This time, taking the job in Singapore, I got more than I bargained for. Being of Asian heritage and moving to Asia was having an interesting effect on me. Sure, I had no prior link to Singapore, only to India and East Africa, a common lineage among British Indians (a famous example being Rishi Sunak, Britain's first non-white prime minister). Don't be alarmed, I am not peddling a misguided Asian version of US race activist Marcus Garvey's 'back to Africa' movement from a century ago. Being Western, British and a Londoner to boot is my identity.

Yet at the same time, if I kept my mouth shut as I travelled in Asia, people tended not to guess where I was from, which I also enjoyed. To tap into my heritage and to feel the winds changing in Asia's favour was quite something. The conversations were fascinating as people opened up to me about what they *really* felt about receding Western power. Not because they were anti-Western; more prosaically because they were non-Western and saw different things of note in a changing world.

I wanted to put the pieces together: to reflect not only on the power dynamics of changing world order but also on identity, and the emotional and intellectual influences flowing outside of and apart from the West with gathering force. A cynic might say there is nothing novel to see here. People always complained about the Western countries – including plenty of Westerners – while enjoying some of their fruits and rejecting others, so what was new? Was I simply learning ever-present truths by living far from home?

Perhaps, but fresh themes were also coming into play. On 1 January 2024, the BRICS countries (Brazil, Russia, India, China and South Africa), an acronym coined in the early 2000s for these emerging economies, expanded to 'BRICS+' as Egypt, Ethiopia, Iran and United Arab Emirates accepted their invitations to join the club, with Saudi Arabia following later on. Western countries were not invited to the annual BRICS summits, where Chinese officials spoke portentously about a new era dawning.

Western sceptics rolled their eyes at this, arguing the BRICS nations' marriages of convenience hardly competed with the West's deeper bonds. I would not dismiss these developments as a failing fad. Significant chunks of the world have *already* started acting as if the West is ceasing to be the dominant force it once was.

Perhaps this was why China's defence minister, even after receiving such a grilling at our event, walked out with a swagger. Yet, the future will not be Chinese. There will however be less of the West in the world.

What is Westlessness?

EVERY DAY, ALL of us see the same sun rise in the east and set in the west. The Earth spins towards the east as it orbits the sun, and people at the Earth's equator – close to where I write these words in Singapore – move at a thousand miles an hour. Further from the equator – in London, where I was born, for instance – the Earth moves at around 650 miles an hour. We don't feel this movement or notice the difference in speed from place to place because the motion is constant. Our natural world offers plentiful metaphors for picturing a fast-changing international order.

Welcome to 'Westlessness'. It is not about the vanishing of the Western world – far from it, since the West is not going anywhere. The expression 'post-Western world' is a misnomer since it doesn't capture this rebalancing. Nor is it about pitting 'the West versus the rest' since there is no inevitability in either Western unity nor in its confrontation with others.

Rather, it refers to the declining slice of the global pie held by Western nations and peoples. In demographic, economic, military and cultural terms, we are hurtling towards a far more diverse global future. Many of our certainties about the present, built on centuries of massive Western influence, are being questioned afresh by people the world over. The receding of Western global influence is speeding up, shaking the ground under our feet.

The crucial syllable is 'less'. Less doesn't mean absent. There will be a surfeit of Western ways of doing things in the West itself, even as other parts of the world become less tethered to the West. 'Less' means the relative decline of the Western world's presence and power to act as gatekeeper and arbiter of the world's affairs. It means the consequent empowerment of other nations, peoples and regions to interact with the West on more equal terms; to agree and disagree among themselves with less Western oversight; and to act and organise themselves with minimal reference to Western ways and mores.

This swims against the historical tides of rising and peaking Western global power. The world that the West has had a centuries-long role in building and influencing is breaking down – but how fast is it changing, and in what ways? Can we distinguish between the spaces in which Western global influence endures from those where it already fades? How will the world now function, if it comprises several centres of power and influence, some located in the West and others elsewhere? And should we fear a less Western-centric world – or could it become a positive opportunity?

This challenges our sense of self as it forces us to recentre the globe away from the Euro-Atlantic world and from the concerns of the Europeans and North Americans. It doesn't matter if you are Western or not, and whether you identify wholly or partially as such, because the transition away from Western-centrism will affect you. Which leads to the most fundamental question of all: are you ready, professionally and personally, to adapt to a much more diverse global future?

The real story of the century will not involve the West's stand-off with the autocracies of China and Russia; it is the *even bigger* story of rebalancing away from the world crafted by the West. China's economic rise is a huge part of this right now but it is also a door opener to other developments we should pay attention to. In surveying this tilting landscape, I welcome you to judge how quickly we are sliding into the era of lessening Western influence – and to consider how this will impact the West itself. We will discover that Westlessness is advancing at pace. In some places it is considerably more advanced than you might think. The question now is just how far it will go.

* * *

The term 'Westlessness' was introduced into the public debate and devised by the Munich Security Conference and Tobias Bunde.[1] 'Westlessness' is a shorthand expression for interpreting the significance of several phenomena that are reshaping our world.

Our mission is to observe the world at a time of transition, not to deliver a polemical castigation of the West. Nor is it about fantastical crystal-ball gazing, scantly backed by evidence. The humility of admitting what we cannot know remains front and centre. For instance: the global shocks yet to come; the paradigm-shifting technologies still in their infancy; and the leaders yet to emerge in response to future events. A decade ago, we would not have predicted the worldwide chaos of the coronavirus pandemic originating in

Wuhan, China; Russia's all-out invasion of Ukraine; and Donald Trump's election as President of the US (to take three examples). Two decades ago, our wildest visions may not have fully imagined just how smartphones would rule our lives. And so on . . . we never truly know what is coming around the next corner until it hits us.

The challenge here is not prediction but tracing the big trend lines alongside which future events will unfold. This involves providing qualitative evidence and hard data where it is available, and moving into conjecture at appropriate points to discern where we are headed. Our task is to explain and estimate rates of change, detecting those areas of social and global affairs where declining Western influence is most tangible, distinguishing them from areas where it is developing more imperceptibly.

We must look far beyond such headline-worthy topics as whether China or the US has the bigger economy. Or India overtaking China as the most populous country. Or Russia selling its oil and gas to Asian rather than to European countries. It is not only about these global behemoths, but about those of us living in smaller countries who are experiencing the impacts of a changing global guard. Moreover, it is as much about hard power truths and pecking orders as it is about identity and the *feel* of the evolving less Western world for inhabitants of countries large and small.

Grappling with so many complex arcs of change is not an exact science, which is why this book makes an offer to the reader. What this book provides is the inspiration, the data and the intellectual scaffolding to support your own mental framework for understanding the aspects of a less Western world that are most interesting to you. Depending on the industry in which you work, your family heritage, your sense of inherited or chosen national identity, and your ambitions, the evolution away from the old world more shaped by the West will matter differently to you. Keep your eyes and your ears open based on your own unique perspective. And do pay attention to how the more extroverted parts of the West are manoeuvring to preserve their influence – while those elsewhere who feel their influence has hitherto been denied make a grab for the limelight. The Western world, with Europe still heavily shielded by the US's power, will not cede its privileges willingly. The West wants managed evolution, not violent revolution, as the guard changes.

Several things are coming together in the mid-2020s as history arcs away from the long era of Western global dominance. Around the world, notably in the 'Global South' countries, there is much anticipation about the changing world. China's rise is not necessarily seen as a rallying call to unite behind Beijing, but as opening up economic opportunities that also encourage fresh thinking about a world more independent of the West. India's rise is also on the cards and countries like Indonesia are touted as future centres of influence. The sum total outcome from this will be diminishing Western influence, a phenomenon I am convinced we will see more of in the coming decades.

In Latin, the *occidens* referred to the west and sunset while the *oriens* was the east and sunrise. This was the etymology of 'orient', the now badly outdated term for places east of Europe. Updating our assumptions about the world is never a wasted enterprise. Right now, with such dramatic changes afoot, seeing the world for what it is becoming is a matter of profound importance. To begin, we can see these themes play out in four vignettes of well-known events, each one illustrating some of the different facets of Western influence facing challenge and at times decline.

From dominance to diversity

If you enter the splendid halls of the Commonwealth Secretariat in London's Marlborough House, a display of historical photographs of old Commonwealth Summits shows an ever-changing cast of national leaders and an ever-present Elizabeth II. She was Head of the Commonwealth until her death. Which leads us to the matter at hand: the passage of time away from a world still within living memory, in which Britain's monarch presided over a vast global dominion, and how dramatically things have changed since then.

What went through your mind when Queen Elizabeth II died in 2022? Aside from the loss of a globally familiar face, her passing marked the end of an era. When she was born in 1926, much of the globe was still shaded pink to denote Britain's empire. The twenty-five-year-old Elizabeth arrived in British Kenya in February 1952 as a princess, but after her father George VI's sudden death, she departed as Queen of Britain and its empire.

Her great-great-grandmother Victoria's nearly sixty-four-year reign (1837–1901) had spanned Britain's ascent to becoming the world's largest empire. Elizabeth II's reign

(1952–2022) spanned the empire's dismantling. Britain, exhausted by its privations and expenditures in the world wars, gave up its largest colony in 1947 with the botched and bloody Partition of the Raj into India and Pakistan. The end of numerous British colonies followed in Elizabeth II's reign. Kenya became independent in 1963, for instance, and the process carried on until the handover of Hong Kong to China in 1997. In place of its empire, Britain set up the voluntary Commonwealth.

Another of her forebears, George III (1760–1820), reigned when America's Thirteen Colonies kicked out the British. 'America is lost! Must we fall beneath the blow? Or have we resources that may repair the mischiefs?' wrote George III.[2] After this schism in the English-speaking world, it took some time for Britain to reconcile itself as the smaller party in the Anglosphere, and to recognise how the rise of the US could be a boon to Britain.

Even by Elizabeth II's coronation in 1953, Britain retained a pretence as a superpower in its own right. However, World War Two had stretched the British Empire's military and economic capacity to breaking point and it was only saved by the US's entry into the war in December 1941. The US, unlike the UK, emerged from the war in 1945 with its economic and military stature rising. The ageing Winston Churchill was in his second prime ministerial stint when Elizabeth II took the throne. Churchill knew from British reliance on US wartime largesse that transatlantic power was shifting, but Churchill's successor, Anthony Eden, acted in defiance of this trend. In 1956, alongside France and Israel, Britain tried to forcibly seize the Suez Canal from Egypt's military government. The war was a disaster as the US chastised Britain and its co-conspirators for invading Egypt. The US had pulled rank: from now on, other Western countries would have to accept the US's leadership (or at least its acquiescence) in matters of waging war.

As the remainder of the British, French and other European empires were dismantled (most African and Asian colonies gained independence in the 1950s and 1960s), the US stepped into the void by building not a colonial empire but an informal empire comprising military bases and alliances all over the world, from Europe to the Middle East and across the Pacific. In the Indian Ocean, the US military used the island of Diego Garcia, a far-flung remnant of the British Empire. The changing of global dominion from one English-speaking nation to another was also evident culturally, as the US's films, music, literature and products like Coca-Cola became known in every corner of the globe. Commonality of language left the UK particularly open to influences from the US.

In her later years, Elizabeth II would have seen the Black Lives Matter (BLM) movement explode in the US in 2020 after the killing by a policeman of an African American man, George Floyd. BLM protests subsequently spread to the UK and other parts of Europe. The common thread of the protests on both sides of the Atlantic was anger towards historical and contemporary injustices against peoples of African and Caribbean descent. One common historical thread linking the British Empire to these matters was the brutal transatlantic slave trade, which Britain partook in until the nineteenth century. Now, tides of opinion in Britain and elsewhere were turning in favour of hearing the stories of the modern descendants of those who had once been enslaved and colonised. In some quarters, there was a fresh desire to question depictions of history that gave the benefit of the doubt to Britain's imperial forebears and to question the origins of their wealth from centuries ago.

The Queen was removed as the head of state of Barbados as it transitioned into a republic in November 2021, a year after a statue of British Admiral Horatio Nelson was removed in its capital, Bridgetown. In April 2022, future heir to the throne Prince William and his wife Kate received frosty welcomes on an official Caribbean trip. After a protest in Kingston calling for reparations for the transatlantic slave trade from Britain, Jamaica's Prime Minister Andrew Holness told William that his country was 'moving on' from a past era of relations with Britain. Sensing a changing tide, in June 2022, future King Charles travelled to the Commonwealth Heads of Government Meeting in Kigali, Rwanda, and, speaking on behalf of the ailing Queen, expressed 'the depths of his personal sorrow' for the historical slave trade.

Prince Harry, the Queen's younger grandson from her oldest son, Charles, provided the Royals with another unwelcome moment of reckoning. After his army career, which involved service in Afghanistan to support the US-led 'Global War On Terrorism', Harry married actress Meghan Markle. Born in Los Angeles in 1981 to a Caucasian father and an African American mother, Markle's background was hardly untypical given Los Angeles's ethnic diversity, but it was just too much for the traditionalist Royal Family to easily digest. In a 2021 interview with celebrity host Oprah Winfrey, Harry claimed that, during Meghan's pregnancy, concerns were raised in the Royal Family over the possible colour of their son's skin. The Queen had to respond to this allegation of racism: 'The issues raised, particularly that of race, are concerning,' she said in an official statement.

Her passing in 2022 was the end of an era, reminding us that Britain's monarchy had previously never felt much obligation to acknowledge the messy historical origins of British power, nor comment on the Royal Family's perceptions of race. Once, it was enough for the monarch to seek comity with peoples of other races via the hierarchy of the Commonwealth. Now, hierarchies of race within white-majority countries were being questioned like never before, while the voices of formerly colonised nations grew louder with the desire to interpret history as they chose, not as it was written for them.

Times had clearly changed during Elizabeth II's famously long lifetime, as Britain moved from dominance to a world of diversity – trends that are hardly going to reverse.

Dial +1 for America

Can you recall a time when the US wasn't the overall world number one? Barely anybody alive today would be able to. A neat symbol of the US's lofty position is offered courtesy of the International Telecoms Union of the 1960s, and the story of the +1 international phone code – the simplest to dial and the easiest to remember – being accorded to the US.

In 1964, the world's national phone operators met under the auspices of the United Nations to establish a system for international calling. The mechanical telephone exchanges of the day made it necessary to assign single-digit phone codes to the biggest continental landmasses. The +1 code was taken by America and Canada. Africa received the +2 series, but no country has this singular code, only elongated extensions beginning with 2. In Europe, the +3 and +4 codes were divided among its countries (+33 for France and +44 for Britain as the easiest to remember, and so on). The USSR received the +7 code, later retained by the Russian Federation.[3] Phone codes are somewhat incidental in an era of internet telephony but dialling +1 for the US is a fitting way to remind us of the habits of mind that naturally arise when you are at the top of the global tree for four generations and counting. Of course, the US is number one. How could it be any other way and can you really imagine anything different?

Having consolidated its strength after its devastating civil war in the 1860s, the US became the world's largest economy roughly a century ago, following the Great War (1914–18) and the consequent self-devastation of Europe's imperial powers. There have been setbacks aplenty along the way for the US but its overall ascent to economic, military and cultural prominence has been stratospheric. Blessed with the immense geographic advantage of continental separation from its modern rivals and enemies, abundant natural resources, and direct access to the two largest oceans, the US has played this blessed hand very well indeed.

Elements of the US's modern experiences have become synonymous with a winner's mentality. Just consider the roll call: the US intervened decisively in both world wars; it was the first country to develop and use the atomic bomb; the first (and so far only) to land its astronauts on the moon; Hollywood makes the world's highest-grossing movies; US athletes often top the medal tally in the Olympic Games; the 'greenback' is the world's most used currency; the US has the most powerful military . . . and so on.

Why learn from others when your country consistently takes pole position in so many fields and attracts so many talented foreigners to its shores? This mentality – 'American exceptionalism' – has birthed phrases like the 'empire of liberty' (Thomas Jefferson), the 'last best hope of Earth' (Abraham Lincoln), the 'indispensable nation' (Madeleine Albright) and, naturally, 'leader of the free world'. Much ink has been spilled by patriotic Americans and concerned well-wishers alike warning of the delusion of taking these aphorisms at face value. American professor Stephen Walt pointed out that 'unchallenged faith in American exceptionalism makes it harder for Americans to understand why others are less enthusiastic about US dominance, often alarmed by US policies, and frequently irritated by what they see as US hypocrisy.'[4] Not all of its citizens buy the American exceptionalism arguments at face value, but the broad sentiment remains tangible in the US's national consciousness. One has to disagree with it to challenge it. As Singaporean writer Kishore Mahbubani observed, 'America has its own sacred cows. One such sacred cow is that America is number one and will be number one forever,' which makes it harder for Americans to debate changing world realities.[5]

This is one underlying reason why America's domestic politics have of late become worryingly untethered from reality. The battle of the septuagenarian (turning octogenarian) presidential candidates, Republican Donald Trump and Democrat Joe Biden, dominated Washington politics in the 2020s. There is so much to venerate in a lifetime of experience, but when lived through an era of US global dominance, it is no surprise that the one thing uniting Biden and Trump in their outlook was a dogged determination to prevent China from becoming number one. During Trump's presidency, the US unleashed trade restrictions against China, ostensibly to protect US workers from unfair competition in the global market. Biden's presidency retained and refined this attempt to contain China's economic and geopolitical rise. Bipartisanism, in perilously short supply in politically polarised America, has been in abundance when it comes to hawkishness on China. The only agreeable topic in Washington's political debates these days is for the US to guard its number-one status.

You dial +86 to reach China (and a derivative number, +886, for Taiwan, despite its code not being initially listed as belonging to a country to avoid offending China's perception that Taiwan was a rogue province). Back when the International Telecoms Union met in 1964 to assign these phone codes, Taiwan still putatively represented all of China in the UN, banishing China's Communist Party (CCP) to diplomatic obscurity. Back then, both Taiwan and mainland China were still recovering from their civil war, which ended in 1949. The Taiwan/China schism remains unresolved, but under CCP rule, China has moved far beyond its agrarian past and grown its military, industrial and technological power so substantially that it can now feasibly challenge the US's dominance in Asia, at least to begin with.

America's winning mentality refuses to accept this; it sees little virtue in China's national story of a modern rise against the odds under one-party rule. For the rest of the world, too, accustomed to only seeing Western nations securing global dominance, it is jarring to think that the leading nation in key aspects of power could be from Asia. It is also a simpler thing to focus on China's nastier authoritarian tendencies and to conclude that it doesn't deserve to be number one – but neither moral opprobrium, nor US military and economic containment, can reverse China's rise, and the impact its rise is having on others all over the world. One way or another, get ready for change.

Waging Westless war in Ukraine

With the prospect of global change comes great temptation to exploit this transition period at the West's expense. Timing is everything. Judging when a moment is ripe – 'Westless' enough – for whatever gambit one has in store is tricky. A clear example of getting it wrong was Russia's invasion of Ukraine in 2022. Russian President Vladimir Putin's catastrophic military gamble to conquer Ukraine was based on three assumptions, two of which were badly wrong.

First was Putin's belief in Ukraine's lack of will to fight, an assumption driven by his perception of Ukraine as an errant Russian vassal state. He was wrong here; the Ukrainians fought back bravely. Second was his belief in Western disunity. Putin was encouraged by events in 2021 in Afghanistan, when the Taliban insurgency routed the

Western-backed government and Afghan Army, forcing the US and its allies to evacuate their remaining personnel from Kabul. It was a tragic and ignominious end to twenty years of US-led occupation. If Afghanistan could be callously abandoned by the West, reasoned Putin, so might Ukraine. Again, he was wrong.

Third, Putin placed a bet on a changing world order, with the US cast as a declining hegemon, and Europe too preoccupied with its own decay to stop his reconquest of Ukraine. Putin bet on the non- Western world. Here, at least, his judgement proved sounder. Russia's invasion clearly deserves moral outrage, but this feeling alone was not the leading reaction in every part of the world.

Why isn't Russia 'Western'? Russia's dual identity as straddling Europe and Asia is symbolised by its old imperial motif of the two-headed eagle, its gaze pointing in different directions. Originating at the edge of Europe but forged also by the historical experiences of nomadic Scythian and Mongol invasions from across the vast steppe, Russia's hybridity of geography and identity are its defining characteristics, and its rulers have defined Russia as being apart from the West.

By invading Ukraine, Russia further sealed its economic fate as an Asian-facing power, as it was cut off by economic sanctions from its Western markets. Seven months into his invasion, Putin delivered a speech almost as far from Ukraine as he could reach in Russia. Taking to the podium in Vladivostok, he addressed the Eastern Economic Forum, a gathering for drumming up investment in Russia's far east. In Putin's assessment, the rise of the emerging economies spelled 'irreversible and even tectonic changes in international relations'.[6] Putin had already banked on Asia after Russia's earlier invasion of Ukraine when it annexed Crimea in 2014; that year, he secured a thirty-year deal for Russian state-run energy company Gazprom to supply China via a pipeline called 'Power of Siberia', which opened for business in December 2019.[7] Russia was already de-Westernising its foreign relations. In doing so, Putin risked creating a 'Sino-Siberia' of Russia's economic vassalage to China, but even this seemed preferable to him than being lectured to and blocked in his imperial ambitions by the West.

Was Putin correct – was the West now a spent force? Not quite. Assumptions about Western disunity in Ukraine were swiftly disproven. The US and UK gunned for a Ukrainian victory and, while unwilling to fight Russia directly (which risked unmanageable escalation), they intervened by proxy, dispatching weapons, intelligence and money to enable Ukraine to fight. Joining this cause via the US-led North Atlantic Treaty Organization (NATO) military alliance, countries like Poland and the Baltic States also armed Ukraine. France and Germany instinctively preferred to maintain economic relations with Russia, but even Paris and Berlin were talked round to dispatching military supplies to help Ukraine. Swedes and Finns, with their own histories of fighting Russian empires, now broke with decades of diplomatic neutrality by joining NATO. So much for Western disunity. Opposing Russian malevolence was in fact galvanising the West.

But in the East and the South, Putin's bet on the changing world order proved sounder. China and India defied Western criticism by purchasing Russian oil and gas, furnishing Russia's war chest with profit. Moreover, Russia secured ambivalence or even sympathy in some African and Asian countries for its war against what Putin described as an encroaching Western hegemony. The United Nations General Assembly vote on 2 March 2022 saw a majority of countries deplore Russia's aggression against Ukraine (141 voted for this motion, five against, thirty-five abstentions, twelve absent) – but while talk in the UN was cheap, so was Russian oil and gas, and plenty of countries carried on trading with Russia.

As Western countries imposed bans and price caps on Russian energy exports, the Global South was largely unmoved. Confused Europeans and Americans wondered why others did not share their moral outrage over Russia's heinousness or consider Ukraine's quest to join the West as sacrosanct.

Consider this conversation, when an ill-prepared interviewer in Munich asked India's Foreign Minister Subrahmanyam Jaishankar about India's refusal to sever its ties with Russia over its invasion of Ukraine: 'So you disagree that the principles [of] the international rules-based order and international law should apply across the world uniformly?' Jaishankar responded sharply: 'I would say principles and interests are balanced, and if people were principled in this part of the world [Europe], they would have been practising [principles] in Asia or in Afghanistan before now.'[8] He told India's Western critics 'to grow out of the mindset that Europe's problems are the world's problems – and the world's problems are not Europe's problems.'[9] He said this while India's trade with Russia jumped by 205% in 2022.

Bollywood wasn't far behind this message. India's highest-grossing movie of 2023, *Pathaan*, cast its star Shah Rukh Khan as an Indian intelligence officer; midway through the movie he heads to Russia and is reminded by his superior: 'Russia is still a friendly country and a crucial ally. A scandal will not be tolerated in Moscow or Delhi.' The fantasy script echoed India's policy on the war: to push peace talks rather than to follow the West's lead on backing Ukraine's army to beat back the Russians.

India and others in the wider world were not convinced that Ukraine's ambition to join the EU and NATO represented a defining battle between autocracy and democracy, as was the wont of many Europeans and North Americans to believe. Indonesia and Brazil got in on the act by suggesting half-baked peace plans for Ukraine as the invasion entered its second year in 2023, reflecting these countries' weariness with the war and its impact on global grain and energy supplies. South Africa led a delegation of African countries to Ukraine in 2023 where they unveiled their own peace plan.

Other major countries refused Western calls to economically strangle Russia. When the US asked Saudi Arabia to increase its oil supply to bring down prices to reduce Russia's oil profits, the Saudi King snubbed Biden by keeping the supply as it was to maintain high prices. In 2022, Saudi's national oil company Aramco raked in profits of $160 billion, a quantum more than ExxonMobil in second place.[10] Turkey played both sides in the war, burnishing its status in NATO by supplying Ukraine with armed drones while welcoming Russian tourists and enjoying an 87% jump in trade with Russia. (Also in 2022, Turkey renamed itself Türkiye, shedding the Latinised name it adopted a century ago when the West truly dominated.) Countries with their own proud histories were asserting their influence in notable ways for the pride of self-expression.

None of this meant Putin's invasion would succeed. Few countries directly backed Russia's fight (aside from Belarus, Iran, North Korea and Syria, already pariahs in Western eyes). On the battlefield, Russia's army was mauled by Ukraine's Western-supplied forces. The West remained capable of sufficient unity if facing adversity on its doorstep, so best not to pick even a proxy fight with America's 'Arsenal of Democracy'. But different lessons played out far from the battlefield: of changing balances of authority between the West and India, China, Saudi Arabia and Türkiye. Westerners who were confident of using sanctions to strangle Russia's economy missed this. Western global leadership on matters of war and peace was a declining asset, creating grave uncertainty around how to punish warmongers like Putin.

Rules of the game in Qatar

Few events attract as much attention as the quadrennial football World Cup, with an estimated 3.5 billion people – almost half of us – tuning in to watch.[11] In 2018, the World Cup was hosted by Russia, and despite Putin's government having already annexed Crimea, the tournament proceeded with very little extra Western criticism of Russia. When the Gulf Kingdom of Qatar hosted the 2022 World Cup, the heaping of moral opprobrium on Qatar for its exploitative use of migrant labourers to build the football stadiums that were used to entertain the world, and the subsequent boycotts by Western dignitaries of the football tournament, were striking.

Football has attracted huge investment and generates considerable income from television and other rights, aside from gate receipts, transforming it from a sport into a space for international business and influence. Famous football clubs are increasingly owned by rich foreigners. For instance, Manchester City has been owned by the deposed Thai Prime Minister Thaskin Shinawatra and latterly by Emirati royal Sheikh Mansour. Given the huge amounts of money that surround professional football, there is also clearly an ugly side to the beautiful game (a phrase popularised by late Brazilian football legend Pelé in his book, *My Life and the Beautiful Game*). One manifestation of this was the susceptibility of football's Switzerland-based governing body FIFA (the Fédération Internationale de Football Association) to accept bids to host World Cup tournaments from countries like Russia and Qatar.

FIFA's president of the day, Gianni Infantino, defended Qatar, which was the first Arab or Middle Eastern country to host the World Cup, against its critics: 'For what we Europeans have been doing around the world in the last 3,000 years we should be apologising for the next 3,000 years before starting to give moral lessons to people,' said Infantino. His history was badly off, since in 978 BCE (3,000 years prior to his speech) Rome hadn't even been founded. But Infantino landed one telling blow: 'How many of these European or Western business companies who earn millions from Qatar, billions, how many of them have addressed migrant workers' rights with the authorities?'

Modern slavery is a serious issue and nasty versions of indentured labour remain a scourge all over the world. Qatar was not alone in this practice, in which workers were paid a pittance to live in harsh conditions while working in the blazing heat. Western media reported migrant labourers from Bangladesh, Nepal, Pakistan and Sri Lanka having died in Qatar in the years leading up to the country hosting the World Cup. In its rush to complete the eight stadiums for use in the tournament, critics of Qatar's human rights record said that migrant labourers were pushed to work in unsafe conditions, and the Qatari state was covering up the true death toll.[12]

This controversy offers a window into a bigger matter: in a less Western dominated world, who has the moral right to criticise who? Can the West *credibly* lead a moralistic charge against breaches of human rights by non-Western states? What of human rights issues in Western countries, whether involving people sleeping rough or living below the poverty line in otherwise rich cities; or migrants turned away at the US border with Mexico; or migrants sailing to Europe's coastlines and left to their fates – could criticism of these social inequities, and of the human consequences of some Western countries' own harsh choices, come back to bite them?

In the *Financial Times*, Janen Ganesh was acerbic: 'To judge by the criticism of Qatar, lots of people are psychologically unprepared for the rest of this century. Whether or not China surpasses the US, the centre of world power is likely to creep away from the established democracies.' Yes, 'sports-washing' is a dubious practice, referring to authoritarian regimes using huge investments in sports teams and events to distract from their own injustices. But how could the West complain about

Qatari sports-washing while buying Qatari liquefied natural gas (LNG)? (Demand for LNG shot up after Western bans on buying Russian gas after its Ukraine invasion.) Ganesh concluded, 'The outrage reveals something about those who feel it,' since 'lots of people have paid lip service to the idea of a changing world, a less Western-skewed balance of power, without reckoning with its practical effects.'[13] What weight does a Western-led moral stand against malpractices elsewhere have anymore?

Moral power is distinct from regulatory power, and Europe has a head start on the latter. As Qatar's World Cup played out, the EU was drafting its sweeping new legislation to clean up the supply chains of companies operating in the EU. In 2022, the European Commission proposed a directive on corporate sustainability due diligence, which 'means more effective protection of human rights' because 'workers must have access to safe and healthy working conditions'.[14] In commissioning the construction of its stadiums, Qatar could have learned from this. After all, why shouldn't these humane standards be applied globally?

The question is just how much appetite is left around the world for receiving Western tutelage. Some in the West had got too comfortable critiquing and tutoring others. Consider this rejoinder in a Pakistani newspaper column about Western media criticism of exploited migrant workers in Qatar: 'There's more than a grain of truth in the accusation, and there's dollops of hypocrisy about it' because 'Western colluders, nearly all of them champions of human rights, have used the oil extracted with cheap labour that plies Gulf economies, to control the world order.'[15] Such anti-Western polemic may be hackneyed, but it resonates differently in an era of lessening Western influence.

One encounter in Qatar that was captured on camera highlighted this. During the World Cup, protests erupted in Tehran against the Islamic Republic of Iran's clerical regime after a twenty-two-year-old Iranian woman, Mahsa Amini, was beaten to death by Iran's morality police for breaching female dress codes by wearing jeans with her hijab allegedly askew. In Qatar, BBC reporter Shaimaa Khalil asked Iran's football team captain about the protests. But Iran's Portuguese coach, Carlos Queiroz, intervened and reprimanded Khalil for posing an unfair question. 'But I'm asking an Iranian player about his own country,' implored the BBC's Khalil. Queiroz was firm: 'To the other cultures why don't you ask [England team manager Gareth] Southgate, 'What do you think about England and the US that left Afghanistan' . . .?' before storming off.[16]

The to-and-fro alleging of double standards is not new. But what of Westerners enjoying a uniquely privileged podium from which to judge the sins of others? This may finally have had its day.

'I suppose everyone finds the despotisms of other peoples hard to comprehend,' mused a character in Amitav Ghosh's novel about the Opium War.[17] In a less Western world, we are going to hear far more about this when it comes to passing moral judgement on others. Even if two wrongs cannot make a right, the power of one side to win the argument will be blunted.

Can 'less be more' in the great global rebalancing?

We are fast passing the peak era of global Western power and influence. The 'collapse of the West' is too sensationalist. More optimistically, this book is about sharing influence and about coexistence between different parts of the world. There is a transition underway from an era of unbridled Western global influence to one of contested Western influence.

This need not spell the West's doom. The possibility that less (as in 'less of the West') could be better utilised to preserve and even gain more influence in certain areas is taken seriously. Innovations in technology will place greater emphasis than ever on quality over quantity in a number of things, in some of which the West and its closest allies in Asia have an important lead already.

Nevertheless, changes will happen. Even the greatest sceptics of China's continuing economic ascent, or of Russia's long-term prospects as an imperial state, or of the viability of the BRICS+ project, have to concede one thing. For the Western countries to perpetuate their global leadership roles in the coming decades they *must* adapt to the changing realities outlined in the coming chapters.

The tactics that once worked for the Western countries in perpetuating their influence are simply not going to suffice under changed circumstances. This is the very minimum admission we should all be able to agree on. We are facing real epochal change as more centres of meaningful power and influence multiply outside of the West's reach. For the West, it will not be enough merely to endure these changes; it needs to actively manoeuvre to preserve its global influence.

Some Westerners would like to gain inspiration from the world wars and the Cold War, where the Western democracies toiled against opposing forces before emerging triumphant, validated and expanded. These are poor analogies for the evolving Westless era, which draws its historical focus from elsewhere, and most notably from troubled past relations between Western and non-Western peoples. When tracking the great global rebalancing, no matter what your preconceptions might be at the outset, be prepared to have them challenged by the evidence.

Part One

WESTFULL WORLD

1

Origin Stories

> The origin myth of the West imagines Western history as unfurling back unbroken in time through Atlantic modernity and the European Enlightenment; back through the brightness of the Renaissance and the darkness of the Middle Ages; back, ultimately, to its origin in the classical worlds of Rome and Greece. This has become the standard version of Western history, both canonical and cliched. But it is . . . both factually wrong and ideologically driven.
>
> Naoise Mac Sweeney, *The West: A New History of an Old Idea* (2023)[1]

MANY OF US are familiar with the story of the rise of the West, but if you are rusty on the details, here is a recap. The West developed an outsized influence on world affairs over several centuries of ascending and peaking global dominance. This ascent was gradual, involving long periods of trading, skirmishing and coexisting with other kingdoms and empires dotted all over the map, before the Europeans eventually overwhelmed most of these other places. As Europe's empires reached their peak powers, they competed more intensively with each other for influence and for colonies. Global dominion passed as if it was a baton being wrenched from the bloodied hands of one European empire by another, before being taken by the European settler colony turned superpower, the US – at which point, the lexicon of 'European' dominion became 'Western'.

Some people at the time thought Europe's rise was divinely ordained, although whether it was seen as a curse or a blessing depended on whether you were a victim or a beneficiary of it all. Europeans and then Americans also considered themselves uniquely advantaged by inheriting the spirit of the Greco-Roman world, which made their elites feel superior to other societies.[2] Today, we have the good sense to better understand the factors that *actually* allowed the Europeans to outpace other societies around the world.

There is an abundance of scholarship debating the key reasons behind Europe's global rise and advancing different theories to this end. For instance, how the uneven hand of physical geography differentiated the development paths of various regions. How transmissible diseases decimated some populations and not others due to prevailing immunities. And how intense competitions between Europe's kingdoms drove their technological and military innovations faster than in other places.[3]

What concerns us here is teleology – using the end of a story arc to assume the inevitability of its outcome. We know the outcome because everyone alive today has lived through West*full*ness, by which we mean the apex of Western global influence. This will be our baseline and our point of departure for tracking its ongoing contraction. The Westfull world was far from inevitable. It is important to see the rise of the West as an uncertain journey that was contingent on many factors to succeed. In short, we need good historical literacy to understand what we are now seeing declining from its past heights. What we don't need is a straw man target of the West as history's omnipresent bogeyman.

What is 'the West'? Despite its name, it is not a geographic cluster but a cultural and geopolitical grouping of countries and peoples in North America, Europe and Oceania. In distant history, European Christendom was a sensible boundary.[4] In modern history, European settler colonialism expanded the Western world. Britain spread the Anglosphere to the US, Canada, Australia and New Zealand, while other settler colonies like Rhodesia did not last. Given its diversity, it is unwise to consider the West as a single 'civilisational space'. Nevertheless, political scientist Samuel Huntington's description in *The Clash of Civilizations* remains useful: 'Historically, Western civilisation is European civilisation. In the modern era, Western civilisation is Euroamerican or North Atlantic civilisation. Europe, America and the North Atlantic can be found on a map, the West cannot.'[5] He controversially excluded Latin America from his idea of the West, despite it sharing Europe's romance languages and Christianity – so in its cultural rooting and in the lineages of many of its citizens, as well as in its hemispheric location, Latin America is Western, but its geopolitics have taken very different paths.

* * *

The West rose from obscurity. Before 1500, during the medieval Middle Ages, Europe was a backwater. The Middle Ages, which lasted between the fall of the Western Roman Empire in the fifth century of the Common Era (CE), until the start of Europe's Renaissance in the late fourteenth century, saw dynamism and wealth located elsewhere, especially in the kingdoms and empires of Asia.[6]

Consider the horse-borne conquests of the Mongols in the thirteenth century. The Mongols took over China and ruled it as the Yuan Dynasty; they reduced to vassalage Kyvian Rus and Muscovy in modern Ukraine and Russia; they advanced into Central Europe, capturing Hungary and attacking Polish and Austrian lands; and they sacked the Abbasid Caliphate in Baghdad, an important centre of learning and religion. In the words of Marco Polo, the Venetian merchant who explored Asia in the late thirteenth century and served Genghis Khan's grandson, Kublai Khan (1215–1294): 'All the emperors of the world and all the kings of Christians and of Saracens combined would not possess such power as this same Kublai, the Great Khan.'[7]

Consider also the propensity of English and French kings to wage the Hundred Years' War in the fourteenth and fifteenth centuries, over disputed claims to France's throne. Recall that there was no Italy or Germany at this time, only separate provinces, city states and the cobbled-together confederation of the 'Holy Roman Empire'. Divided, obsessed with its own wars, in thrall to Papal authority, and panicked by Mongol and Muslim invaders, it is no wonder the word 'medieval' retains its traction in modern English for denoting that which is pre-modern. Among this era's great conquerors was the Ottoman Empire, founded in Anatolia in 1299. Among the world's great civilisations was China's Ming Dynasty, which ruled from 1368. Christian Europe did not get a look in and it was the losing side in 1453, when the Ottomans sensationally seized Constantinople from the old Eastern Roman Empire, also called the Byzantine Empire.

Now widen your gaze to the wider world of 1500: sophisticated societies existed in Asia, the Americas and Africa like the Ming, the Aztecs of Mexico, and the Kingdom of Benin. For Europeans, hemmed into their own continent, a largely unknown world awaited. As veteran scholar Wang Gungwu explains, 'the Muslim powers were by the fifteenth century in control of most of the world's trading routes on land and sea. Thus, the Europeans found themselves unable to trade directly with China and India. So they turned to the Atlantic. It was not an accident that it was the peripheral Portuguese who led the way south along the African coast.'[8]

The Portuguese were the heralds of Europe's breakout. Portuguese explorers like Henry the Navigator (1394–1460) sailed along Africa's coastlines, building on Venetian and Genoese nautical traditions of exploratory maritime trade.[9] In 1499, Portuguese explorer Vasco da Gama returned to Lisbon from his pioneering voyage past the Cape of Good Hope on Africa's southern tip, reaching India's Kerala coast. In 1500, another Portuguese armada set sail under the command of Pedro Álvares Cabral, who visited four continents, travelling to Brazil before retracing da Gama's route past southern Africa and on to India. Also during that year, the Genoese explorer Christopher Columbus returned from his third Spanish-funded voyage; this time he had sailed beyond Cuba, Hispaniola and the Caribbean islands, reaching South America, his furthest venture yet.

These seminal events marked Europe's coming of age as mastering ocean-spanning exploration. Advances in nautical techniques for long-distance sailing, pioneered by the Portuguese and Spanish, were shrinking the globe. Historian John Darwin reminds us that beforehand 'it might have taken a whole season to reach Malacca from Gujarat', referring to voyaging between the Malay and Indian coasts, and that 'in general, intra- rather than inter-continental migration was the rule'.[10] But this did not spell a sudden European takeover of other places.

Only toeholds of European control were being established in Africa and Asia at this time. The Portuguese and then Spanish captured the coastal North African city of Ceuta in 1415 (Spain rules it to this day), but this was not immediately followed by big inland European conquests in Africa. As for India, European sailors reached its south-west coast, but this merely scratched the side of an unknown world. China was another world away from Europe, although in 1511, voyaging Portuguese captured the strategic port of Malacca on the Malay Peninsula, which hosted a settled Chinese expatriate population.

Ming China did not sail to the defence of Malacca. Indeed, its ruling dynasty had foresworn its own maritime voyages after the last of Admiral Zheng He's treasure fleets ended in 1433. Zheng's naval mastery is much spoken about today since it showed China's potential to have rivalled the Europeans as ocean-going masters. Zheng's voyages traversed the Indian Ocean to reach Sri Lanka and East Africa, but the Ming allowed its maritime prowess to wither. Undoubtedly the major land power of East Asia, China's rulers lost interest in interacting with distant cultures and had no interest in establishing formal maritime colonies. By comparison, Europe's various kingdoms were fervently trying to outcompete each other in their capture of far-flung riches.

Asia remained tough to open up for the Europeans. Take for instance the story of Portuguese explorer Ferdinand Magellan. He sailed past South America's southern tip, and his name was later given to the 'Strait of Magellan' in Chile. Crossing the Atlantic to the Pacific, in 1521 he reached the Philippines. Here he met a sticky end, killed while converting the locals to Christianity. Portugal may have captured the lucrative Asia-to-Europe spice trade, but its control in Asia remained confined to the coastal edges.

The only world-changing European conquest at this time was in the Americas. Columbus, convinced he had sailed to India, mistakenly gave to the Spanish a permanent misnomer of their new subjects in the Americas by calling them 'Indians'.[11] The historian Fernando Cervantes recounts that after Columbus, 'A flurry of expeditions followed, culminating in the conquests of two formidable civilisations: the Aztecs of Mexico, conquered by Hernan Cortes in 1521, and the Incas of Peru, conquered by Francisco Pizarro just over a decade later.' These self-styled 'conquistadores' overwhelmed the existing populations through warfare and disease, seizing their territories and building 'monasteries, convents and cathedrals; churches and cemeteries; palaces, mansions and commercial enterprises'.[12]

The Iberian conquest of the Americas was simply unprecedented in terms of the distances involved and the scale of the conquest. This transoceanic projection of power had gone so much further than the late medieval voyages of the other Europeans. Its world-altering effects had only begun.

* * *

By 1600, other European eyes were filled with jealousy at seeing Spanish and Portuguese profiting from gold in the Americas and spices from Asia. That year in England, Elizabeth I granted a royal charter to the East India Company (EIC). Two years later in the Netherlands, the Dutch East India Company (VOC, after its Dutch name) received its charter. The EIC and VOC were company-states, operating privately to violently claw out a share of the profit in Asia, free from political control but with official approval from their respective monarchs. The arrival of these company-states supercharged the transoceanic race for influence between Europe's kingdoms.[13]

Spain was the superpower of the day, enriched by profits from its New World conquests – a 'new world' to the Europeans, of course, not to its existing inhabitants. Spain's monarch also ruled a huge realm in Europe by holding the Habsburg and Holy Roman titles. Spain and Portugal even joined forces in the Iberian Union (1580–1640). Both were Catholic monarchies, and after the Protestant Reformation in the 1500s, competing ideologies wedged Europe apart. As the Protestant English and Dutch broke from Catholic Papal authority, bitter wars ensued. Famously, in 1588, Spain tried to invade England with its failed naval armada. The Dutch waged a long revolt against Spanish rule which lasted eighty years and ended with Dutch independence in 1648.

It was in this context of Spanish superpower that the English and Dutch East India Companies went into action to challenge Portuguese and Spanish trading monopolies. The Dutch were the great disruptors, as historians Jason

Sharman and Andrew Phillips recount: 'Between 1595 and 1602, approximately fifty ships leaving from Amsterdam alone undercut the Estate da India [Portugal's trading company], returning to Europe laden with Asian luxury goods.' From the early 1600s the VOC captured Portuguese outposts in the Spice Islands, Malacca, Ceylon (modern-day Sri Lanka), at the Cape of Good Hope, along India's coasts and in Taiwan. Even if 'the VOC's military capabilities paled in comparison with Asia's leading empires, they were sufficient to command the high seas in Asia', wrote Sharman and Phillips.[14] Dutch trading posts sprang up across the Java Sea and the Indonesian archipelago, centred around old 'Jayakarta', which the Dutch renamed as Batavia.

An incident that took place in 1603 off modern Singapore's east coast illustrated the Dutch rise. Dutch ships were trying to break Portugal's trade monopoly along the Malacca Straits and in the process captured a Portuguese ship, the *Santa Caterina*. The incident prompted the Dutch jurist Hugo Grotius, then a legal counsel to the VOC, to author two tracts, *Mare Liberum* ('The Free Sea') and *De Jure Praedae* ('On the Law of the Spoils'), which laid foundations for the modern notions of international waters, freedom of navigation and maritime trade – and justifying war to uphold these principles.

The English were slower off the mark in East Asia; they were forced out of the Spice Islands by the Dutch, so the English refocused their commercial interests in South Asia. But England's major success was on the other side of the world, crossing the Atlantic to North America. The Virginia Company received its royal charter in 1606 and sent settlers to establish the Colony of Jamestown in Virginia the following year, named after King James I. So began the colonisation of North America's east coast.[15]

This intensified the horrors of the transatlantic slave trade. Slave-taking for forced labour was an age-old practice. For instance, the Omani Sultanate took captives from East Africa's coast as it built its empire in Zanzibar and Mombasa. But Europeans were by far the most brutally systematic slave traders, and European-run plantations in the Americas would not have been profitable without slave labour from Africa. The Portuguese and Spanish had been shipping slaves taken from West Africa to work in the Americas in the early 1500s. The English and Dutch soon got in on this grisly business. John Hawkins led the first royally endorsed English slaving mission from West Africa to the Caribbean in 1562. A century later, England's Royal African Company established itself as a major player in transatlantic slaving. West Africa was where Europeans struggled to settle, often succumbing to disease; and it was the land they systematically depopulated to boost profiteering in the New World colonies.

Contemporary debate about the slave trade has intensified in the West. The *New York Times* began its '1619 Project' to highlight two centuries passing since 'a ship appeared near Point Comfort, a coastal port in the English colony of Virginia' containing '20 enslaved Africans, who were sold to the colonists' – the start of the slave trade in North America, albeit after it was already well established in South America.[16] Writer Howard French explains how the slave trade abetted the rise of the West, setting the 'Europeans onto a path that would eventually propel their continent past the great civilisational centres of Asia and the Islamic world in both wealth and power'. Europeans did not possess any kind of innate superiority to rule the world, reasoned French, and relied on exploiting slaves from Africa to make their New World colonies profitable. 'Without African peoples trafficked from its shores, the Americas would have counted for little in the ascendance of the West.'[17]

This is a powerful point. At this time, the great Asian and Islamic empires still followed their own story arcs, generally untroubled by Europeans. The Ottoman Empire was at its peak, its population reaching 30 million by 1600. The Safavid Empire ruled Persia from its capital, Isfahan, waging a long war with the Ottomans in the middle of the century. The Mughal Empire's conquest of India's subcontinent accelerated under emperors Akbar, Jahangir, Shah Jahan and Aurangzeb. In China, the Ming Dynasty was overthrown by its Manchurian neighbours, who from 1644 ruled China as the Qing Dynasty. Shogunate Japan, reeling from its catastrophic invasion of Korea in the 1590s, ordered by Toyotomi Hideyoshi from his capital in Osaka, in 1603 began a new chapter in Edo – Japan's new capital under the Tokugawa Shogunate, and later renamed Tokyo.

It is nonsense to suggest that these non-Western peoples lived untroubled lives before Europeans came in force. Far from it, since wars and brutal successions dominated their regal affairs. But while the Europeans had developed oceanic dominance, Asia's and Africa's inland riches still remained largely out of their grasp.[18] For how long would this balance hold?

* * *

By 1700, Europe experienced a vital reprieve: the Great Turkish War finally ended, after repeated failed attempts by the Ottoman Empire's army to sack Vienna. In 1697, they were defeated once and for all by a multinational European alliance called the Holy League, leading to the Treaty of Karlowitz in 1699, which permanently ended Ottoman plans for further conquest in Europe. Thereafter, the Christian kingdoms were less fearful of attack by a Muslim empire, freeing more of their energies for their own expansion. The 1700s show the appearance of important features that remain recognisable today.

Russia's expansion from the city of Muscovy and across Asia is one such feature. The Russians had tried their hand at being a seafaring empire, with the city of St Petersburg envisaged by its founder Peter the Great as a base for maritime power, but they did not get further than the Baltic and Black Seas. As empire-builders, Russia's destiny was to conquer adjacent lands, heading into central Asia and across Eurasia where the biggest opposition they met was in the weather and terrain. After reaching the Pacific Coast, which was a continent away from Muscovy, Russia annexed the Kamchatka Peninsula (situated north of Japan) in the early 1700s.

Its vast expansion further embedded Russia's complex split identity, as an Orthodox Christian European power that built a contiguous land empire in Asia. This has complicated any attempt to characterise Russia as 'Western', since Russia's evolution was abidingly influenced by its encounters with the peoples and environments of Central Asia, Siberia, the Pacific, and by the vast expanse of territory it has retained to this day.[19] Russia's modern rulers can and do always hark back to this imperial mindset.

Other European ambitions for conquest were still somewhat circumscribed in 1700. Apart from the coastal territories, Europeans had not yet conquered North America's expanse. Comparable situations existed on other continents. John Darwin explains that 'as late as 1750, across much of the world the European's presence was either confined to the coast or meekly dependent on the fiat of Asian or African rulers', not least since some of these rulers were strengthened by their trading relations with Europeans. So much so that 'in the 1750s few seemed vulnerable to a European takeover' and 'the great Asian monarchies of the Ottomans, Safavids, Mughals, Ming, Qing and Tokugawa had looked impregnably safe from European domination.'[20]

The mid-1700s is when the balance of military and industrial power really tilted in European favour. We can see how so many other parts of the world were impacted by Europe's Seven Years' War (1756–1763). This was in fact a series of wars waged principally by Bourbon France, Britain and Europe's other imperial powers. It was waged by Europeans but became truly global, fought in the Americas, India, the West Indies and Philippines. Rival European empires were expanding at each other's expense and the existing inhabitants were increasingly co-opted and caught in the middle.

The Indian subcontinent was the next major European conquest. The ruling Mughal Empire were local conquerors, having expanded bloodily into the subcontinent from their base in Afghanistan in the 1500s. After two centuries of rulership, the Mughals were by now weakened by their own wars in the subcontinent, becoming increasingly vulnerable to predation by the English and the French. The EIC pounced most effectively when Clive of India's army inflicted a huge defeat on the local Indian ruler (and his French allies) in Bengal in 1757. The outcome of this battle opened up the rich state of Bengal to British influence. In the wake of Clive's victory, the EIC's trading post in Calcutta (now Kolkata) became the centre of a growing imperial realm across the subcontinent.

What was changing? Industrialisation, as pioneered by the British across the late eighteenth and early nineteenth centuries, was key. Steam power when used for ship propulsion enabled the Europeans to deploy their soldiers more speedily and into hard-to-reach locations, superseding the sailing ships still being used by non-European powers.[21] Industrialisation also helped in the development of more destructive gunpowder weapons with which to wage wars of imperial conquest.

New ideologies were also part of the new Western canon, appearing in seminal developments including the US's Declaration of Independence in 1776; the Treaty of Paris, which formally created the US in 1783, thus opening a new branch of the Western world; and France's revolution in 1789, which rendered it (as the US was founded to be) a republic free from monarchy. Altogether, the British industrial revolution, and the French and American political revolutions, provided the ideas, the territorial heft, and the industrial fuel for the emergence of the modern West. In the wider world, balances of power teetered ever more in favour of the Westerners.

* * *

Evident by 1800 was one the most vital features of the world hereafter: the expansion of the US. The following year, Thomas Jefferson became the US's third president, leading a state still in its infancy and largely confined to its east coast. France retained the colony of Louisiana and New Spain belonged to the Spanish. In 1803, Jefferson secured the Louisiana Purchase, buying 530 million acres of territory from France for $15 million in the price of the day, and doubling the US's size in the process. France was keen to divest itself of its North American holdings, having recently been defeated by a slave revolt on Saint-Domingue (now Haiti) and evicted from this colony, while at the same time waging its revolutionary wars in Europe. The US was the great beneficiary of France's distractions.

Elsewhere, France was still energetically expansionist. In 1798 Napoleon Bonaparte led a French invasion of Egypt, briefly conquering Cairo and Alexandria. This served a foretaste of the humiliations later suffered by the Muslim kingdoms in North Africa and the Middle East at European hands. France's imperial glory was short-lived, however, and by 1801, France's occupation of Egypt was over and Napoleon was preoccupied once again with France's wars in Europe at the expense of its far-flung colonies. France was eventually defeated in the Napoleonic Wars in 1815 by a coalition of opponents. Britain played a leading role in this coalition and, by doing so, opened for itself the path to becoming the preeminent maritime colonial power. Britain soon overtook not only France but also the Netherlands and Spain.

The conquest of India became the centrepiece of Britain's burgeoning empire. By 1800, India had increasingly fallen under British control as the EIC defeated one local principality after another and marginalised French influence. In 1799, the EIC's most strident local opponent, Tipu Sultan of Mysore, was killed in the Fourth Anglo–Mysore War, which resulted in the overthrow of his kingdom. Thereafter, the EIC controlled a large chunk of southern India. The British built naval stations in Madras, Calcutta and Bombay (now named Chennai, Kolkata and Mumbai), as well as in Singapore and Penang on the Malay Peninsula. This network of ports gave Britain an unmatched ability to launch naval power in Asia.

As an indication of its maritime reach, Britain's first settlements in Australia were established at this time. Britain's 'First Fleet' arrived on 26 January 1788 at Sydney Harbour, now marked as 'Australia Day', and the New South Wales penal colony was established that year.[22] Although the British sailor James Cook had annexed Australia's east coast back in 1770, Cook's voyages did not initially interest his paymasters. Only after losing its American colonies did the British embark on building major settlements in Australia, eventually creating another thriving white-settler outpost at the expense of the locals and setting themselves up for further conquests in the Pacific Ocean.

Meanwhile, in 1799, the Dutch changed tack, consolidating their colonial winnings by annexing the Dutch East Indies from their own East India Company which had been declared bankrupt, dissolved and nationalised. By now, Britain had displaced the Netherlands as the largest European trader with China. There was one obstacle: the Chinese did not want anything Britain had to offer. So British traders grew opium in India in industrial quantities and then sold it to China, encouraging mass addiction among the Chinese populace to maintain demand (the Dutch also sold opium but not at this scale). The scene was set for the Anglo–Chinese conflict and the Opium Wars that began in 1839 and ended in 1860 when the Chinese tried to curb the sale of opium and resist the terms of trade being foisted onto them by outsiders. The Chinese were defeated in the Opium Wars and their descendants continue to mark this as the start of China's 'Century of Humiliation'.

British imperialists during the Victorian era even mooted turning China into 'another India' but decided against this. As the historian Ronald Hyam explained in *Britain's Imperial Century, 1815–1914*, fully colonising China was debated at this time, but the reasons that mitigated against it included the likelihood of the other European powers piling in, causing a general war over the spoils, plus British fears that China's total conquest may have been impossible anyway. The British stuck to exercising informal control over China while seizing Hong Kong and persisting with selling opium.[23] Meanwhile, formal control was extended over India when in 1858 it became the Raj, an official British colony directly ruled by the British state. (The EIC, having served its purpose, was divested of its holdings and dissolved in 1874 – company-states now gave way to state-run colonisation.)

These disparate developments in different parts of the world had a cumulative effect on world power. Spain and France had been completely eclipsed as imperial powers by Britain, which had as its centrepiece the Raj in India and a series of naval stations on the routes to China and Australia. In North America, the victory of the white settlers in their conquest of the continent and their adopting English as their primary language transformed the Atlantic.[24] The balance of world affairs had tipped decisively not only in European favour but in favour of one specific branch of the European world, namely the Anglosphere, with other Europeans now following in their wake.

Around the world, a new vision of 'free trade' was being spread at the behest of European imposition. Examples of this included the one-sided trading arrangements that were now routinely being foisted on non-European empires and kingdoms. For instance: Britain's 1838 free trade agreement with Egypt and the Ottomans; its 1842 and 1858 treaties with Qing China after the Opium Wars; the 1855 Anglo–Siamese treaty over the ruling Thai kingdom; and the 1858 Ansei Treaties, to open Japan's ports for the benefit of Britain, Russia, France, the Netherlands and the US.[25]

The floodgates had opened to an unprecedented era of European dominion, spearheaded by the British but now involving the US, its rise representing a defining victory for white-settler colonialism.

* * *

Liang Qichao, a Chinese intellectual (1873–1929), wondered why the China of his day had fallen so far behind the West: 'It is not true that the Great West is now wealthy and powerful, stronger than all the other continents, because Heaven finds its particular favourite among people there. I once made a study of this situation and discovered that everything started with Bacon, the English gentleman [whose influence led to] new laws and reason, new instruments and technology.' By citing Francis Bacon, Liang was referring to the evolution from the pre-empirical to the empirical age and hence to the European Enlightenment. Liang also noted the impact of political ideas: 'Therefore in today's situation if we want to counteract the national imperialism of all those world powers so as to save the country from total catastrophe, we must develop a nationalism of our own.'[26]

By 1900, the West was fast becoming the main game in town. This was the apex of Britain's imperial power and it also saw the emergence of the US as a superpower in its own right. Near the turn of the century, in the Spanish–American War (1898), the US defeated the last vestiges of Spanish power, seizing its colonies in Cuba, Puerto Rico, Guam and the Philippines. This capped off a century of continental expansion for the US. After 'Winning the West' at the expense of the Native American tribes, who were displaced from their land into reservations, often at enormous cost to their lives, so the white settlers could use their land to feed and house their own growing populace, the US expanded up to its Pacific coast and now projected its influence into Latin America.

In the world's other continents, old-fashioned inland empires became increasingly vulnerable to predation by offshore Western imperialists. The Mughal, Ottoman and Chinese dynasties had mastered the art of conquest in their own regions, but by now fell behind the Western colonists' new-found industrial and naval might. By 1900, Africa's kingdoms also became the target of European conquests, a notorious example of which follows.

Still retold today, the story of the 5,000 or so artefacts known as the Benin Bronzes, famous among Africa's treasures, were looted in 1897 when British soldiers attacked the Kingdom of Benin. Bronze items, sculptures, ivory, wooden and coral artefacts dating back centuries were stolen, all part of the Britain's march into West Africa aimed at ending the Benin King's trade monopoly around the Niger Delta. Some of the stolen artefacts were given to Queen Victoria, others were sold for profit. This notorious story of cultural theft has come to symbolise the rapaciousness of British colonial conquest.[27]

The carve-up of Africa was well underway. At the Berlin Conference held in 1885, fourteen European countries agreed to divide the African continent between themselves to exploit the land and for the pride of expanding their own colonial empires. Even the minor European kingdom of Belgium gained a foothold with the Congo Free State, which existed from 1885 to 1908 as the King of Belgium's personal possession, inflicting such damage on the Congolese in these two decades that its people still struggle to recover from it. Newly unified Germany was another late entrant in the race for colonies. It perpetrated the Herero massacres in modern Namibia (1904–07), then called German South West Africa, which began after the Herero tribe led a rebellion against the colonisers by killing scores of German settlers. German troops under Lothar von Trotha issued an extermination order, having failed to encircle and defeat the Herero rebels and instead using his soldiers to drive the Herero into concentration camps and into the desert to die of thirst.[28] Another colonial newcomer, Italy, tried to conquer Ethiopia in the 1930s and used chemical weapons against their Ethiopian opponents.

The controversies around these wars remain alive today, and governments in France, Germany and Belgium, and the Dutch monarch, have latterly officially apologised for thefts and massacres perpetrated in their one-time African colonies. Handling these controversial legacies continues to bedevil modern European relations with African states in particular, but elsewhere too, wherever the Europeans have colonised and looted in the past.

From Africa to Asia, the Europeans were ascendant. Consider this speech delivered by German monarch Kaiser William II in 1900, as he approached the middle of his thirty-year reign. German troops were sailing to China as part of the 'Eight Nation Alliance', which intended to march to Beijing to save besieged foreigners during China's Boxer Rebellion. To inspire them, the Kaiser invoked the worst of his age, when Europeans routinely fought to punish recalcitrant foreigners:

> The Chinese have overturned the law of nations; they have mocked the sacredness of the envoy, the duties of hospitality in a way unheard of in world history. It is all the more outrageous that this crime has been committed by a nation that takes pride in its ancient culture. Show the old Prussian virtue. Present yourselves as Christians in the cheerful endurance of suffering. May honour and glory follow your banners and arms. Give the whole world an example of manliness and discipline. You know full well that you are to fight against a cunning, brave, well-armed, and cruel enemy.[29]

The international troops of the Eight Nation Alliance, which comprised European, US and Japanese soldiers, were wading into a complex civil war. The Boxer Rebellion (1899–1901) was waged by the Righteous Harmony Society, which sought to kick out Western influences from China and to limit the spread of Christianity. The Boxer rebels blamed the Qing Dynasty, which by now had ruled China for well over two centuries, for weakness in the face of foreign influence. One interesting perspective on the Boxer Rebellion is that, unlike in Europe, which exported its young, restless and violent men to fight in its colonies, China did nothing of the sort and was thus prone to bitter domestic wars.[30] In the end, the Boxer rebels were beaten back by the Eight Nation Alliance. Imperial troops of the Qing Dynasty even sided with their erstwhile Boxer enemies to fight off the foreign invasion, but the whole sorry episode humiliated and weakened the Chinese Empire, furthering its slide to total collapse a decade later.

Imperial Japan was the only Asian nation to recreate key ingredients of Western success. Given the island mentality of its people, Japan became a maritime empire in its own right. In 1895, Japan's navy defeated Qing China and captured the island of Taiwan in its spoils. In 1905, Japan's navy defeated Russia in a sea battle that was also significant for showing the world that an Asian power could be triumphant. Japan was increasingly confident that its imperial culture and military prowess would allow it to displace Western power in Asia, for instance, by conquering the Dutch colony of Indonesia. The high point in its imperial campaign came in 1942, when Japan's army marched down the Malay Peninsula and forced the humiliating surrender of Britain's imperial army in Singapore. The nadir came in 1945, when Imperial Japan's spell over its nation was finally broken by America's atomic bombs, dropped to end World War Two.

Before this cataclysmic final act, all across Asia, people looked with astonishment at Japan's rise. Rabindranath Tagore concluded that 'I, for myself, cannot believe that Japan has become what she is by imitating the West.' He saw other old civilisations like India and China being transformed into nations, as nationalism was 'hurled with all this force upon the naked skulls of the world of No-Nations', while reminding us that 'all the great nations of Europe have their victims in other parts of the world'.[31]

Contemporary writer Pankaj Mishra considers how this might have felt at the time, writing of:

> . . . a long line of bewildered Asians: men accustomed to a divinely ordained dispensation, the mysterious workings of fate and the cyclical rise and fall of political fortunes, to whom the remarkable strength of small European nation-states would reveal that organised human energy and action, coupled with technology, amount to a power that could radically manipulate social and political environments. Resentfully dismissive at first of Europe, these men would eventually . . . arrive at a similar conviction: that their societies needed to attain sufficient strength to meet the challenge of the West.[32]

Thereafter, modern history morphed into stories of imitation and assimilation of Western ways of doing things. If non-Western cultures were to survive and thrive, no matter how proud and insular they may once have been, they needed to look to the West for inspiration, for their money, especially in the case of rebuilding Japan, and often for its blessing. The Westfull world had dawned.

* * *

The 'West' as we now know it only took forms and shapes that we can readily recognise after its scientific, economic and political revolutions from the eighteenth century onwards, even if its Greek and Roman inspirations date to much earlier eras.

After the Iberian conquest of the Americas, and the subsequent transatlantic slave trade, a great deal of time elapsed before the Europeans decisively controlled Asia and Africa. Only in the eighteenth century did balances of power tip decisively in European and later in the US's favour. Until around 1800, the internally driven growth experienced in parts of Asia was as impressive as in Europe.[33] In the grand sweep of history, the West's ascension to become the first ever globally dominant civilisation is a recent phenomenon, but one that feels older than it is because nobody alive remembers otherwise.

European and Western global influence grew and diminished in cycles. In Latin America, it came and receded earlier. In Asia, it developed gradually through the Portuguese conquest of Malacca in 1511, the founding of Dutch Batavia in 1619, and the British conquest of India that began in 1757. In Africa, it endured in colonial form into the 1960s. Just as it did not arrive in a 'big bang' moment, the trends of history strongly suggest Western global influence in its modern forms will not suddenly vanish, but will recede and rebalance just as gradually, doing so in piecemeal fashion, faster in some places than in others.

Until now, dominion stayed within the Western world. The only credible modern non-Western pretenders, the Ottoman and Japanese empires, ended in 1922 and 1945 respectively. No non-Western power ever gained and held supremacy again. All great powers rise after breaking out from containment by their rivals: the Dutch from a Spanish stranglehold; the British from the Spanish and French; the US from the British, and so on; but all these powers came from the West. Even the USSR, despite its Asiatic territories, originated as a colonising European project that later spurned the West. We have no experience in modern history of a power transition involving dominant fully non-Western powers.

History is indeed written by winners, and so long as the winners keep winning, the narrative can remain fundamentally unchallenged. To close, a noted American historian of Islamic studies, Marshall Hodgson (1922–68), wrote sardonically of the canonical 'rise of the West' story:

> We know how the traditional story runs: history begins in the 'East' – in Mesopotamia and Egypt; the torch was then passed successively to Greece and Rome and finally to the Christians of Northwest Europe, where medieval and modern life developed. During the Middle Ages, Islam temporarily was permitted to hold the torch of science, which properly belonged to the West, until the West was ready to take it over and carry it forward. India, China, and Japan also had ancient civilisations but were isolated from

> the mainstream of history and 'contributed' still less to it (that is to Western Europe). In modern times Western Europe expanded over the rest of the world, so that Islam and India and China have ceased to be isolated, and have entered the orbit of the ongoing Western Civilisation, now becoming a world civilisation.[34]

There can sometimes be a tendency to backcast the West's latter-day dominance into mistakenly thinking that its peoples were *always* somehow superior. Get ready to reinterpret the history books. The next chapter in world affairs will differ so much from what came immediately before that the older stories of Western dominion will inevitably be seen in a new light. Overemphasised narratives of past Western benevolence and leadership will be even more coherently challenged than they are today, including within the West itself. Our future origin stories will more habitually accommodate a fuller range of perspectives, changing their tenor and tone. Until one day in our near future, the era of unbridled Western dominion will itself be spoken of as a passing chapter in world history.

2

Westfullness

> For as long as any of us can remember, to be modern has meant to be Western, and to be Western has meant being at the forefront of pretty much everything – of science, of social change, of culture, of affluence, of influence, of power in all its forms. Not everyone has liked this state of affairs, even inside Western countries themselves, but regardless of sour grapes or ideological discontent this Western dominance of modernity has become such an established fact that we have lost sight of quite why it is so.
>
> Bill Emmott, *The Fate of the West*[1]

UNTIL VERY RECENTLY, 'Westernisation' was still a term people used interchangeably with 'modernisation'. Just imagine a Westerner in decades gone by holidaying in a far-flung place who returned home to report that where they visited had flushing toilets, few potholes on the roads, locals speaking our language, and wasn't it all very 'Western'? I recall thinking in these terms during my annual family trips to East Africa as a child to visit grandparents there. With some justification based on their technological advancement, the advanced nations of the West presented themselves as global benchmarks for the progress that others aspired to.

Arguably, this claim already feels outdated when looking at the gleaming new infrastructure popping up in different parts of the world. Few today would use Westernisation as a synonym for modernisation without fact-checking for instance the sorry state of some infrastructure in New York, Paris or London. These grand cities retain their unique historical cultural charms, something that is the literal opposite to snazzy and soulless shopping malls or new high-rises. But this is a different kind of appeal, more vintage than it is future-focused.

In many ways the leading Western countries remain rich, influential and advanced. How have they maintained this lofty position? How was the Westfull world built? We must explore this question before we can survey the *relative* rather than *absolute* decline in the West's global standing. What is the world now adjusting away from? What was Westernisation and how did it spread around the world?

Westernisation is a shorthand for the global diffusion of Western influence. It has involved other societies of the world adopting the practices and cultures of North America and Western Europe, whether by free choice or compulsion.[2] Not all of this was forced through the barrel of a gun. Compulsion doesn't have to involve threats and violence. It might just as readily refer to the costs of remaining aloof being so prohibitive that a society is forced to partake in what the West is advocating in order to thrive. It is not just a fear of missing out, but a fear of failing to function at all in a world where some of the key levers of control were designed by and operated in Western countries. The old adage holds: 'If you can't beat them, join them'.

We intuitively know this because, until now, we have all lived in a world full of advocates of a broad-brush Westernisation of global systems, values, consumer habits, and suchlike. The West has not turned the rest of the world into a pastiche of its own image – far from it. As Western influences were absorbed, they mixed with local or traditional influences, coexisting and producing hybrid outcomes. Moreover, the West absorbed influences from elsewhere too. As Samuel Huntington wrote in his article, 'The West Unique, Not Universal': 'The heart of a culture involves language, religion, values, traditions, and customs. Drinking Coca-Cola does not make Russians think like Americans any more than eating sushi makes Americans think like Japanese.'[3] A fair point regarding consumer tastes, and one that adds perspective to anti-globalisation catchphrases of the 1990s warning of a 'McWorld', or of 'Coca-colonisation'.[4]

Polemics against Westernisation are commonplace and you don't need another here. Instead, we can trace the overlapping historical processes that collectively shaped the modern world at the behest of different forces emanating from the West. It is a mistake to see them as disconnected, for instance, only fixating on the US's rejection of the wicked colonising ways of Europeans. Or seeing the US's Cold War stand against the USSR as apart from the concurrent end of Europe's colonial empires. Westerners naturally fixate on the schisms and contrasts *within* the Western world. But think of how it looks from the outside – the torch was passed from old Europe to the US at the changing of the guard in the West. The outcomes for everyone else were clear as the world overflowed with a myriad of Western influences.

***

In the West, we tend to consider the big chapters of the twentieth century as involving the world wars followed by the Cold War triumph over communism. Much of the rest of the globe – Asia, the Middle East, Africa – experienced these events through the prism of colonialism and independence. Countries we recognise on the map today in these regions only came to be in the twentieth century as empires ended. Westerners often drew the map lines and sometimes departed so hastily that newly independent nations struggled to adequately prepare their security, economy and national cohesion. Even after independence, consider the advantages Europe's one-time colonisers possessed.

Imagine colonising far-flung places and peoples and later having to leave, as the tides of change now wash against you, the occupier, after the locals become sufficiently empowered to see you off. Although you may dress up your departure as a supreme act of benevolence, you wanted to remain in control if you could. At the very least, you wanted to depart with your head held high, reminding all and sundry – not least yourself – that colonisation was a grubby but necessary job. And that you shall be entitled to salvage lasting advantages as the curtains fall on the colonial enterprise.

Versions of this saga played out for Europe's old imperial powers, which is why the very term 'de-colonisation' was itself a misnomer. Recovering from the great imperial hangover was a long process for all concerned. Even after independence, sinews of colonial influence lingered.

Canny France maintained currency ties with the newly independent nations of its former empire in North and West Africa. Stubborn Portugal clung on to Goa until they were forcibly kicked out by India in 1961 and only gave Macao back to China in 1999. Wily Britain kept Hong Kong until 1997 and during the drawn-out end of their empire, nourished the linguistic, legal and parliamentary commonalities with their ex-colonies, even rebranding the 'British Empire Games' the Commonwealth Games. Not all of this was sinister or conspiratorial (even if some of it undoubtedly was). It reflected the natural instinct of the colonisers to secure the most favourable terms of departure.

Colonialism had allowed Europeans to pursue a two-tier approach to the world. For themselves, the rules of sovereignty should be respected. Way back in 1648, the Peace of Westphalia brought the Thirty Years' War between Catholic and Protestant nations to an end. The treaties that ended this war became a key European reference point for codifying the legal status of national borders, and the associated norms by which states govern their own territories but ought not to intervene in the affairs of other states. Europeans paid heed to these principles in their own continent and punished violators like Napoleon and Hitler who tried to conquer Europe, while treating the rest of the world as a borderless free-for-all, ripe for competitive colonisation.[5]

As historian Vijay Prashad asked, 'Why did the French forget *liberté, egalité, fraternité* when they went into the tropics?' India's first prime minister, Jawaharlal Nehru, asked the same question of the Raj, wondering why it was the 'England of the savage penal code and brutal behaviour' that came to India, not the England 'of noble speech and writing and brave deed, of political revolution and the struggle for freedom'.[6]

The modern system of states – the political world map that we are so accustomed to looking at – bore these imprints. Between 1920 and 1939, just sixty-three countries were members of the League of Nations, the precursor body to the United Nations. Many others were colonies and dominions (Britain had League memberships for Australia, New Zealand, Canada, India and South Africa but excluded its Middle East and Africa colonies; the French didn't bother with separate memberships for their colonies). US President Woodrow Wilson famously called for the self-determination of nations after the Great War ended but, as historians Jane Burbank and Frederick Cooper write, 'Wilson intended self-determination to apply to white people only. Not surprisingly, many people of colour did not see it that way. Anxiety that the principle might be extended haunted some designers of the [1918] post-war world.' Specifically, 'Wilson's Secretary of State, Robert Lansing, worried that the President's declaration posed "the danger of putting such ideas into the minds of certain races".'[7]

This two-tier mentality over who deserved freedom was still hard to shake after 1945. Historian Margaret MacMillan recounted that since 'self-determination occupied such a venerable place in the annals of many "civilised" powers themselves', it became harder to keep denying freedom to others. 'Third World revolutionaries were fond of reminding the US of the role of liberation struggle in its own history.'[8] Today, there are

193 member states of the United Nations, a number that has risen as waves of independent countries were created or freed themselves in the latter half of the twentieth century.

The terms of freedom from colonialism are worth dwelling on. As the political scientist Benedict Anderson wrote in *Imagined Communities*, 'The world historical era in which each nationalism is born probably has a significant impact on its scope. Is Indian nationalism not inseparable from colonial administration . . . after mutiny?'[9] Versions of this are true for many ex-colonies: local anti-imperial struggles and revolutionary leaders defined their national stories, but their newly independent nations still had to fit into the Western-designed family of states. Few countries remained aloof like Cuba, which cut itself from the Western world in the 1950s after its communist revolution. Most former colonies have reconciled themselves in some way to the rules of the global game as defined by their ex-colonisers.[10]

An astonishing 133 of today's non-Western states gained independence after most recently being ruled by a Western country (in most cases by European colonisers, plus a few instances of direct US occupation, as in the Philippines). The USSR occupied or otherwise dominated the affairs of twenty-two countries (fifteen Soviet Republics, including Russia, and seven members of the Warsaw Pact, the involuntary Soviet-dominated military alliance of the Cold War). Prior to the USSR, the Ottoman Empire was the long-time occupier of several nations (including Albania, which withdrew from the Warsaw Pact in 1968, Bulgaria and Romania). Japan occupied Korea. Some countries have modern histories of occupation by non-Western imperialists.

The Ottoman and Japanese Empires were defeated in the Great War and in World War Two respectively, and their colonies were carved up, some falling into Western hands (Japan itself was occupied by the US after its defeat in 1945, regaining its sovereignty in 1952). The immensity of the USSR meant that swathes of Eastern Europe and Central Asia have experienced a lingering and often malignant Russian imperial influence even after the USSR collapsed in 1991. By comparison, Western rule had an incomparably wide spread as far and wide as from Belize to Iraq, and Mozambique to Indonesia. By far the most numerically significant recent occupiers – and consequent bequeathers of independence – were the Western states.

It is not as simple as saying 'the West made the modern world'; qualification and caveat is always required. Former settler and slave communities in South America broke free much earlier in the early nineteenth century, and more time has elapsed out of direct Spanish and Portuguese rule as compared to more recent stories of independence from European rule in Africa, the Middle East and Asia. The experience of each ex-colony was always unique but there were common legacy themes: borders drawn by the colonisers; European languages deposited; Christianity sometimes spread; and enduring patterns of trade established by the ex-colonisers.[11]

With this Western influence came an infusion of Western values. Scholar Wang Gungwu, who was born in 1930 and experienced the dissolution of British Malaya, recounted how 'it was only in the nineteenth century that international law made sovereignty something that could be legally tested.

Where Asia was concerned, it was only with the establishment of the UN in 1945 and in the context of decolonisation that sovereignty became crucial to enable countries to justify their post-colonial borders.' He highlights another important feature of post-colonial Westernisation, of 'the European assumption that international law was built on common Christian heritage'.[12]

All systems bear their creator's mark. Values are consciously exported or baked into the design. Tom Holland wrote in *Dominion* that 'the West, over the duration of its global hegemony, had become skilled in the art of repackaging Christian concepts for non-Christian audiences. A doctrine such as that of human rights was likelier to be signed up to if its origins among the canon laws of medieval Europe is concealed.'[13] For the Indian writer Deepak Lal, 'Christianity has a number of distinctive features' of which 'the most important is its universality. Neither the Jews, the Hindus, nor members of the Sinic civilisations were claiming to be universal. You could not choose to be a Hindu, a Chinese, you were born as one.'[14]

There have been different phases to what we can call 'the Evangelical West'. Converting others to its values was once the job of the missionaries. Writer Ben Ryan explained how modern Western political ideologies have evolved 'through a distinctively Christian, Enlightenment, European intellectual prism', underpinned by 'universalism' and a belief that progress towards a moral endpoint 'could be fostered in any society of the world'. Religious Europe saw the endpoint for non-Western peoples as Christianity; the modern secular West has seen it in achieving liberty and democracy. 'This sense of necessary progression – from barbarism and backwardness to civilisation and a republican future – is inherited above all from the West's Christian past,' Ryan writes.[15]

The Europeans became transoceanic colonisers partly thanks to having industrialised earlier, as everywhere else played catch-up. Essential to justifying colonialism was the lexicon of 'civilised' and 'non-civilised' worlds. After empire this mentality persisted in new forms. The West placed itself in the privileged positions of setting rules, shepherding success and defining terms of progress for others. In the twentieth century the lexicon shifted to the 'developed' and 'developing' worlds. Given how diminished the Europeans were after the world wars, however, a new Western champion was needed as the lead influencer.

* * *

We have just lived through the American Century; it cohered in the twilight of European empire and in turn we now consider its own twilight. As the chief standard-bearer of contemporary Westernisation, the US has morphed it with Americanisation, reflecting more of its own world views and its chosen prescriptions for others. As Bill Emmott observed, 'The US is not the West. But the West would be severely diminished, even finished, without the US.'[16] This dependency is not all one way. Where would the US be without having exercised its leadership over Europe's post-World War Two recovery via the Marshall Plan and by stationing its army in Europe with NATO? If the US had retreated from Europe after 1945, it would have evolved in a more culturally and strategically isolated way. Conversely, where would the Europeans have ended up without the US? Likely, much more damaged, if not defeated outright, in their Cold War stand-off with the USSR across divided Germany. Europeans and Americans have benefitted from each other during America's century even if their transatlantic bonds require nourishment for each new era.

The US's singular stature in the Western world has elevated the importance of the Anglosphere, eclipsing the linguistic diversity represented by other Western countries. Churchill's multivolume *A History of the English-Speaking Peoples* likely inspired the British historian Andrew Roberts, when he wrote that:

> Just as we do not today differentiate between the Roman Republic and the imperial period of the Julio-Claudians when we think of the Roman Empire, so in the future no one will bother to make a distinction between the British Empire-led and the American Republic-led periods of English-speaking dominance between the late-eighteenth and the twenty-first centuries [because] they have so much in common – and enough that separated them from everybody else.[17]

Perhaps this is going too far for some, but it raises the importance of continuities between *Pax Britannica* and *Pax Americana*. Such continuities were not a foregone conclusion; it took some time for the original Anglo–American split of 1776 to heal. Some English elites were so mean-spirited about the fledgling USA's success that 'such men did not conceal their glee when the American Civil War broke out in 1861, nor seek to hide their identification with the "aristocratic" South', historian Ronald Hyam recounted.[18] Eighty years later, all was forgiven by Britain's ruling classes when the US bailed them out of defeat in World War Two. On 14 August 1941, Churchill and President Franklin Roosevelt jointly delivered the Atlantic Charter, which stated the US post-war aim to 'respect the right of all peoples to choose the form of government under which they will live', with 'sovereign rights and self-government restored to those who have been forcibly deprived of them'. With the end of the British Empire in sight, it would fall to the Americans to reboot Westernisation for a new era.

Successful reboots cannot ditch their source material entirely. Tracing the intellectual origins of US global dominance, Stephen Wertheim writes that 'For most of their history, Americans have claimed their nation was exceptional because it did *not* covet armed supremacy over the rest of the world.' By pursuing global supremacy without formal colonies, the US certainly distinguished itself from the Old World – but it also chose this path because the means of pursuing global dominion had changed thanks to the newest technologies of transport and communication. The US astutely judged that it no longer needed to keep annexing colonies to maintain a preponderance of world power. 'Americans ever since, from experts to ordinary citizens, have considered world dominance to be their nation's natural role', concluded Wertheim.[19]

The incredible rise of the US to become a world-beating power in just over a century had convinced Americans that they had cracked the code to modernity. This has provided the underlying justification to the US's twentieth-century foreign interventions, such as acquiring extensive treaty rights with international partners; mounting interventions to unseat unfriendly leaders such as the coup in Iran in 1953 instigated jointly by the US and the UK; and mounting economic interventions aimed at foisting free trade on other nations to 'liberate' them in the long run by making them more prosperous.[20]

The US's network of international security alliances and partnerships have been central to its influence. There are concentric rings to the US's partnerships, the innermost core being the 'Five Eyes' of the Anglosphere nations (US, UK, Canada, Australia and New Zealand) forming their own tight-knit security partnership. The US has treaty obligations to defend thirty-two members of NATO in Europe and Canada; mutual defence treaties in Asia and Oceania with Japan, South Korea, Thailand, Philippines, Australia and New Zealand; and the Rio Treaty of 1947, which on paper binds the US in the collective defence of Central and Latin America (although this has proven controversial for countries fearing unwelcome levels of US influence: Mexico, Bolivia, Nicaragua and Ecuador withdrew from the Rio Treaty in recent decades; while Venezuela and Uruguay also left, only to rejoin later).

The US has operated a global network of military bases and arrangements to use the ports and airstrips of other friendly nations. Supporters of this US 'global security architecture' argue that it has helped to keep the peace by often (if not always) deterring would-be aggressors all over the world for fear of inviting US reprisals. Opponents of the US global role fixate on the human and military disasters that followed its Vietnam, Afghanistan and Iraq invasions as evidence that the US is a self-interested, war-addicted and culturally blind superpower, intoxicated by its own myths of moral superiority.

We all know this well-worn debate – our concern here is not to refight it, but to consider afresh its significance in a less Western world. We will return to this theme but, as an opener, let us consider a key historical example of how the US has sought legitimacy for its leadership with non-Western peoples.

The signature accomplishment here was Japan's 'recruitment' to the West after seven years of US post-war occupation (1945–1952). General Douglas MacArthur, the mastermind of the US victory in the Pacific War, acted as Viceroy while the Emperor of Japan retained his ceremonial status (Japan's Emperor was ceremonial even under the old feudal Shogunate and Daimyo system, so this was in line with Japan's political culture). Japan has fully aligned with the US in geopolitics ever since, and by hosting a large US military garrison on the subtropical southern Japanese island of Okinawa, Japan has protection against the threats it has perceived from China, Russia and North Korea. Meanwhile, Japan can continue to be Japan, balancing its geopolitical alignment with the US and the West while remaining economically ambitious and culturally apart.[21]

Japan's membership of the geopolitical West is significant on other levels too, namely in terms of how the West can present itself. By successfully including a powerful non-European heritage society in the US's club of close allies, 'white' is replaced by 'West' as the approved stamp of civilisation. Japan is the pre-eminent case study in how 'the West' has evolved beyond its origins in race, in Atlantic geography and in empire, to encompass a wider set of ideals under US global leadership.

There is greater imperative than ever to appeal to non-Western countries to align with and join the West, because the US's and Europe's share of global resources and influence is shrinking relative to the last century. To this end, it is in the US's interest to advertise how multiracial and welcoming its version of global order is to all, so others can sign up to it and enjoys its fruits, like Japan and South Korea have done (South Korea too is bound to the US by hosting another large American military garrison). But, as US domestic politics turn toxically on immigration policy debates and on complex matters of racial equality, the US struggles to tell a convincing story to the wider world about the limits of its inclusivity. As a branding challenge, this is a significant one.

History is once again instructive. The original mindset behind the US's globe-straddling posture was forged during its shift from isolationism after the Great War to internationalism after World War Two. Back then, Wertheim writes, 'America's foreign policy elite saw themselves as part of a small cohort of people who governed the world, where they understood world governance to be a principally American, Anglophone, white, Western or civilisation project,' casting themselves 'as one of a handful of guardians of civilisation tasked with disciplining lawless savages and lawbreaking aggressors.'[22] The US would not describe itself like this today, but you can see the journey it has been on to modernise its image and its justification for leading others. To perpetuate its influence into the Westless era – given the racialised era in which its power originated – the US needs to keep updating its sales pitch to the world.

Today, the idea of world order orbiting the American sun is beset by uncertainty. Totalitarian states in Russia, China and Iran are defiant; erstwhile US allies or partners in Türkiye and Saudi Arabia are disobedient; rising countries like India and Indonesia cannot be assumed as being in thrall of the US. Casting itself as the best hope against tyrannical authoritarianism in Russia, China and Iran in our current age is one thing. It remains to be seen if other parts of the world accept this framing, or continue to recall much that was also objectionable to them in the American Century.

* * *

If America has stolen the limelight of Westernisation, we mustn't downplay the *Pax Europa*. Europe had to recover and rebuild after the world wars, doing so during the Cold War, which divided its continent into rival blocs. These events paralleled the end of Western European colonisation and the start of the European Economic Community. The Berlin Wall fell in 1989, and the European Union formed in 1992, replacing the EEC. Despite the many setbacks faced by the EU, the modern European continent has been reshaped by the advent of its joint economic bloc and common currency. Without the

EU, the European countries would simply be too small to make any independent global impact at all.

The EU has made two unique contributions to modern Westernisation. First is the EU's role in Westernising Europe itself by helping to spread democratic political systems and associated liberal values. Democracy in Spain, Portugal and Greece arrived after dictatorships. Portugal's democratic transition took place in 1974–76; Spain's democratic transition began after dictator Francisco Franco's death in 1975; and Greece was ruled by a junta in 1967–74. The EEC and later the EU rehoused these countries during their democratic transitions into the European economic area. Moreover, EU enlargement has taken in former Warsaw Pact countries and some former Soviet Republics, beginning the Westernisation of Eastern Europe. Successive waves of EU enlargement in 1995, 2004 and 2007 saw the EU's membership grow, bringing the tools and values of Westernisation to rehabilitate the former dominions of the USSR, now freed from the shackles of Soviet rule.[23]

The era of EU enlargement has not been without controversy and setbacks. The UK left the EU for domestic populist political reasons, formalising its departure in January 2021. Numerous European countries have contended with their own populist political forces, with Hungary ruled by a government that has been happy to accept the advantages that come with EU membership while railing against the centralising impulses coming from Brussels. Croatia joined the EU in 2013 but the other Balkan states remained in the antechamber of EU accession at the time of writing. Moreover, the prospective EU memberships of Ukraine and Georgia have become vexed matters due to violent Russian resistance, while Türkiye's EU membership prospects, which were alive in the 2000s, have since run aground.

Nevertheless, the overarching trend lines have shown modern Western civic, democratic and economic values spread across most of the continent. Europhile Timothy Garton Ash wrote in 2009 that 'Europe's history over the last 65 years is a story of the spread of freedom. In 1942 there were only four perilously free countries in Europe' whereas 'most Europeans now live in liberal democracies. That has never before been the case; not in 2,500 years.'[24] To which I would add that, aside from its missing parts in the UK, Norway, Switzerland and part of the Balkans, the EU brings much of Old Christendom into modern union. Although the EU is not a Christian club, its member states are historically predominantly Christian nations, which provides a strong dose of historical and cultural binding. It also explains why Muslim Türkiye's frozen EU accession bid had signalled among other things the importance of these cultural factors behind EU enlargement (and despite Türkiye's NATO membership).

The EU's expansion was another peak of the Westfull era: in the 1990s and 2000s it became possible to speak of 'Europe' writ large as belonging to the West, which was impossible during the Cold War. The EU reunited much of Europe in economic terms, while the concurrent enlargement of NATO brought more of East and Central Europe into the transatlantic security alliance. Faith in the articles of democracy, capitalism and American military power had seemingly replaced Christianity as the bonding ideology of Westernised Europe.

Which brings us to the second of the EU's big Westernising contributions: projecting its values outside of its borders. The EU's real superpower resides in something vital to the modern world: how it influences trade and regulatory standards worldwide. In *The Brussels Effect: How the European Union Rules the World*, academic Anu Bradford explains that:

> . . . notwithstanding all its challenges, the EU remains an influential superpower that shapes the world in its image [through] the EU's unilateral power to regulate global markets. The EU today promulgates regulations that influence which products are built and how business is conducted, not just in Europe but everywhere in the world . . . through its ability to set the standards in competition policy, environmental protection, food safety, the protection of privacy, or the regulation of hate speech in social media.[25]

This still carries something of the genealogy of Europeans educating the world, albeit now in the dull art of regulatory compliance. As she continues: 'Trading with the EU requires foreign companies to adjust their conduct or production to EU standards – which often represent the most stringent standards globally.' The EU can directly regulate its own huge common market comprising some 450 million people. The EU's regulatory power around the world is rather more indirect, since multinational corporations often try to standardise their products globally, rather than produce specific models for each market. Which means that multinational companies are incentivised to adhere to the EU's standards, which in turn become the global standards, so long as they are doing any of their business in Europe.

These standards cover a lot of things, from product safety to digital data protection, and from environmental standards such as banning produce garnered from unsustainably deforested land, to human rights standards and prohibiting modern slavery in the supply chains of companies that wish to do business in the EU. It has led some people to accuse the EU of practising 'regulatory imperialism', but one must also applaud the ingeniously technocratic use of European market power to enforce modern standards of ethics and safety on what is otherwise unfettered global capitalism.

Westernisation changes with the times. For the Europeans, influencing the world beyond their Mediterranean, Anatolian and Russian frontiers has required newer forms of persuasion. Without the military ballast of the US, Europe is remarkably defenceless. But without Europe, the US has no claim to represent the Western world. As ever, the West remains greater than the sum of its parts.

* * *

Globalisation has been the main mechanism of modern Westernisation. Americans primarily but also Europeans became the keepers of the standards of global commerce, while the US military served as the security force for defending the international trading system from harm or hijack by any would-be usurpers. Globalisation has been Western-led, building on the maritime colonial era of the nineteenth and early twentieth centuries by encouraging the interconnection of the world through trade, through technology, the spread of multinational companies and the rules for governing international capital flows and exchanges.

If you recall the 1990s, you will remember the West's sense of unbridled validation by its victory over communism, leaving the US in a commanding position in world affairs with Europe following on its coat-tails. As a student in early 2000s Britain, I read what were then cutting-edge books about the triumph of transnational corporations and entities like the EU, alongside receiving my expected dose of Francis Fukuyama's 'end of history' thesis, which provided an intellectual explanation of the global spread of liberal democracy and capitalism due to the bankruptcy of Marxism as a means for organising society. Back then it was tricky to see beyond the West's ascent. Challenges from elsewhere were only very small specks on a distant horizon. Even China's rise was more an abstraction than an actuality.

Unease was evident in some quarters over the ways in which Western leadership had defined the terms of globalisation. Economist Joseph Stiglitz captured this mood in *Globalisation and Its Discontents* (2002). He argued that free trade as being advocated by the West was a misnomer since 'most of the advanced industrial countries – including the US and Japan – had built up their economies by widely and selectively protecting some of their industries until they were strong enough to compete with foreign companies.' While they 'preached – and forced – the opening of the markets in the developing countries to their industrial products, they had continued to keep their markets closed to the products of the developing countries, such as textiles and agriculture.'[26] It was a double standard that could only work because the West had its hands on the steering wheel of the world economy.

This power sat with the so-called Bretton Woods institutions, referring to the location of the United Nations Monetary and Financial Conference of July 1944, which planned the rebuilding of the European continent after the devastation of war. The International Monetary Fund (IMF) originated here, as did the practice of the IMF's boss always being a European while the boss of the World Bank was an American. The World Bank's full name was the 'International Bank for Reconstruction and Development', reflecting its original mission. Once their post-war purpose had been served, they were put to a very different use, and Stiglitz recounted that 'dramatic changes in these institutions occurred in the 1980s, the era when Reagan and Thatcher preached free market ideology in the US and UK. The IMF and World Bank became the new missionary institutions, through which these ideas were pushed on the reluctant poor countries that often badly needed their loans and grants.' The 'Washington Consensus' as it was known referred to the coordination between the IMF, World Bank and the US Treasury to set the terms for lending money to other countries for infrastructure projects and structural adjustment loans, based on IMF-approved conditions for receiving this help. It also involved spreading Western economic systems around the world, creating a single global economic system.

As the West exercised its immense financial and institutional power over other countries, the Indian economist Amartya Sen captured the controversy that followed: 'Those who take an upbeat view of globalization see it as a marvellous contribution of Western civilization to the world' and as 'a gift from the West to the world' whereas 'from the opposite perspective, Western dominance – sometimes seen as a continuation of Western imperialism – is the devil of the piece'.[27] Over this matter there would never be a consensus, and how could there have been?

I am not denying agency to non-Western parts of the world, only arguing that the other regions have developed in the context of Westernisation. For instance, several East Asian states were huge beneficiaries of globalisation. After this Asian economic miracle, the 'Asian values' debate saw statesman Mahathir Mohamad of Malaysia and Lee Kuan Yew of Singapore try to reconcile Islam, Confucianism and Hinduism and advance a Pan-Asian vision of modernisation that didn't just involve aping the West. But they could never compete with Westernisation for coherency and influence, since even the most successful 'Asian tiger' economies were playing catch-up. In 1997 they suffered a major economic crisis and turned to the IMF for assistance. First-mover advantage was formidably exploited by the West to stay ahead of any competitors.

This chapter has brought us to the peak of the Westfull world. Not to be confused with the US 'unipolar moment', which began after it had seen off the USSR, the 'Westfull era' is the far grander sum of a quarter-millennium of European and US predominance. Western civilisation's export potential has been immense and the world has overflowed with its many influences.

At the turn of the millennium, the US stood tall in its

leadership of the Western world. But in the aftermath of Al-Qaeda's 9/11 terrorist atrocities directed at New York's World Trade Center and Washington DC's Pentagon – symbols of US capitalist and military might respectively – America had only a poverty of responses to offer the world, waging a misbegotten war in Iraq and a doomed twenty-year occupation of Afghanistan. After the 2007–08 financial crash, many questioned the reliability of the US financial system, and this is our point of departure to what comes next.

3

Status Shift

This – the inward and outward fulfilment, the finality, that awaits every living Culture – is the purport of all the historic 'declines', among them that decline of the Classical which we know so well and fully, and another decline, entirely comparable to it in course and duration, which will occupy the first centuries of the coming millennium but is heralded already and around us today – the decline of the West. Every Culture passes through the age-phases of the individual man. Each has its childhood, youth, manhood and old age . . .'

Oswald Spengler, *The Decline of the West Volume I: Form and Actuality* (1918)[1]

QUESTIONING THE ORIGINS and durability of its global dominance, and peering over the precipice of its decline, is once again of interest in the West. You don't need to search far in contemporary Western history writing to detect the concern. One common coping mechanism deployed in literary Western circles is to look to the Romans and search for analogies in their imperial decline. Allusions to the classical world tend to make their enunciator sound eminently cultured but beyond this I am not convinced the Roman analogy holds much use for fathoming the era of diminishing Western influence. This is because the question for the West today is not about collapse – it is about sharing power.

Far from doomsayers, writers who invoked Rome were coming to terms with what the origins of Western power suggest about its nature and possible demise. Niall Ferguson's *Civilization: The West and the Rest* (2011) presented the 'six killer apps' that hitherto guaranteed Western supremacy while considering how to maintain them. Ferguson has been no shirker when articulating Western accomplishments and he has been keen to sound the alarm around Western civilisational decline.

One of his references – as is so common in orthodox Western historiography – was Edward Gibbon's Victorian-era account of the fall of the Western Roman Empire. 'Today, many people in the West fear we may be living through a kind of sequel,' wrote Ferguson, given that Rome's fall resulted from 'economic crisis; epidemics that ravaged the population; immigrants overrunning imperial borders; the rise of a rival empire – Persia's – in the East; terror in the form of Alaric's Goths and Attila's Huns. Is it possible that, after so many centuries of supremacy, we now face a similar conjecture?' Ferguson was alarmed by the West's 'worst financial crisis since the Depression' unfolding 'while many of the Rest are growing at unprecedented rates' and 'meanwhile, a rival empire is on the rise in the East: China'.[2] His book's blurb makes it clear that the end of Western ascendancy is a thing to be feared.

Western historians in Gibbon's age and in our own invoked a counterfactual account of history, wondering how the world would have been different if the Western Europeans had been beaten and enslaved by others. Gibbon himself wondered what would have happened if instead of Charles Martel leading the Franks (the ancestors of the French and the Germans) to victory at the famed Battle of Poitiers in 732, the Franks had been beaten by the Muslim army they faced. 'The Arabian fleet might have sailed without a naval combat into the mouth of the Thames. Perhaps the interpretation of the Koran would now be taught in the schools of Oxford,' he wrote.

Another US-based British historian, Ian Morris, opened his book, *Why the West Rules – For Now* (2010), with his own colourful counterfactual story: of Chinese warships docking in Victorian London, after helping fund a British victory in the Napoleonic War, before imprisoning Albert in the Forbidden City and leaving Victoria to wither under the Chinese yoke. Morris asked: 'Why did history follow the path that took Looty [a dog looted by British soldiers from China's Summer Palace] to Balmoral Castle, there to grow old with Victoria, rather than the one that took Albert to study Confucius in Beijing? Why did British boats shoot their way up the Yangzi in 1842, rather than Chinese ones up the Thames?'[3]

Parallels with Romans are evocative for a certain Western-minded readership, as are allusions to the inevitability of all empires and civilisations one day crumbling to be reclaimed by the undergrowth.[4] Picture the vast sprawl of the Angkor Wat temples of the Khmer Kings in modern Cambodia, or Machu Picchu, built by Incas in modern Peru. Like the climax of the 1968 American movie *The Planet of the Apes*, we may imagine the Statue of Liberty as one day collapsed and buried in the sands of a dystopian future, our way of visualising the final fall of the US and the Western world that it guards.

Such visions of doom lurk in the Western subconscious but, barring some unforeseen global apocalypse, this is not going to happen. Western ways of doing things are too hard-wired into the fabric of global commerce and cultural exchange to vanish entirely or to be supplanted fully by alternatives. Nevertheless, what goes up must one day come down, whether it comes down by a little or by a lot; the uncertainty of what comes next is stoking paranoia in some quarters. Unlike the end of the Western Roman Empire, or the later shattering of the Byzantine Empire, the West is not facing collapse – it is facing readjustment. The better lessons are around sharing power, not losing it in a seismic collapse, but the stories and analogies for sharing are not yet common parlance in the West.

The very idea of sharing global power is anxiety-inducing. In America today, there are genuine strategic and economic reasons for challenging China's rise – but doing so is also animated by a fear of future loss of status in sharing the pedestal of being the world's primary influencer. When politicians and commentators in the US take umbrage with China, they often work through the standard talking points of a China hawk: they bring up China's repression of Hong Kong's pro-democracy protests; China's forcible re-education of the Uighur people in Xinjiang; some Chinese tech companies posing threats to American society; and the possibility of the People's Liberation Army invading Taiwan. Each of these matters is important in its own right, pointing to areas of actual or potential Chinese wrongdoing. But by habitually raising these issues, rather than any number of the other injustices in the world today, these anti-China hawks are keen to highlight any matter that embarrasses China or weakens its rise by persuading others to spurn Beijing's advances.

Exaggeration is common when making this point. At a private event taking place in Asia, I heard a long-standing former Trump cabinet member confidently declare that 'China is the greatest ever threat to Western civilisation.' (I will leave you to guess which ex-Trump official it was.) Sceptical at his words, I wondered how China, half a world away from Europe and the US, could credibly bring down Western civilisation. I can only guess the speaker meant *Western civilisational dominance* was threatened by China, which seems a more credible concern as some countries look to China and less to the West for their key economic partnerships.

If you are American, you may be aware that your country is still coming to terms with the New World no longer being especially new and losing some of its lustre. Those Americans who already accept this may have experienced their compatriots labelling them as defeatists for not believing their country's greatness. Which Trump has made into his 'Make America Great Again' rallying call. If you are from Old Europe, while you may readily grasp the sense of world power having drained from your continent in the previous century, you may not personally recall the vulnerabilities felt in Europe immediately after World War Two and at the end of colonial empire.

Putting aside the melodramatic notion of a complete Western civilisational collapse – which is not going to happen no matter how many times the collapse of the Western Roman Empire is invoked – even the realistic prospect of relative decline is tough to comprehend. Westerners have no recent precedents of real power-sharing with the rest, and this makes it harder to sensibly and sedately discuss the implications of what is coming without always feeling the need to hark back to classical tales that are as comfortingly evocative as they are irrelevant.

***

Looking out at the horizon from the peak of global power can be vertigo-inducing for some Westerners. It is tough to keep perspective when you (and those directly descended from your immediate ancestors, and with whom you share kinship) have been number one for so long. From this pedestal the mind plays tricks, conjuring fears of civilisational decay from within or an unceremonious dethroning from without; of slow decline followed by a precipitous toppling and bracing for a hard landing as the West is overtaken by others.

Decline is not only material – it is also experienced emotionally and intellectually. Anxieties in the Western world come in different vintages. The Western European nations have had far longer to accustom themselves to their changing global status, as their fall from colonial mastery was cushioned by other post-war developments like joining NATO and the EEC (later the EU). It is a much newer feeling in the US to sense one's own peaking world mastery. Some in the US deny it is happening and others think they can reverse it by 'beating China' in the quest to remain world number one, but the anxiety underlying how these matters are discussed is palpable.

A sense of impending doom due to a fear of decline has periodically gripped Western minds. To place today's Western anxieties in context, it is worth briefly casting our minds back a century to German intellectual Oswald Spengler's world. Spengler (1880–1936) published his two-volume work on *The Decline of the West* in 1918 and 1922. Chilling to its European readers in the wake of the Great War, by the late 1920s, Americans may have shared these pessimistic sentiments after the Wall Street Crash and the ensuing Great Depression brought their country into the doldrums.

Spengler discoursed on the lifespan of empires and civilisations, his focus being 'the only culture of our time and on our planet which is in the phase of fulfilment – the West-European-American'. He called it 'the Civilization which at this present time has gripped the earth's whole surface'. No apologist for Western hegemony, he considered Eurocentric perspectives as inimical to studying world history, criticising 'this current West European scheme of history, in which the great Cultures are made to follow orbits round us as the presumed centre of all world happenings'. Spengler thought that we should admit 'no sort of privileged position to the Classical or the Western Culture as against the Cultures of India, Babylon, China, Egypt, the Arabs, Mexico'.[5] This is a captivating point: what if the other major world cultures were more equally weighted in the Western world's understanding of historical accomplishment? Such a rebalancing may yet be forced upon us.

Spengler theorised that dominant civilisations experience their youth, maturity and decrepitude over roughly a 1,000-year period. The lifespan of dominance has been an enduringly popular topic. The British soldier-scholar Sir John Glubb in *The Fate of Empires* (1978) observed that throughout history empires remained at their peak for 200–250 years before experiencing protracted declines and sudden final collapses.[6] Recently, the US investor Ray Dalio wrote about the lifespan of empires to give context to the slipping material dominance of Western countries in relation to China's rise.[7] Whenever the West feels as if its dominance is slipping, the theme resurfaces more prominently in the discourse of the day.

Whatever the theory and the calculation, it is clear that everything ends in one way or another. If a leading civilisation does not collapse entirely, once it has enjoyed is expansion phase, it must at some point evolve into something new and unrecognisable, shedding its skin and taking on a new guise to elongate its lifespan in changed global circumstances.

The mortality of Euro-American world influence started to rise again in our attentions after the financial crisis of 2007–08 which betrayed structural weaknesses in America's financial system.[8] Former Australian Prime Minister Kevin Rudd placed the financial crisis in its global context when he explained that 'for the first time, the world needed economic solutions that were beyond America's ability to provide alone. As a member of the G20, China was sharing the world stage as an engine of global economic recovery', making it clear 'how significantly the centre of global economic gravity was shifting. China had finally arrived at the top table of global affairs.'[9] After the financial crash, at the behest of leaders like President Barack Obama and Prime Minister David Cameron, China played a big role in the global response since the Western economies could never have done it alone.

Other worldly Westerners have observed these trends unfold and reflected on their implications for heralding a changing world order. A former ambassador of France to the UN, Jean-David Levitte, offered this view a decade after the 2007–08 financial crisis, which began in the US before spreading globally:

> From this moment on, there is a challenge to the Western order. This challenge stems from the BRICS club but also goes far beyond. It can be summed up in the following terms: emerging countries say yes to modernisation. They say yes to globalisation of the economy. But they say no to the Westernisation of their societies. During the triumphant decade of 1991–2001, we Westerners had the conviction, or at least the hope, that gradually all emerging market countries would adopt not only the rules of the market economy, but also the values that underpin it and that underlie the Western order. Today, this illusion has disappeared.[10]

Another astute observer, former British diplomat and parliamentarian Rory Stewart, presented his view to Chatham House in 2023. After the 2007–08 financial crisis destroyed the West's reputation around building prosperous economies, other assumptions and claims made by the West were also disproven. 'The link between prosperity and democracy was effectively destroyed by the rise of China; it became bigger than the British economy as recently as 2005,' said Stewart. Around the same time, 'the idea of the liberal global order was destroyed by the humiliations and messes of Iraq and Afghanistan'. Since then, 'Social media tore us apart in terms of the idea of consensus and it created polarisation' within Western societies that held liberal democracy as sacrosanct.[11]

Such self-awareness is not yet widespread in the West, weaving together links between the politics of populism, and the relative decline in key aspects of the West's global standing. The messages may be less difficult to convey from a European perspective given how long ago its countries experienced their own declines, placing them behind US leadership. Admitting that your part of the global community no longer enjoys its former dominance is an undesirable message to convey – if heard in a certain way, it sounds less like realism and humility and more like defeatism.

Contemporary politicians and opinion formers in Washington DC, London, Paris, Brussels and Berlin have tended to come of age and professional maturity sometime in the 1970s, 1980s and 1990s. So they experienced the peaks of Western influence and triumphalism at formative moments in their own lives. They may admit at an intellectual level that change is now afoot. Acknowledging societies' relationship with status anxiety, while taking on board a myriad of still alien non-Western perspectives, may come less naturally to many. Some may wish the West could carry on partying like it was 1997 again, so to speak, in terms of the comparatively unbridled levels of Western influence and optimism from back then.

In the coming decades, the West will experience a generational 'software update' in its prevailing world views, to use the analogy of a computer operating system that needs to be rewritten to keep up with the demands of the day. Those yet to come to maturity will do so imbued not with tales and experiences associated heavily with Western triumph, but of Western coexistence with others on a more equal level than before. This update will only take effect with time and, until such understandings are more widely held, the anxieties are likely to worsen.

* * *

As the West comes to terms with losing its near-monopolisations of global power and influence, there is the other side of the coin to consider. Those who are playing catch-up with the West are wracked with their own emotions surrounding their exclusion from the top table of global decision-making, admixed with lingering resentments from old historical humiliations. At its worst, playing catch-up with the West could morph into score-settling. The West's most ardent critics will be sharpening their knives. Some voices will cheer loudly as the world becomes less Western-dominated, thinking they are saving their societies from the corrupting Western influences and that they can fill the power vacuum.

The West is not aways to blame; those sitting atop the pedestal of success are always targets for the resentments and jealousies of others, whether these sentiments are justified or embellished. While there are some genuinely felt lingering grievances against past Western deeds, we ultimately see what we want to see in history. If you fixate on the West's 'original sins', you will conclude that history is finally catching up with those dastardly Westerners who for centuries have held the rest back.

I am sensationalising things for dramatic effect, but this forces us to contend with an important distinction: *Westlessness* is different to *De-Westernisation.* Let me explain. The former refers to the steady erosion of global Western influence, and the latter to dedicated attempts to uproot past Westernisation. Hence, a steadier drift away from the West will contrast with more aggressive drives to de-Westernise. Accordingly, we should distinguish the 'Western-sceptic' from the more implacably 'anti-Western' view.

Living and working outside of the West, I've heard a range of emotions expressed. Everything from: abject fear that the West might retreat; to mild scepticism and disappointment around how the West has so disappointingly fulfilled its global roles; to all-out ranting in which the West can do no right. The important habit of mind is to remain objective in spite of the passions that are aroused. Sure, you can sit in one camp if you like, 'ruing the loss of Western leadership because it is still the last and best hope for humanity'; or conversely, 'dishing out just deserts for the Western world's past misdeeds', to caricature the extreme perspectives on either side. It is wiser to understand the passions giving rise to these sentiments while avoiding becoming a prisoner to them. We can spot from a safe distance the advocacy arguments that encourage us to adopt them, lest we all be turned against each other. This is far too expansive and too provocative a topic to simplify our responses in such a binary fashion.

This comes to life as we survey a range of Western-sceptic and anti-Western views. Starting at the temperate end of the scale, Pankaj Mishra's book, subtitled *The Revolt Against the*

West, offered a fair critique: 'From a Western standpoint, the influence of the West can seem both inevitable and necessary, requiring no thorough historical auditing' because 'Europeans and Americans customarily see their countries and cultures as the source of modernity and are confirmed in their assumptions by the extraordinary spectacle of their culture's universal diffusion.'[12] All it asks for is some self-awareness.

Others see only mischief and conspiracy in Westernisation. Samir Amin (1931–2018), the Marxist Egyptian-French academic, wrote a book called *Eurocentrism*. It delivered this broadside, calling Westernisation 'a project of homogenisation through imitation and catching up', an impossible feat since 'wouldn't the extension of the Western way of life and consumption to the nearly seven billion human inhabitants of this planet run against absolute obstacles, ecological among others?'[13] As the planet surpasses eight billion people, this is far from an idle concern. Amin saw global capitalism as a Western ruse to dominate the rest by encouraging them to 'catch up' in a race they could never win. He asked, can the West 'contribute to the building of a truly polycentric world in every sense of the term, that is to say, a world respectful of different social and economic paths of development?'[14]

Now that China really is catching up, arguments like Amin's appear in a new light. Critiquing the West is an old hobby that left-wingers in Western countries have long indulged themselves with, enjoying the freedom of speech to do so. But more articulate arguments have added gravity in this era of transitioning power. Which is why in 2011 Martin Jacques took this swipe in *When China Rules the World*:

> Having been hegemonic for so long, the West has, for the most part, become imprisoned within its own assumptions, unable to see the world other than in terms of itself. Progress is invariably defined in terms of degrees of Westernisation, with the consequence that the West must always occupy the summit of human development since by definition it is the most Western, while the progress of others is measured by the extent of their Westernisation.[15]

Captive audiences exist for these kinds of messages. There are some people who will be greeting any hint of rebalancing away from Western influences like a long overdue friend, late to the party but welcome all the same. Which brings us to the misuse of these messages and the horrifying possibility that they could be used to incite hatred and violence.

Reaching the aggressive end of the scale, it is worth recalling the horror of brutal past de-Westernisation campaigns. Terrorists and insurgents of the Al-Qaeda and Islamic State (ISIS) jihadist movements invoked mass murder not only in the name of religious sectarianism, but to humble the West and to purge its puppetry of post-colonial states in the Middle East, Africa and Asia. Their fight against Westernisation blurred with their fight against modernity. But this is not only about one specific set of ideologies. My mind is taken to another very different example: Zimbabwe and Robert Mugabe, who led the country from its independence in 1980 until his death in 2017. Mugabe unleashed mob violence against white farmers and families to encourage them to flee Zimbabwe so that their land could be reclaimed. Mugabe's response to the vestiges of colonialism in what had been the white-settler colony of Rhodesia only further scarred the country. Like any radical cause that plays on grievances and insecurities, the idea of expelling people of Western heritage and purging Western influences could unleash great hatred in certain contexts.

This is why alarm bells sounded loudly in May 2014 when Chinese President Xi Jinping seemed to publicly say, 'Asia for Asians'. Ironically, Xi's speech was delivered to a 'Conference on Interaction and Confidence Building Measures in Asia', but something was being lost in translation. Xi's precise wording was that 'Asian affairs should be ultimately run by the people of Asia; Asian issues should be ultimately handled by the people of Asia; Asian security should be ultimately maintained by the people of Asia'.[16] This was a standard Chinese government talking point, but it was seized on by China's own nationalist hawks as a call to arms, given their appreciation of arguments such as this one:

> When China becomes the world's leading nation, it will put an end to Western notions of racial superiority [because] all the nations in recent history that have become the world's leaders have been nations founded by Westerners. When China takes its leading position, it will prove that Asians can lead the world as well – that it isn't the exclusive purview of Westerners. Whatever Westerners can do, Asians can do just as well or better.

This passage appeared in Chinese army Colonel Liu Mingfu's book, *The China Dream* (2010), in which he wrote that 'the West is entering a long period of painful self-adjustment' because 'for two centuries, Western nations have been the most prosperous nations in the world, but a historic change will take place when China, a developing nation, slowly overtakes the Western economies.' He calls status anxiety 'America's champion's anxiety', although he also sees much for modern China to emulate in how the US increased its strength to superpower levels in the nineteenth and twentieth centuries.[17]

Could disparate Western-sceptic and anti-Western ideas from different places coalesce and forge new connections? Colonel Liu provided a foretaste when he wrote that 'The original sin of the West was in shaping a backward Africa to create a developed Europe' through the transatlantic slave trade; while earlier in history, 'Spain committed the original sin of religious persecution' when the Conquistadores forced Christianity onto the native populations. It takes no leap of imagination to understand why there are concerns in Western circles of such messages being passed between China and its African or Latin American interlocutors to build comity in their modern interactions.

There are some seriously radical perspectives out there if you know where to look. The title of Chandran Nair's *Dismantling Global White Privilege: Equity for a Post-Western World* says much about the emotions at play for the author and his readership. Nair's formative years in the British colony of Malaya made him 'highly attuned to how white people acquired special status and privileges wherever they went in the non-western world'. In Nair's view, 'dominating the world remains the principal objective of Western powers' and it is still based on a belief that 'races who lived in other parts of the world were inferior and could be tricked, cheated, or just exploited.' Some people may dismiss this as Marxist claptrap, but I found Nair's suggestion that we should recheck some of our terminology useful. He wrote of how he cringed when being called a citizen of an 'emerging market' or coming from the 'Global South' since they are 'archaic and condescending Western narratives about development and growth, very much rooted in a sense of superiority. Emerging from what? Poverty, deprivation, backwardness, incompetence, and drudgery?'[18]

Remember when, as president in 2018, Donald Trump casually denounced Haiti, El Salvador and parts of Africa as 'shithole countries'? The racism and historical illiteracy in Trump's comment provoked justified outrage in the US and far beyond. The West does itself no favours by becoming the very worst that it could be, especially now, when swathes of global opinion are fertile for reconsidering their old realities in light of new power shifts.

* * *

The mere anticipation of change has the power to provoke all kinds of anxieties. As with an abstract painting, we can see whatever message we want to see. Some can make out a heroic Western-led stand against the perennial evil of totalitarianism, now in Chinese, Russian and Iranian incarnations. Others see an overdue humbling of the West after its historical hegemony and its modern hypocrisies. No one side is going to monopolise global debates unless their purveyors fool themselves into believing so by only preaching to the converted.

We naturally derive different meanings from the same things because of our unique heritages and from what we stand to gain or lose. Our reference points are wildly varied as a result. Taking a well-known example from the current power shift, Kevin Rudd pointed out that 'Americans typically believe that their country's approach to China has been driven by high ideals in defence of democracy, free trade, and the integrity of the global rules-based order', but 'in China's perspective, this is reflected in 150 years of US commercial efforts to penetrate China's domestic market – from the age of opium to the age of Apple'.[19] I cite this passage because it is another reminder that some see continuities between the British Empire and today's US in ways that do not always occur to others.

Can we hold both thoughts in our heads, that Westernisation has clearly brought to different parts of the world benefits *as well as* inequities? In an ideal world we could look carefully at its many sides and encourage temperance, but the world is far from ideal. The emotions at play are too complex, the stakes are too high, and people often jump to conclusions about complex matters anyway.

'All non-Western peoples were crucially defeated at some point or other and compelled to admit Western superiority in terms of brute force,' wrote the historian Theodore Von Laue (1916–2000), before explaining how later and more temperate interactions with the West also held appeal. 'Women in China, Japan, or Africa, for instance, admired the respect and freedom enjoyed by women in the West; by comparison, their societies offered even less equality with men. Consumers everywhere liked Western goods suitable for local consumption. To the educated elite Western ideals like freedom, equality, and fraternity were even more attractive.' In the end, however, 'most potent surely was the appeal of political and military power, the remedy against humiliation'.[20] What a cocktail of emotions and inheritances: defeat and humiliation; hard-won female empowerment still in progress unevenly around the world; consumption and education; and the tantalising promise of catching up with the West. Now, catching up is finally in sight, even if only patchily and for some parts of the 'rest' – but even just closing the gap with the West will transform all of our realities.

Globe-straddling influence is hardly built with humility. Hubristic moments have been natural and plentiful in the West, and the idea of sharing your perch with others can be fear-inducing. Adjusting to change is both a psychological and material undertaking. When the exclusivity of high status starts to slip, and even if it is never violently wrenched away, those who once proudly held it will feel bereft.

4

Fusion Cuisine

> The word 'fusion' is greeted with suspicion these days. This is odd, really, since ideas travel across the world at the speed it takes to refresh a mobile phone screen, and many chefs and home cooks seem perfectly happy to dabble in plenty of mixing and matching. When done considerately, cross-cultural hybrids can be both eye-opening and delicious.
>
> Celebrity chef Yotam Ottolenghi, *Flavour: A Cookbook*[1]

THERE IS A myth surrounding the origins of pasta that is amusing to recount even if it is totally untrue. So, it was said that when Marco Polo travelled from Venice and sailed along the South China Sea in the thirteenth century, one of his crew rowed ashore for supplies and discovered a local family preparing long slender ribbons of dough. Marco Polo took this recipe for noodles back to the Italian Peninsula, resulting in the invention of spaghetti. The myth originated in a 1920s trade magazine published in the US for the pasta industry, which contained an advert written in the form of a long historical fable.[2]

The truth is much more interesting. Pasta was developed separately in China and Italy, called the 'two great pasta civilisations' by Silvano Serventi and Francoise Sabban in *Pasta:*

The Story of a Universal Food. As they recount, wheat was discovered in ancient China and used to make pasta long before it was popularised in Europe. Wheat farming took place in Europe in the Roman era, but bread overshadowed pasta as the classical-era carb of choice. Each civilisation, Chinese and European, developed its culture of preparing pasta in distinct ways and at its own pace. 'China was far ahead of Italy, but since it never had durum wheat, it remained a civilisation of fresh pasta, made by artisanal methods,' they write, and it is only in recent times that China also became the world's leading manufacturer of instant noodles. In contrast, Italy 'over the course of time perfected its mastery and understanding of wheat, developing at the same time a highly diversified production of fresh pasta and a dry pasta based on durum wheat'.[3] Joint honours are due when it comes to the development of pasta, shared between China and Italy.

As this perfectly innocent story reminds us, there may not be a single path of development when making useful advances, although there could be a race to claim the credit. Does it matter if different places develop their own approaches to the same things in parallel? What if we take inspiration from each other and add our own local spin? Where are the lines drawn between imposition, inspiration, imitation and theft? Fusion complicates simple notions of 'us and them', or 'closed versus open', or 'West versus rest', because it reminds us that whether things develop in isolation or in parallel, we inspire and borrow from each other all the time, accumulating various influences as we go. Combining ingredients to form new and hybridised outcomes is essential to how ideas and processes spread around the world.

Entire industries exist to protect against the theft of inventions and carefully developed industrial processes. An intellectual property lawyer would offer to patent their client's technological inventions against imitation, just as a counter-intelligence officer guards their nation's innovation hubs against theft from foreign espionage. Companies and countries alike sensibly guard their best ideas. Even then, we still inspire and borrow from each other. The world is an interesting place precisely because we develop similar things by following different paths.

Fusion dishes combine contrasting culinary traditions in one dish. We have all seen versions of this. I came across 'Laksa Linguine' – the Laksa flavour comes from Malaysia, Singapore and Indonesia, while dropping Italian linguine into the pot is not much of a stretch from the noodles that are otherwise used. It is a nice claim for uniting European and South East Asian tastes in a single dish, as we mix and match from across the great global buffet of varied choices.

This helps us to better understand what a relative decline in Western influences actually entails. Our overall direction of travel is the world shifting from Westfullness to Westlessness. In some cases, it is a shift by degrees, a little at a time. The outcome is not necessarily outright replacement by non-Western ingredients, but a different blend in which the Western ingredients remain but are ever more diluted.

Some people argue that we are actually headed towards a world of different opposing camps. Recently, the term 'de-globalisation' has emerged to describe the cumulative effect of rising geopolitical tensions, economic protectionism, internet censorship in authoritarian countries, and other phenomena that make us less open to the globe-straddling interactions we saw develop at the height of globalisation. In the 2020s, these headwinds have slowed down the globalisation trends we saw thirty years ago.

But unlike in Marco Polo's time, when it took a maverick traveller – and the embellishments surrounding his travels – to spread stories of the Far East to Europeans, most of us no longer live in continental isolation. Word spreads faster than ever and many commercial supply chains follow the logic of 'profit wherever it leads'. The question now is whether some around the world will lose a little of their taste for the Western versions of things, as the range of quality offerings expands healthily.

* * *

Since the declining dominance of the West is not dependent on its total collapse, what are we looking out for when observing it in motion?

We are not expecting whole civilisations to try to conquer each other in the manner of old settler colonists, but the risks of land-grabs are rising. Russia's all-out invasion of Ukraine in 2022 so far remains a modern aberration but there are no guarantees it will remain so. The possibility remains of China taking military action against Taiwan, which it considers a rogue province. Elsewhere, governments might see fresh opportunities to threaten territories that were created by what they interpret as historically unjust borders. In 2023, Venezuela's government raised the spectre of seizing Guyana's resource-rich region of Essequibo, prompting the UK to dispatch a warship in a show of solidarity with Guyana (a British colony until 1966). The heightened risk of more wars breaking out between countries during this era of transition is one of its most important features, to which we will return in later chapters.

Barring a truly calamitous descent into World War Three, the real tussles will be over influencing how the world works. Do not expect too many outright victories for one way of doing things over another. If you want one set of countries to 'win' the current rivalry for influence between the West and the powerful parts of the rest, or if you think it best for certain countries to 'decouple' and wall themselves off from others by cutting their businesses and their cultural practices off from each other, that is your prerogative. But you will likely be disappointed with what ensues, and you won't get very far in deciphering the nature of the current transition period.

Instead, we can expect intense competition for influence featuring mixes of Western and non-Western players. When fusion takes place in a less Western world, we would expect to witness *dilutions* of predominantly Western influences as Western inputs are matched or overshadowed by other influences to a greater extent than before, and as Western monopolies over certain global goods are broken up.

Just as the West is too hardwired into the sinews of global exchange to be fully uprooted and is far too loud a voice in the global commons ever to be muted, its principal rivals are not going to vanish either. Unlike in the Cold War, when the US prevailed over the USSR's collapse in 1991, a similarly seismic triumph over the People's Republic of China is unthinkable. The USSR was an economically moribund behemoth weighed down by its clunky imperial system, while China has learned lessons from the USSR's failure and is now too embedded in the world economy to ever be fully marginalised by its opponents. China does not need to recruit ideologically compliant disciples and allies to rebalance world order – it just needs enough other nations to trade with it to continue growing its global stature.

Instead of a grand victory by one bloc or civilisation over the others, we are entering an era of shared winnings between a myriad of Western, Western-aligned, Western-sceptic and anti-Western centres of power and influence, all coexisting for the foreseeable future. Those wishing to permanently hobble China's rise by decisively stymieing its influence over other nations, do be warned. As Singapore's then incoming president, Tharman Shanmugaratnam, put it at Chatham House in 2023:

> We must avoid thinking that the final outcome is going to be some great triumph of one system over another. It is most unlikely that we are going to see the triumph of one system, one method of government over another; one system of values over another. We are going to have to coexist in ways that serve the interests of our own populations . . . both sides have to recognise China's size, and the fact it is not going to go away, and that it will keep climbing the innovation ladder. It eventually rises anyway, but when it finally gets there, it will know who made it extremely difficult for it to get there, and this leads to a fundamentally unstable world.[4]

Not angering either side comes naturally to Singaporean politicians; it is the very essence of small-state manoeuvring. If there is truth in Shanmugaratnam's forecast then the titles of a plethora of books will be disproven as prophecy. Clearly, Jacques's *When China Rules the World* and Parag Khanna's *The Future is Asian* cannot be literal, while Mahbubani's *Has China Won?* is saved by posing a question. Conversely, the warning by ex-US intelligence officer Michael Pillsbury in his book's subtitle, *China's Secret Strategy to Replace America as the Global Superpower,* is too binary to reflect what is likelier to develop.

There is an understandable tendency to pick out absolute winners and losers when fathoming where this era of transition is headed. Such a winner/loser portrayal is tempting because it validates one set of political, economic and civilisational standards over others. It is why some people backing the US's global leadership role have converged around the 'democracy versus autocracy' formula to describe the modern dividing lines of global competition, placing the US's democratic partners on one side, including the European states, Japan, South Korea, Taiwan and others, all facing off against the threats posed by autocratic China and Russia. Where the Kingdom of Saudi Arabia fits in the equation, as a longstanding US economic and security partner while also being a monarchic autocracy, is never answered in this overly simplistic formula. Rather than a rallying cry, 'democracy versus autocracy' becomes a gross distortion of the complexities of the less Western world.

This is second-nature knowledge around the world. For instance, India clearly benefits heartily from the US being at the top table, given their cooperation in sharing advanced technology, their deal on sharing know-how in civilian nuclear power and their rising bilateral defence cooperation. At the same time, India has carried on buying Russian oil and defence supplies to maintain its old Russian and Soviet vintage tanks, planes, warships, Kalashnikov assault rifles and suchlike. As I once heard a retired Indian admiral retort, to a criticism around India keeping its ties open with Russia despite Putin's war in Ukraine, India had every right to do so for its strategic interests – just as the US has supported Israel through thick and thin, no matter the controversy of the day (such as after 7 October 2023 when, after the Palestinian armed group Hamas engaged in the deplorable mass murder and abduction of Israelis, the US government instinctively backed the Israeli military reprisals against Hamas and the accompanying mass killings of Palestinians in the Gaza Strip). Returning to the retired Indian admiral, as retorts go, one has to admit it was effective.

For countries like India, this era is about feeling confident that the changing world presents fresh opportunities that did not exist before, fusing whatever they can get their hands on by mixing their partnerships between the West and the rest without feeling much compunction to choose one club over the other. It is why much of the wider world is *not* rallying to a Western-led bloc to confront Russia and China, even if they consider either country warily.

Nor does the BRICS group of countries represent a monolithic anti-Western bloc, since the diversity of views between its members precludes this. Even if Russia is openly anti-Western, Brazil, India and South Africa could only be classified as Western-sceptics on some issues more than others. At the fifteenth BRICS summit in Johannesburg in August 2023, when the BRICS+ expansion announcement was made, South Africa's President Cyril Ramaphosa's opening speech made this point: 'Our world has become increasingly complex and fractured as it is increasingly polarised into competing camps. Multilateralism is being replaced by the actions of different power blocs, all of which we trade with, invest with, and whose technology we use.'[5]

Later that year, I had the chance to ask Ramaphosa's deputy president Paul Mashatile about this in an on-the-record discussion. Mashatile described the world as operating on the basis of 'geopolitical inequality', using this turn of phrase without giving specific examples. So, I asked him if the BRICS+ announcement in Johannesburg was intended to address this inequality. 'It's not anti-Western,' he said, but about 'the more you can play on an equal stage in the world', before qualifying that 'we will continue to engage with Western countries'.[6] Each BRICS country is clearly out to use this club to get the best deals it can. But in South Africa's case, the country's tangled Dutch and British colonial pasts, and the racist apartheid system that lingered long after it became an independent republic in 1961, would certainly influence its interpretation of a less Western world.

Even if China would like to use the BRICS as a vehicle to bring other emerging countries into a Beijing-centred vision of the world, it is difficult to see how it could do this in practice. China can hardly stop India from trading with the US – just as the US failed to stop India from trading with Russia. The trick with the Westless approach is to avoid fishing for a clear winner and loser, and seeing the world in terms of fixed blocs. The aim is to guide us into thinking about a more mutable world in which the West remains vibrant in its own right but becomes less able to decisively influence the rest and to choose their friends for them.

* * *

The nations and peoples of the world are the products of numerous past fusions into which the West has poured enormous influences. Minimising Western influences may be viable in some circumstances; purging Western influences outright will often be impossible (aside from the quixotic aforementioned Taliban-style approach of eradicating not only Westernisation but modernity in its many guises). Indeed, Western influences are so deeply embedded in the foundations of so many places, especially those once colonised by Western countries, that we can observe a layering effect throughout history.

Many post-colonial countries are the literal outcomes of colliding worlds, of Western and other immigrant and indigenous traditions mixing during the eras of colonialism and globalisation. The levels of contemporary Western influences in their cultures and peoples of course varies and can change over time. But you cannot prise Western influences out of the world, even if the terms by which they first fused with local traditions were deeply unequal. The interesting question is how fusions of influence will manifest and change in the Westless era from place to place.

Día de los Muertos – Day of the Dead – is celebrated annually in Mexico as a communal festival in which families gather to honour their deceased ancestors. Scholars are divided on its roots between pre-colonial and European settler influences. It is celebrated with the Roman Catholic holy days of All Saints' Day and All Souls' Day, reflecting the Catholicism brought by the Spanish conquest in 1521. Catholic Mass is now a less famous part of the holiday, and most attention goes to the carnival of the macabre involving skeletons, skulls and caskets reflecting on themes of mortality. The Day of the Dead is the outcome of a fusion with Mexico's native traditions from thousands of years ago, in which Aztec and Toltec peoples did not mourn the dead so much as view their passing as part of the continuum of life, with the dead remaining part of society in spirit. Latterly, the holiday has become closely associated with Mexico's national identity as distinct from the country's Spanish and US influences.[7]

The Mexican poet and Nobel Prize winner Octavio Paz (1914–98) wrote an essay on the 'Day of the Dead' in his 1961 book, *The Labyrinth of Solitude*. 'At one time I thought that my preoccupation with the significance of my country's individuality – a preoccupation I share with many others – was pointless and even dangerous,' he wrote. Paz also reflected on how the festival distinguishes Mexico from the West. 'The word death is not pronounced in New York, in Paris, in London, because it burns the lips. The Mexican, in contrast, is familiar with death, jokes about it, caresses it, sleeps with it, celebrates it . . . True, there is perhaps as much fear in his attitude as in that of others, but at least death is not hidden away: he looks at it face to face, with impatience, disdain, and irony.'[8]

Fusions of popular cultural events like the Day of the Dead is one matter. The profoundest fusions of all involve the marriages of people of different racial and cultural heritages. Mexico's demographics illustrate these fusions, with Mestizo people of European and Native ancestry being in the majority, followed by White Mexicans, then Native or Indigenous Mexicans, with the smallest group being the Afro-Mexicans. The arrival of Europeans drove the increase in the Mestizo population, and socio-economic opportunities have since favoured certain groups over others. Mexico is far from unique in being the product of its past fusions. Consider countries like South Africa or Singapore, mentioned earlier – it is unfeasible to pull apart the Western and non-Western components of history, identity, population, heritage, and so on.

With the examples of these other countries in mind, it is striking how much an aberration China has remained. China currently competes for global influence while keeping its own doors closed to outside influences. The CCP is the archetypal opponent of fusion. There is ample evidence for this, with its internet firewall; the clear delight of its government in limiting the travel of its citizens during the Covid-19 pandemic; and its Han ethnocentrism, which holds in greater regard the majority Han Chinese people over and above its minority cultures. The nationalist political climate in China has turned the country into an increasingly self-referential place where some foreign influences are becoming less welcomed, with Westerners trying to do business in China sometimes reporting frostier welcomes in recent years. Since Xi Jinping's rule in China began in 2013, the state has encouraged greater shows of domestic nationalism. China's repression of the pro-democracy protests that took place in Hong Kong in 2019–20 added further weight to the sense of China closing itself off.

The perils of walling one's nation off from all foreign innovations is well known to the Chinese. The final Chinese imperial dynasty, the Qing, collapsed in 1912 because it had studiously ignored the fast-moving outside world, whereas nearby Japan adopted enough Western innovations to later invade China. The current closed mentality in China is not as head-in-the-sand as the so-called Hermit Kingdom of North Korea, truly embracing its isolation from the Western-dominated world order. In the twentieth century, and even more so after the Cold War, it was potentially fatal to ignore the success of the West, and those who spurned their chance to learn from Western success often fell behind.

Westerners point to the comparative openness of their societies as offering a competitive advantage to China's closed-door mentality, even if countries like France, the UK and the US have their own assimilationist expectations and majoritarian cultures, and their own tense political debates around accepting immigrants, but only in certain numbers and in certain ways. The point still stands, however, which is that China is deeply uneasy with cultural fusion between its people and foreign, especially Western, influences. The Chinese government fears its populace questioning state-sponsored narratives on the basis of pro-democracy narratives from abroad. (Technological or industrial fusion involving the adoption of foreign technologies is another matter, and it is welcomed in the name of assisting China's economic rise.)

Mind you, Japan has also been resistant to foreigners integrating into its society, albeit not in an authoritarian way but by picking and choosing from the many fruits of globalisation (i.e., Japan has wholeheartedly enjoyed and proved highly adept at exploring the trading opportunities for importing the technologies it needed during its post-war recovery and subsequent economic growth, but it has resisted mass immigration despite its plummeting birth rates).

'Imitation is the sincerest form of flattery that mediocrity can pay to greatness,' Oscar Wilde is supposed to have said. Some Western-sceptics and implacable anti-Westerners still partake in the rampant hypocrisy of buying European luxury goods, buying properties in Europe and North America and also choosing to educate their children in the West – while still denouncing the West, sometimes using European languages to do so. The West still influences even those who dislike it. The question is for how long.

Paying tribute to Western-propagated markers of modern success is still a feature of how the world turns. As Fukuyama observed: 'If one needed proof of liberalism's positive impact as an ideology, one should look no further than the success of a series of states in Asia that went from being impoverished developing countries to developed ones in a matter of decades.' Gradual fusion with local proclivities was clear since 'Japan, South Korea, Taiwan, Hong Kong, and Singapore were not democracies during their high-growth periods, but they adopted key liberal institutions like protection of private property rights and openness to international traders to take advantage of the global capitalism system.'[9] These Asian success stories started in the last century. Mahbubani writes that 'One reason the West can no longer dominate the world is that the rest have learned so much from the West. They have imbibed many Western best practices in economic, politics, science, and technology.'[10]

The extent to which the Westernisation of political systems, institutions and social norms still hold wider appeal – and more vitally, whether they remain the keys to economic prosperity – is a more contested topic now than at any point in the post-World War Two and post-colonial eras. On this topic, one thing is already clear. Fusions of Western and non-Western influences will still define the coming era, but on terms that are increasingly less weighted to their Western ingredients. The real kicker for the predominance of Western influences will come as more parts of the non-Western world trade and interact increasingly with each other, ignoring Western preferences around who to ostracise, and learning directly from each other's examples. Moving from the Westfull to the Westless world, influences will meet and blend differently, creating the conditions for global exchanges of goods, ideas and peoples that slip ever further from the more exclusive grasp of the Western world.

5

Peak West

WHAT GOES UP must come down. Sir Isaac Newton's third law of motion is a phrase that finds itself applied to everything from the rise and fall of stock markets, to those moments of personal success that we wish would last forever but know cannot. Coming from the hard science of physics, theories of gravity remind us that the natural world is heavily governed by ironclad laws that are in principle open to prediction and calculation. Unlike apples falling from trees, however, past precedent is no predictor of future performance when it comes to changes in world order, which adds to the sense of uncertainty and risk when passing from one epoch to the next.

How can we guide our thinking? There are the softer social sciences to study the available data around political and economic trends. We have the humanities to better understand the relevant historical and cultural contexts. And we have the practical wisdom that can be gleaned from observing human behaviour in action. Even armed with this scholarly and practical wisdom, the best we can hope for is to study broad trajectories in world affairs with the full expectation of being blindsided by the future shocks that we never saw coming.

Given these limitations in our predictive powers, self-fulfilling prophecies are important parts of future thinking. The phrase tends to be used with financial markets in mind, where optimistic groupthink can have us keeping faith in certain things climbing upwards while collective panic can send things tumbling down. Something similar also applies to guessing and gauging the different possible outcomes for the future world order. Because we cannot know for sure, we are highly susceptible to persuasion. Our confidence in certain outcomes being likelier than others can be manipulated by clever arguments.

Just as with the stock market, by saying loudly and repeatedly that something is heading down into the doldrums, its descent becomes confirmed in people's minds; treating this outcome as a foregone conclusion, they will act accordingly. The inverse is true: by portraying something as a winning proposition, people flock towards it in the hope of sharing its spoils. We naturally like to be associated with success while giving failure a wide berth.

With this in mind, the *Economist* newspaper tried to calm Western nerves with its feature in 2023 heralding 'Peak China', illustrated by an exhausted-looking golden dragon rendered as a flatlining growth chart to portray China's economy as a busted flush. It also depicted President Xi riding a snail to point to China's slowing (but still impressive) economic growth rates. 'The country's historic ascent is levelling off', explained the *Economist*. 'The rise of China has been a defining feature of the world for the past four decades,' lifting many of its people out of abject poverty and making it the world's second largest economy behind the US. But 'whereas a decade ago forecasters predicted that China's GDP would zoom past America's during the mid-21st century (at market exchange rates) and retain a commanding lead, now a much less dramatic shift is in the offing, resulting in something closer to economic parity'.[1] Anyone anxious about China's seemingly unstoppable economic rise would have been relieved to read this and would be armed with the data and the arguments to persuade others accordingly.

This prediction was partly inspired by a book written by a pair of US political scientists. In *Danger Zone: The Coming Conflict with China*, Hal Brands and Michael Beckley argued that 'China will be a *falling* power sooner than most people think' because 'for more than a decade, China has been concealing a serious economic slowdown that existentially threatens the ruling regime.' Moreover, China is becoming isolated because 'the CCP has now violated the first rule of global politics for the past century: Don't make an enemy of the United States.'[2] Behind this baiting flourish, there were arguments of substance to consider.

The race to stop China overtaking the US and displacing it as a global hegemon will bother some of the brightest minds in Washington for a generation to come. Brands and Beckley wrote that 'China had it all – the mix of endowments and environment, peoples and policies to take off as a great power. But once-in-an-epoch windfalls don't last forever. During the past decade . . . many of the assets that once lifted the country up are fast becoming liabilities weighing it down,' before they list the reasons for China's impending economic doom: dire predictions of the impact of an ageing population on its further economic growth; a stiflingly autocratic political environment scaring domestic entrepreneurs, thus harming China's ability to innovate; and geopolitical tensions with the West that have encouraged multinational companies to relocate their supply chains away from China. As they asserted, 'building an Orwellian police state is hardly the hallmark of a vibrant economic superpower'.

A more sedate version of this prediction – 'Plateau China' – was articulated by the head of the EU's Chamber of Commerce in China when he completed his role in 2023. His plateau prediction was that for the next two decades China's economic prospects would be flat, forcing it to become more preoccupied with looking inwards and focused on alleviating the various factors stymieing its economic growth.[3] We do not yet know if China's future growth rates means that its economy has peaked or plateaued. Even if its population ages and declines somewhat in size, and its economic growth slows, China will be huge regardless, its rise already having had a transformative impact on how world order is evolving.

One of the consequences of these predictions is to associate China with a sense of failure and with a downward trajectory, encouraging the rest of us to bet against China and to cease being awed by its economic ascent. Predictions of this nature are standard fodder for jostling superpowers as rivals try to do each other down. They miss the far more interesting point: even if we have reached 'Peak China' or 'Plateau China' (which remains to be seen), we have also passed the moment of 'Peak Westernisation'. The US–China rivalry may well be the single most important geopolitical question of the twenty-first century, as we hear in the media or from politicians, but a complete picture only emerges when inquiring about the wider world too.

This is why the coming of a more multipolar world is the more significant development in which China's power is only one component of a more general rebalancing against Western influences. China's rise has galvanised other parts of the world to think afresh about their own national interests, cultures and unique histories, while also empowering them to reconsider their relations with the Western world – even if these other countries have no great affinity for China's government. These relations with the West, which were decidedly unbalanced for much of the last century of rising and peaking US hegemony – as they also were during the prior century of Europe's colonial empires – will be more readily rebalanced in the wake of China's rise. But crucially, this is not because China will alone lead the charge against the West.

China's leaders would surely love to take the lion's share of the credit for the rebalancing in world affairs. President Xi once declared China to be 'blazing a new trail for other developing countries to achieve modernisation'.[4] The other BRICS countries baulk at the idea of falling in rank behind China and the future is likely to be more multifaceted than Xi's sloganeering suggests. The framing offered by Singapore's former foreign minister George Yeo seemed more on the mark when he said 'China's rise will crystallise multipolarity by helping all the ships to rise.' Yeo argued that asking if China will 'take over the world' was the wrong question since China has never been globally hegemonic in the sense of conquering far beyond its immediate environs.[5] Kevin Rudd, himself a Sinologist, pointed to 'Beijing's decades-long advocacy of multipolarity as the preferred form of global governance'. Moscow too has long hankered for a 'poly-centric' world order, as has India. This is what the BRICS states are preparing for, rather than for a solely China-led new world order.

Even if China's rise slows down due to a combination of its internal limitations, and dedicated efforts by the US to trip it up, regardless, the world is becoming unrecognisable to what it was thirty or forty years ago. If we remain obsessed with the 'rise of China' above all else, we miss the biggest picture. Even 'rise of Asia' is too narrow: where does that leave the non-Asian BRICS countries and other emerging economies? What about Africa's leading countries and the future international allegiances of its growing populaces several decades from now?

The underlying trend is Westlessness, itself a hydra-headed set of phenomena that cannot be reversed entirely, and one that not even the gargantuan Chinese state will be able to harness for its own benefits. This is not simply the moment we have reached 'Peak China' – it is also the era of 'Peak West'.

* * *

There is no singular set of metrics by which to track changes in global power and influence. We are looking on the one hand at hard material power and on other hand at the appeal of ideas and the new possibilities of cultural diffusion. We are purposefully mixing apples and oranges, so to speak, in combining measurements that appear to have no complementary value as part of the overall equation of influence. This is the final part of the mindset for tracking Westlessness: *being open to mixing various indicators of influence.*

We want to build an intellectual scaffolding by combining qualitative and quantitative sources. Data and forecasts (quantitative) are essential. So are the political, moral and social justifications that have been invoked to explain, justify or condemn Western influence over the rest of the world (qualitative). Creativity is key in pulling it together into a compelling and convincing whole.

For inspiration in this undertaking, I have looked back to 1982, and reopened American author John Naisbitt's book, *Megatrends.* He identified and analysed several underlying trends driving the most salient changes in late-twentieth-century America (which was his focus). He presciently explained several developments that we take for granted today but were still in their infancy in 1982, like the US economy moving from factory production to the knowledge economy; and why people would rely less on the institutional help offered by authority figures like educators or the government by moving to a new era of consumer self-help. In his words:

> These larger patterns are not always clear. Helped by the news media, especially television, we seem to be a society of events, just moving from one incident sometimes even crisis to the next, rarely pausing (or caring) to notice the process going on underneath. Yet only by understanding the larger patterns, or restructurings, do the individual events begin to make sense. This book focuses on the

> megatrends or broad outlines that will define the new society. No one can predict the shape of that new world! Attempts to describe it in detail are the stuff of science fiction and futuristic guessing games that often prove inaccurate and annoying. The most reliable way to anticipate the future is by understanding the present.[6]

These are perennial truths when tracking the big trends of the day and sussing out the overall direction of travel, while spotting the possible tipping points that could speed up the process of change.

Westlessness is an aggregate underlying reality, and to some extent it will continue happening *anyway* regardless of whatever other events unfold. When we think of change and uncertainty, we think most immediately of the big newsworthy items that are affecting business, society and geopolitics, such as the technology revolutions in artificial intelligence, or US–China tensions. And we will continue to be stopped in our tracks by cataclysms such as Russia's invasion of Ukraine. So, it is a bold thing to say that *underlying all of this is the broader Westless drift.* We are talking about nothing less than the overall gradient of the world tilting and of this affecting how everything else is playing out.

Being bold is important but so is being humble about what cannot yet be gleaned. Even if we can expect a Westless drift, its form and shape is not an inevitability, nor is the speed of its onset since it will be hastened by some developments and slowed by others.

We are tracking multiple sub-trends, which implores us to ask – which are the trends that are shifting from Western control and influence in the quickest time frame? Or are they all slow-burning? Is the West holding on to its influence in some areas more than in others? These are the questions to be asking, and we will revisit them in the concluding chapter, at the end of our journey into the world of changing and declining Western influences.

An important caveat is necessary. No one can be a deep multidisciplinary expert in a dozen areas of study, and I certainly do not claim to be. In the chapters that follow, I rely on the published work and my own conversations with area specialists. Naisbitt encountered this problem and added his own caveat: 'I risk displeasing the experts and subject specialists who can argue that to take the leap of describing the world in terms of ten shifting categories [as per his selection] is too simplistic. In their way, they are probably right. Yet, I think it is worth the risk.' Some experts may be displeased with how I have approached analysing certain trends and may offer their own views on particular chapters, which I wholeheartedly welcome. Like Naisbitt, I'd rather take the risk of studying numerous sub-fields, gaining fresh insights by bringing several disparate trend lines together.

To close the circle on Naisbitt, he was also a keen observer of how dramatically the world had changed during his lifetime. When he wrote *Megatrends* in 1982, it seemed as though 'the driver of change was and would remain the US', something that was 'easy to accept for any American but also to embrace for Asians, especially the Chinese, as their orientation for progress was towards the West, mainly America. Even Western Europe, which never had too humble a mindset, accepted America's lead'. Overall, 'for the past 200 years, the West was the dominating region in the world. It was the driver of economic, cultural and technological advances. It also claimed the right to set standards in the business and political spheres.'[7]

This was surely a common perspective in the Westfull early 1980s, when the former Hollywood film star Ronald Reagan entered the Oval Office, and the US exhibited a new-found post-Vietnam War confidence in its brand of market economics, its global military machine, and its power to captivate the imaginations of swathes of the world's people with its cultural power.

A few years before Naisbitt died in 2021 at the grand old age of ninety-two, he co-authored a new book with his wife Doris, in which they reflected on what was to come:

> Western hegemony has been diminished from various directions . . . Its claim to own the global growth format of democracy and free markets is no longer sustainable. The Westerncentric world is fading into a multicentric world in which many countries and even a 'world of cities' will set the tone in global matters. It is a great opening up to a mix of opinions, of economic and cultural diversity and, in a longer time frame, new governing models. The game changers will be the countries of the Global Southern Belt, reshaping our world in decades to come [because they] have discovered that instead of being directed by the West they could just as well support each other.[8]

This offers up a worthy set of propositions to put to the test, and to carry on the study of the underlying trends governing the changing world. In the chapters to come, always keep in mind the ultimate aim of the exercise. We know that a great global rebalancing is already underway. What we don't yet know is the full span of what it entails and how far it will go.

* * *

It is not necessarily the strongest, but the ones most capable of changing when it is needed, who survive. Survival is only the minimum accomplishment. To actively thrive in an age of transition requires honing the senses to notice the most important changing circumstances. Or else, if we succumb to inertia, acting as if nothing is happening, or if we mistakenly believe that the essential trends can be reversed, then we risk suffering the obsolescence of holding outdated assumptions, and being left behind in a world of evolving balances of power and influence.

Only then can we engage in sensible discussions about whether our choices are in harmony with how the world is changing, or whether we are burying our head in the sand, like the proverbial ostrich, out of obstinacy and ignorance. This does not mean giving up on the West – it means reinventing some of our assumptions around what the West stands for and how its influence is felt.

For nations, questions of security and prosperity are the most essential. There is vast significance for governments when global power balances change: as patterns of global wealth and demography shift, the attention of governments will be devoted to horizon-scanning for new opportunities and threats, shoring up alliances and adjusting trading relationships to reflect newer realities.

For businesses with international reach, the consequences are also profound. The opening of different markets and the changing composition of customer bases will inevitably turn the heads of CEOs and their C-suite executives. Already, as geopolitical rivalries have intensified, many companies have had to reconsider how their global supply chains function.

For individuals who have a worldly outlook, preparing one's children or training younger people in other contexts for a changing global environment focuses the mind. There is nothing quite like seeing the world through the coming generation's eyes for pushing our own thinking far beyond the concerns of today, and becoming as intrigued as we ought to be about the future beyond our own lifetime.

Part Two

PEOPLE

6

Demography

> Asia continues to be the largest continent throughout the century but most population growth is taking place in Africa. By the end of the century most of the world's population will live on those two continents. Of the shifting rankings among the most populous countries, India is expected to overtake China in or around 2022. Nigeria will overtake the USA eventually, probably by 2050 . . . at that point Nigeria will become the third largest country in the world.
>
> Professor John Wilmoth, Director of the United Nations World Population Division[1]

STRENGTH IN NUMBERS is one part of achieving global influence. During the ascent of Western power, the European nations experienced big population growths and became exporters of their people to the Americas, Africa, Australasia and elsewhere. The demographic heft of the world will now reside far from the West. This is not automatically a boon for these countries. Fast-growing populations create pressures and without adequate development opportunities at home people become frustrated, resulting in migratory patterns as people move abroad to better themselves. This is precisely what poorer parts of Europe once experienced and what other regions now experience.

There is a striking headline message about the changing population balance between regions. As a percentage of the total human populace, the share of people in Western countries has been dropping markedly. Whereas in 1950, almost 30% of humanity lived in Europe, North America and Australasia, this is projected to drop to just 12% by 2050. In absolute numbers there will still be plenty of Westerners, but far fewer in relative terms. Rapid population growth in other regions, and ageing populations in the Western countries, provide the general explanation for this trend.

Behind this headline observation, the demographic destiny of our species conveys much about the less Western world. Demographers can highlight huge milestones for humanity, such as when, in April 2023, India's population matched the population of China at 1.4 billion before surpassing it. And by alerting us on 15 November 2022 that the world's population had reached 8 billion, meaning that it has more than tripled since 1950.[2] Over this span of time, improvements in the quality and availability of medicine and sanitation, in crop yields and in food distribution have reduced mortality rates and improved life expectancies, as generalised for our species as a whole (individual countries start from very different points and face their own ongoing challenges regarding food distribution and mortality).

Humanity is still growing at an incredible rate, albeit unevenly in different countries and regions. Astonishingly, as the world's population continues to rise, around half of this total projected growth up to 2050 is expected to occur in just *eight* countries: Democratic Republic of Congo, Egypt, Ethiopia, India, Nigeria, Pakistan, Philippines and Tanzania. Conversely, the demographic trends are heading in the opposite direction in Europe, North America and Japan. Populations in Eastern European countries, Italy and Japan are already ageing and shrinking, while other Western European countries have barely sustained their population sizes through immigration. The US's demography was once far healthier than Europe's, but in the last thirty years it has also aged considerably – its population can now only grow through immigration, which is a politically toxic matter for US politicians of all stripes. Hence a singular focus on China's ageing population (the key fact backing the 'Peak China' thesis, as discussed earlier) distorts our view of wider global demographic realities.

We know much of this thanks to the United Nations World Population Division. Established in 1946 and initially tasked with studying populations in large regions, it started projecting the populations for select individual countries in 1968 by using their census data. It has since expanded its data set to cover the world, allowing us to make historical comparisons between countries and regions.

Demographers are masters of a complex profession, grappling with estimations involving huge orders of magnitude while also conducting precise analysis of current population data. The UN Population Division can project population trends into the immediate future with high confidence. Near-term projections are more certain because the fertility rate and current age profile of countries provide a solid basis for calculations. The 'replacement rate' is understood as being the average number of births per female that is required to sustain the population, and the replacement rate varies between countries based on its levels of development, infant mortality rates and suchlike.

Demographers can only make speculative projections into the far future. Consider the UN projection for overall population growth, which estimates that from our current 8 billion people there will be 8.5 billion of us by 2030; and 9.7 billion around 2050; with humanity reaching its peak in the 2080s at around 10.4 billion people, before remaining at around this size for the rest of the century.[3]

The French economist Thomas Piketty cast healthy scepticism on placing excessive faith in such projections since 'No one at this point can seriously claim to know what demographic turnaround may occur in the twenty-first century. It would therefore be presumption to regard the official UN prediction as anything other than a "central scenario".' But, Piketty added, 'the central scenario is nevertheless the most plausible, given the present state of our knowledge.'[4] Professor John Wilmoth, who has led the UN World Population Division since 2013, offered a similar observation: 'obviously there's a lot of uncertainty in the last few decades of these predictions', he reflected with the 2080s in mind.[5]

The UN projections provide a statistical basis for examining changing regional balances. As of 2022 the most populous regions were Eastern and South Eastern Asia, which contain 2.3 billion people (29% of humanity) and South and Central Asia with 2.1 billion (26%). Since China and India each have 1.4 billion people, they account for the lion's share of people in these regions. Up to 2050, sub-Saharan African countries will contribute to over half of all population increase and will account for a growing share of the world population up to 2100. Conversely:

> Europe and Northern America is projected to reach its peak population size and to begin experiencing population decline in the late 2030s due to sustained low levels of fertility, which has been below 2 births per woman since the mid-1970s and, in some countries, high emigration rates. [Hence in] the next three decades, the regions of the world will experience different growth rates of their populations. Consequently, the regional distribution of the population in 2050 will significantly differ from that of today.[6]

Asia has always been highly populous, but whereas North America, Europe and Australasia still constituted a very sizeable chunk of humanity until around 1950, their share has since been totally dwarfed by faster-growing sizes of Asia's and Africa's populations. In 2022, Europe, North America and Australasia collectively represented 14.5% of world populace. Using the UN's 'medium scenario', in 2030, these regions collectively drop to 13.7%, and by 2050, they are projected to account for just 12% of world population – hence the striking hundred-year trend, because back in 1950, the Western countries constituted 28.5% of the world's population.[7]

Although some Western countries may sustain their population sizes, or manage only marginal declines, on aggregate the most populous regions of the future will be located elsewhere. Let us put more context around what these headline population trends mean for changing Western influence.

***

Demographic history gives us a fresh perspective on humanity's successive eras. Populations flourished initially around rivers, the wellsprings of life. Ancient civilisations thrived around the Nile, Tigris and Euphrates rivers in North Africa and the Middle East, the Indus and Ganges rivers in India, and the Yangtze and Yellow rivers in China. Agricultural societies harnessed these waterways for irrigation and crop growth, boosting the human population into the tens of millions before the Common Era (BCE). By the start of the Common Era (CE) humanity had grown to hundreds of millions, but even around 1500, population growth remained slow compared to modern standards due to high death rates.

It was not until around 1800 that humanity reached 1 billion, thanks to developments like better agricultural yields resulting in more food and better hygiene in water supplies. The second billion was reached around 1930, and as sociologist Gregg Lee Carter explains, the twentieth century saw 'less developed places importing and acquiring in a few decades the death-controlling technologies (public sanitation, vaccinations, agricultural improvements) that had taken more developed nations centuries to create'. Thereafter, humanity has grown rapidly, reaching its third billion by 1960 and then adding a further 1 billion people roughly every decade (these benchmarks were reached as follows: 4 billion by 1974; 5 billion by 1987; 6 billion by 1999; 7 billion by 2011; and 8 billion in 2022).[8] Europe was a driving force in these earlier growth phases but is playing an increasingly back-seat role today.

Urbanisation was the key to early population growth. In ancient times, city dwellers relied on agricultural surpluses to be fed, and early cities in Asia and Mesopotamia thrived thanks to water sources that facilitated strong crop yields. Eighteenth- and nineteenth-century Europe took this to new heights as its industrialisation boosted agricultural production, in turn feeding faster urbanisation. Although cities faced the challenges of crime and cleanliness, they fostered productivity by concentrating greater numbers of people in close proximity. The division of labour allowed a greater range of individual abilities to be harnessed for efficiency in big cities, while economies of scale allowed urban populations to develop collective systems of resource utilisation and become more productive.[9]

As Western Europe enjoyed first-mover advantage with industrialised urbanisation, its labour demands grew. So did its propensity to export people globally. Having already mastered oceanic travel through sail, the Europeans later harnessed steam- and coal-powered vessels in their empire-building. European migration and settlement around the world became a defining trend from the eighteenth until the early twentieth century. Europe's flourishing populations also had the means to travel globally.

Company-states like the English EIC and the Dutch VOC had already sent Europeans abroad in large numbers. For instance, the VOC recruited not only Dutch but also German, Irish, English and Scottish for service in places like Indonesia where it sent an estimated 1 million Europeans to run its operations.[10] Not all these recruits settled permanently, but the taps had already been opened to global flows of Europeans who travelled to make their profits in plantations around the world.

This migratory flow became a torrent as Europe's population grew and grew. Massimo Livi Bacci, a professor of demography, has explained that 'between 1750 and 1850, European population growth accelerated. The annual rate of growth, barely 0.15% between 1600 and 1750, grew to 0.63% between 1750 and 1850.' This was despite the devastation wrought to Europe by Napoleon's wars, in the 1816–17 famine, and by outbreaks of typhus and cholera that ravaged Europe; its population growth remained so vigorous, and the opportunities at home so few, that more and more Europeans opted to leave. As Bacci summed up, 'the migration of tens of millions of people from Europe to transoceanic destinations' involved the movements of people 'from a continent rich in manpower and poor in land to regions rich in land and poor in human resources'.[11]

The spread of its people massively expanded Europe's global influence. Historian Ronald Hyam explained that 'one of the main features of nineteenth century world history was the populating by Europeans of large territories: Australia, the Mississippi Valley, Brazil, the Canadian prairies. By 1900 two-thirds of the English-speaking peoples lived outside Europe.'[12] The overall rates of Europeans emigrating from their continent continued to pick up, with an estimated 2 million leaving in the 1860s, 3 million in the 1870s and 8 million in the 1880s.[13]

There were numerous reasons for these migrations, such as the Irish fleeing the potato famine in the mid-nineteenth century by travelling to the US. Italians with poor prospects would have been tempted by cruise liner companies offering tickets to the Americas for newer opportunities. Vintage posters encouraging emigration can be seen in the maritime museum in Genoa, where it explains that 'Italy in 1861 is a rural country, poor and backward' and 'after the Unity of Italy migration involves not only young men but also all the families. Families sell their land to buy a ticket for a new, unknown, future.' In 1876, Argentina decided to attract more Italian workers to boost its economy and offered incentives that resulted in 2 million Italians settling there by 1914. When Brazil ended the formal slavery of non-whites in 1888, its demand for voluntary workers grew, and Italians were encouraged to emigrate there en masse with free family tickets.

Most of these emigrating Europeans hardly lived lives of luxury, but the overall trend was clear – Europeans were settling globally in larger numbers than ever before. Bacci explained the scale of this:

> The following are estimates for European transoceanic migration between 1846 and 1932 from the major countries of departure: 18 million from Britain and Ireland, 11.1 million from Italy, 6.5 million from Spain and Portugal, 5.2 million from Austria-Hungary, 4.9 million from Germany, 2.9 million from Poland and Russia, and 2.1 million from

> Sweden and Norway . . . Between 1861 and 1961, net Italian population loss due to emigration was 8 million.[14]

In addition to Europe's own poor travelling far and wide, Europeans played a commanding role in voluntary and forced migrations of other peoples. Four hundred years of the trans-atlantic slave trade forced an estimated 12 million Africans to North America, the Caribbean and South America. In the colonial era, indentured labourers were moved between different parts of maritime empires, such as in Asia, where the Portuguese and British moved Indian, Chinese and Malay merchants and workers across the Indian Ocean and when the British moved Indians (including my ancestors) to East Africa. Not only were Europeans migrating far and wide, but their industrialised economies and militarised colonies were dictating the migrations of other peoples too. White settlement was prized above other migrations. In North America and Australasia, indigenous populations were subdued and often killed as these continents were turned into European offshoots. All over the world where European settlement took root, local populations dropped down the pecking order of privilege, were involuntarily removed or, in some disastrous cases, subjected to slaughter.[15]

Modern migratory trends hence represent a full-circle moment in history. Take the example of France: whereas its past colonialism involved French settlers, civil servants and soldiers emigrating to its African colonies, the migration flow reversed when France recruited labourers and soldiers from Africa in the early twentieth century. Later in the twentieth century, after its colonies gained independence, European soldiers and officials moved back to their countries of origin, and scores of African-born descendants of the colonial settlers came with them, followed by economic migrants searching out their own opportunities in France and across the European continent.

Since the end of colonisation, many former subjects and their descendants have headed to the old imperial metropolises. Britain received people from South Asia, East Africa, Hong Kong and the Caribbean; France received Algerians, Moroccans and Vietnamese; the Dutch received Indonesians; and so on. Europe was a huge exporter of people from around 1600 until the early twentieth century, but since the 1950s it has needed to import people.[16] In 2010, the EU absorbed 1.2 million migrants and the figure was 2.3 million in 2021. When you also account for rising Central and South American emigration to the US, which is driven by the pursuit of greater economic opportunities in North America, all of this is part of the West's changing relationship with the rest of the world, different versions of which are being experienced on both sides of the Atlantic.

* * *

What does a demographic decline feel like? Statistics can be abstract and it is not until you wander around somewhere with an ageing population that you visibly notice the lack of younger people. While travelling through Japan with my young family, I found another indicator: buying infant nappies and baby food in cities like Tokyo, Osaka and Kyoto can be a challenge. Many shops and even supermarkets don't stock these items in abundance since the demand just isn't there. Japan's birth rate experienced its seventh consecutive year of decline in 2022 (Japan's health ministry reported the fertility rate as 1.2565 – far lower than the rate of 2.07 necessary to maintain its population size).[17] This is what Europe, North America, Japan and China all have in common: highly industrialised developed countries with falling birth rates. To take another example, Canada's birth rate had dropped to 1.4 by 2020.

The process driving changes in population size and age profile is the 'demographic transition'. All countries experience it, starting from when they tend to have larger families with low life expectancy, and transitioning to smaller families with high life expectancy. As countries experience this transition, their demographic profile changes. Populations fall in size when gains in life expectancy, achieved through better medical care, diets and lifestyle, can no longer compensate for the falling birth rate, and when migration is insufficient to bridge the gap. The speed at which this occurs varies, and in some places, it takes a long time, such as in Western Europe, where it occurred over hundreds of years. In other places it is compressed into shorter time frames, such as in China and Africa.[18]

An ageing population means reproduction is occurring at or below replacement levels. Fertility is the engine of population growth, and if demographers know how many women there are in a country between fifteen and forty-nine years of age, and they also understand the fertility rate (the average number of births a woman will have over her lifetime), calculations can be made around replacement-level fertility.

Younger populations enjoy a built-in momentum for future growth. Migration also boosts fertility since younger people tend to be the ones to migrate in the greatest numbers.[19]

As Professor Wilmoth explained, 'Growth happens because we control the death rate. We extend life and we keep people alive – children don't die in childhood and women don't die in pregnancy,' whereas 'what causes the growth to slow down, that's the reduction in the fertility level. People come to perceive for a variety of reasons that there isn't the motivation to have really large families.' A couple that has two children who survive their parents will only replace themselves and contribute to zero growth. There are numerous reasons for having fewer children, such as the rising economic costs of doing so, and as the position of women in society changes. People delay starting families by a few years in order to secure better education and increase their value in the workplace.[20]

Whereas Europe and its North American offshoots experienced their rapid population growths a long time ago and have since seen the process go into reverse as birth rates fall, Asia and Africa are at very different stages of their demographic transitions, with their high birth rates resulting in population explosions in the last hundred years. For example, Egypt had 10 million people in the early 1900s and now has almost 110 million. Nigeria had about 20 million people a century ago and is now well over 200 million strong. Whereas the sharp population rise experienced by the US, from 3 million in the 1780s to over 300 million today, was driven by migrations from Europe and the slave trade from Africa, the modern growth of Asian and African populations has resulted from domestic births exceeding deaths.[21]

All populations age, and even in sub-Saharan Africa, the average age of populations has drifted upwards, albeit from a very young median age. Some predict that Africa's population growth will be much lower than the UN projections, but these predictions are based on population surveys, whereas the UN demographers analyse data and draw a median line. 'If you have a certain age structure you can predict with accuracy the future of a population,' an officer at the UN Population Division explained to me, before reiterating that 'the demographic future belongs to Africa even if we are off by some way' in estimating the precise rate of population growth.[22]

What do these demographic realities suggest about a world of changing Western influence? The demographic expansion that drove European settlement is clearly over, and the contending trends in global demography are in all likelihood irreversible. Most obviously, the West and its closest allies are becoming a less numerically significant portion of the human populace. In the Western democracies, social trends and changing economies drove these changes, whereas in China, it was state-imposed policy.

China only officially ended its one-child policy in January 2016. Chinese authorities stuck with the policy after warning lights were flashing (much like its Covid lockdowns, the Chinese government shows a clear liking of stringent social controls). China's one-child policy was introduced in 1980 as a reaction to a population of 800 million and famines in the recent past. India also tried a forced sterilisation policy in the 1970s for men after fathering three children, but only Maharashtra passed the law, and the backlash helped to oust

Indira Gandhi from office. Around the 1960s, discussions around population control to ensure economic growth and political stability in the developing world gained more traction.[23]

For China, to continue its economic growth and to sustain its growing geopolitical ambitions while managing its changing demography will be a challenge. One estimate suggests that, by 2050, China may have 500 million people over the age of sixty, which will burden its working-age population. The effect will be magnified because Chinese working culture has stigmatised people who work beyond sixty. The current low retirement age and associated social norms will have to change to accommodate an ageing population.[24] Even if China's population drops and stabilises at 1.3 billion, there will still be more people in China than in the Western countries combined.

The demographic component of Westlessness is a bigger matter than China's ageing population, as other non-Western populations will grow significantly. The gap in population size between China and India will only grow. Uttar Pradesh is India's most populous state with 200 million – far more than Guangdong, China's most populous province with 126 million. These numbers are mind-boggling, with these regions containing more people than most countries. Urbanisation and massive rural-to-city migration have been major catalysts for population change.

What use is huge population growth if countries lack the means to provide for these people? Unfettered population growth is a source of weakness and what matters is absorbing and turning this population into an economic asset. Good government institutions, economic opportunities, education, domestic development and more is needed to cater for growing populations. Conversely, a country that cannot develop the infrastructure to handle many more people faces immense burdens.[25] Emerging economies with the governance and economic strength to ensure these people are absorbed productively will race ahead of the others.

***

The demographic weight of global influence increasingly resides outside the West. The largest consumer markets, the most common tastes and preferences, and the dominant geographical and historical reference points, will change as the weight of world population shifts further to the east and south of the world map.

In the coming decades, the rankings of the biggest countries will be reordered due to different population growth rates. We can anticipate big changes out to 2050: Japan is projected to drop down the rankings and Germany to drop out of the top twenty most populous countries, leaving no European country in the list and the US the only Western country in the rankings.[26]

Does it matter that most of the world's most populous countries of the future had emerged in their modern form after being colonies of the Western countries? This includes India, Nigeria, Pakistan, Democratic Republic of Congo, Bangladesh, Egypt, Philippines, Tanzania, Vietnam, Uganda, Kenya, all of which are expected to be in the top twenty by 2050. Western colonisation in the twentieth century defined the modern circumstances of each of these countries. You have to travel back to the nineteenth century for Mexico's and Brazil's freedom from Spain and Portugal respectively, while the USA's freedom from British rule came in the eighteenth century. Russia, Japan, Iran and Türkiye have their own imperial histories, eventually being on the losing end against Western challengers.

A greater share of the world's population than before will reside in nations with historical memories and national stories forged in part through complex and sometimes bloody past interrelations with the West, while at the same time owing at least something to the West for facilitating aspects of their modernisation since then. Such a mixed-up story leads to complex feelings and relations. Some people in the non-Western world hold benign or favourable opinions of the West, with the most Westernised among them happily so in their tastes and habits, their Western influences forming one layer of their multilayered identities. Others may have love–hate relationships with the West, while others may be more accepting of out-and-out rejectionists of Westernisation, and be able to do so with numbers on their side.

Another set of implications is explored by Mauro Guillen of Cambridge University's Judge Business School, who explained that by 'around 2030 Asian markets, even excluding Japan, will be so large that the centre of gravity of global consumption will shift eastward. Companies will have no choice but to follow market trends in that part of the world, with most new products and services reflecting the preferences of Asian consumers.' As Europe, North America and East Asia experience fast-declining birth rates, while Africa,

South Asia, South East Asia and the Middle East do not, this rebalances the world's economic and geopolitical power. 'Consider: For every baby born in developed countries, more than nine are being born in the emerging markets and the developing world.' As the world population is distributed differently around the globe, patterns of consumption will also evolve. 'The US and Europe house the majority of the world's middle class now, but by 2030, China, India, and the rest of Asia (excluding Japan) will be home to more than half of global consumer purchasing power.'[27]

For the West, there is a rather abstract question to consider. What does it mean to belong to a minority of the world's populace? This is an intangible question since our sense of the relative numeracy of our kin is derived at the community and regional levels, by seeing those around us rather than by consulting the data. Even country-level population statistics can remain intangible, let alone continental- and global-level headcounts. Right-wing populists in Western countries play on tropes about those that they are appealing to being 'outnumbered' by immigrants, especially in big cities, even if the statistics do not necessarily bear this out.

Zooming out from the parochial European and American populists to the global level, purely in statistical terms, it is true that to be Western will mean something very different in the future than in the past. Barring some kind of major civilisation-altering event, there will be no way to turn these trends around. With Westerners dropping in percentage terms from making up nearly three in ten of people in the 1950s to closer to one in ten after the 2050s, other things will start to change too, as we are about to see.

The numbers game is not everything. Quality in living conditions, access to technology, stability of societies, cleanliness of air and suchlike is what makes a place fulfilling to live in. Quantity cannot be dismissed, however. Civilisational strength comes in many forms, but strength in numbers, with youth and vigour, has its own virtues.

7

Lingua Franca

> As we seek to forge new and deeper relationships with other countries worldwide, will there be demand for a wider range of world languages? And crucially: will our future international partnerships be determined by the extent to which other countries are willing and able to use English as a medium of communication?
>
> British Council, *Languages for the Future*, 2017[1]

HAVE YOU TRIED to learn a challenging new language in adulthood? It can be a painstaking endeavour as grasping a brand-new vocabulary renders us into using truncated childlike expositions. All but the most committed students look for shortcuts. Translation apps on our mobile devices that are powered by artificial intelligence may obviate our need to fully master other languages. No matter the sophistication of the translation technology soon to come, the following remains true.

The languages we inherit – and the languages we dream in – animate our imaginations. They give substance to our cultural self-identification. And they allow us to access certain concepts and idioms that might reflect certain cultural proclivities over others. Changing patterns of language usage can duly inform our understanding of the evolving Westless world.

The languages that people are likeliest to speak in the future mirror our fast-changing world: enduringly shaped by the West while increasingly diversifying from its influence. English currently remains the language with the most non-native speakers worldwide whereas Mandarin has the greatest number of native speakers, albeit concentred in China. This is not the only competition that matters. Future AI-powered interpretation tools may in fact embed the role of the Western languages – most notably English – as the global lingua franca, providing some people with new incentives not to learn other complex and widely spoken languages like Mandarin or Hindi. When it comes to languages, Westlessness may be held at bay for now.

England can legitimately claim to have bequeathed a common tongue to the four corners of the world. The British have much to thank the US for: passing the torch to the *Pax Americana* has preserved English as a language of global exchange. For many non-native speakers, an increasingly Americanised English has been their language of study, business, pop culture, globalisation and mutual comprehension with others. 'It is the language in which the Brazilians speak to the Dutch and the Japanese speak to the Italians,' wrote Rosemary Salomone in *The Rise of English*. Indeed, there are far more non-native English speakers than native speakers. 'Of the 1.5 billion of the Earth's population who speak English, fewer than 400 million (less than 25%) use it as their first language,' she notes, because English has become 'an economic skill, a marketable commodity and a form of cultural capital.' However, this apparent advantage is a double-edged sword: 'The unstoppable spread of English is not a win-win for Anglophone countries. It's isolating them in a way that harms their economic and political interests'.[2]

This is an intriguing thought and one that will be put further to the test in a less Western world. The use of English on every continent, alongside other widely spoken European-origin languages like French, Spanish and Portuguese, owe their initial spread to the colonial past. English has outstripped them all thanks to American-led globalisation.

This question piqued the concern of the British Council, an organisation that promotes the UK and the English language globally by providing learning opportunities to non-native speakers. The year after the British public voted for Brexit – a nativist turn in which the UK cold-shouldered the European continent by leaving the EU – the British Council published its 'Languages for the Future' report. It posed tough questions of the British 'as individuals, as a nation or in business' because 'without language skills', it warned, Britain risked both 'a failure to appreciate that other cultures have different ways of doing things and a potential tendency to overestimate the global importance of British culture'. It reported that only just over one in three Britons could hold a conversation in another language.[3]

Questioning Anglophone complacency was a welcome far cry from the following notorious passage in Thomas Babington Macaulay's 'Minute on Education'. Delivered on 2 February 1835 – at the end of the Georgian era, just as Britain became the world's biggest empire – Macaulay argued that teaching in Indian schools should be delivered in English. His rationale reads shockingly today:

> I have no knowledge of either Sanscrit or Arabic. But I have done what I could to form a correct estimate of their value. I have read translations of the most celebrated Arabic and Sanscrit works. I have conversed, both here and at home, with men distinguished by their proficiency in the Eastern tongues. I am quite ready to take the oriental learning at the valuation of the orientalists themselves. I have never found one among them who could deny that a single shelf of a good European library was worth the whole native literature of India and Arabia [and] when we pass from works of imagination to works in which facts are recorded and general principles investigated, the superiority of the Europeans becomes absolutely immeasurable.[4]

Macaulay was a leading politician of his day, beset by the biases of two centuries ago. The British have thankfully come a long way from his views. But Anglophones still tend to be complacent because when the wider world learns your language, you don't need to bother learning theirs. Needs must, however: as global wealth moves elsewhere and demographics shift, so must our assumptions around languages.

In the US, the increasing prominence of Spanish has created its own momentum for linguistic diversity. By 2050, it is estimated that one in three people in the US will speak Spanish due to immigration from South and Central America adding to the already substantial populace with Hispanic roots. According to a US Census Bureau report, 'the number of people who spoke a language other than English at home nearly tripled from 23.1 million (about one in ten) in 1980 to 67.8 million (almost one in five) in 2019', with Spanish being the most common non-English language spoken in US homes.[5] According to a Pew survey, 75% of US Latinos reported being able to speak Spanish fairly well or very well. Even more considered it important for the US Latinos of the future to speak Spanish. Non-Spanish-speaking Hispanics also reported being 'shamed by other Hispanics for not speaking Spanish'.[6] Whether domestic bilingualism translates into more informed engagements between the US and Latin America, let alone with the wider world, is uncertain.

In countries like France, Sweden and Germany, learning English remains the principal second language, vital to participating fully in the Anglophone West. These Europeans will be better able to empathise with non-native English speakers of the world regarding the trickiness of mastering English. The flip side is the angst within the institutions of the EU around the predominance of English as a working language, and the struggle for the EU authorities in Brussels to recruit sufficient numbers of interpreters and translators to diversify the EU's working languages.

The global success of English cannot be assumed as guaranteed into the future. One provocative argument posits that English will one day suffer the fate of Latin, as the one-time dominant language that becomes obsolete after the empire that spread it has crumbled.[7] Alongside Latin, also consider the varying fates of Greek, Sanskrit and Arabic. Latin and Sanskrit remain languages of deep learning and are foundational to modern tongues, but they are no longer in everyday use. Greek is now confined to its country of origin. Conversely, Arabic, with its innate connection to Islam, remains in use across Africa, the Middle East and Asia. Of these fates, English will clearly endure in the Anglosphere, which is defined by its usage, as it will elsewhere in the West – but some parts of the world outside the West may experience changes in their relationship with the English language in the coming decades.

* * *

The six official languages of the UN are Arabic, English, French, Mandarin, Russian and Spanish.[8] Their selection reflects the world a century ago. When the UN was founded in 1948, the British and French empires still covered huge swathes of the world. The UN's official languages still map reasonably well onto a modern list of the world's most spoken languages but the big mismatches are clear. Why not include Hindi, the third most spoken language in the world?

The rankings are compiled by Ethnologue to include people who speak these languages as their native tongue or as their second languages, showing *total usage* worldwide.[9] The rankings remind us of India's linguistic diversity, given that five languages widely spoken in India aside from English appear in the top twenty.

The rankings are different when tallying languages by the greatest number of *native speakers* only. A native speaker has learned this language first – it may not be the only one they speak, but it is their primary language of first learning and of linguistic inheritance. Mandarin Chinese has by far the most native speakers, with Spanish in second place, and Hindi not far behind English. This measure is a useful adjunct to the *most overall speakers* tally, illustrating the relative size of the core linguistic group from which the language has diffused.

Many of us use language tuition apps like Duolingo, and the company running the app offers another perspective on language learning trends. Duolingo published an annual report that analysed the language choices of its global user base of over 500 million language learners in 2022. Its top ten most studied languages around the world on its app were English, Spanish, French, German, Japanese, Italian, Korean, Chinese, Russian and Hindi. Duolingo found that:

> In 2022, the number of countries studying English as the first or second most popular language was basically unchanged (130 total in 2021 and 131 in 2022) . . . The number of countries studying Spanish as a top language dropped overall (81 in 2022 vs. 90 in 2021), while French increased from a top ranking in 90 countries last year to 96 . . . Because English, Spanish, and French are so dominant around the world, interesting trends emerge when we consider the second most popular languages studied in each country.[10]

The ranking for second most popular languages included French in 74 countries; Spanish in 47; German in 16; Japanese in 12; English in 11; Korean in 7; Chinese in 6; Russian in 5; Italian in 3; and Arabic, Danish, Finnish, Hindi, Irish, Norwegian and Swahili in one country each.

Duolingo is far from a perfect measure of language learning trends, since it has more downloads in some countries than others (Vietnam was apparently its tenth biggest user market at the time of this report), but its insights are useful into persisting European-origin language influence around the world. In principle, this makes cultural products and messages of Western origins comprehensible and potentially appealing in their original form to many people around the world. Mastery or even a partial grasp of the languages of the Western world are the basis of forging cultural connections with Westerners.

Conversely, there appears to be a lower uptake in people learning Mandarin or Hindi outside of the broader Chinese and Indian global cultural communities. Learning Mandarin has for the last two decades been considered a ticket for accessing Chinese-centric global business opportunities. Latterly, the escalating geopolitical tensions between China and other countries (not only Western, but also Japan, South Korea, India and others) has reduced the perceived appeal for some people of putting in the immense time commitment required to fully master Mandarin. Confucius Institutes were set up by China's authorities as cultural centres for teaching Mandarin globally. But they have been accused of peddling Chinese propaganda by Western countries and some were duly shut down. They have had more success in countries that receive high levels of Chinese investment. For instance, between 2003 and 2018, the number of people in Africa studying Mandarin rose from 1,800 to over 81,500. In 2020, Mandarin started being officially taught in Kenyan schools as a language option, as it was in Uganda in 2018 and in South Africa in 2014.[11] Language learning trends are never static but the European-origin languages are showing no evidence yet of waning in their wider appeal compared to the alternatives. Can we assume that this will continue in perpetuity?

* * *

European languages became embedded in every continent as languages of settlement and assimilation, while traditional languages continued to be used in more familiar contexts. After the 1500s, thanks to European mastery of transoceanic commerce and settlement, 'the sea becomes the main thoroughfare of language advance, and its spread can be global', observed the historian of languages Nicholas Ostler. With the consolidation of European empires in the 1800s, linguistic dominance became indistinguishable from military and commercial power. This altered again in the 1900s as telegraphs, radio and TV meant native speakers no longer needed to migrate en masse to ensure their languages were used remotely.[12]

With these origins in mind, we can pose two more questions: will the utility of European origin languages continue to trend upwards? And can their usage still be considered a synonym for Western influence – or have they outgrown and transcended their originators?

Portuguese is only trending upwards in usage because of Brazil, where most of its 214 million people use it as their first language. Hence, roughly 90% of the world's native Portuguese speakers reside in Brazil, offering a clear example of a former colony outstripping its former coloniser as the primary language user, since Portugal's populace is just 10.4 million.[13] Angola, Mozambique, Goa, Cape Verde, Guinea Bissau, São Tomé and Príncipe, and Timor-Leste make up the remainder of Portuguese speakers, a lasting testimony to Portugal's old imperial outposts.

Spanish has 475 million native speakers worldwide and official status in twenty-one countries (Argentina, Bolivia, Chile, Colombia, Costa Rica, Cuba, Dominican Republic, Ecuador, El Salvador, Equatorial Guinea, Guatemala, Honduras, Mexico, Nicaragua, Panama, Paraguay, Peru, Uruguay, Venezuela, Spain and Puerto Rico). Mexico's 130 million populace accounts for a quarter of all Spanish native speakers, and the US's 42 million Spanish speakers for nearly 10%. After Catalan is taken into account, Spain has similar numbers of native Spanish speakers to the US! Spain's empire began falling apart 200 years ago, and since then the Spanish language has fully transcended its European roots.

Not all colonisers were language spreaders. The Dutch were largely indifferent to spreading cultural influence in this way and used existing Malay languages in the East Indies and Malacca to foster trade and to supply slaves. Bahasa Indonesia (an evolution of the Malay language) remains in official use in Indonesia, even if more Indonesians speak Javanese. Dutch is the official language in Suriname and a few Caribbean islands, and an evolved version of Dutch – Afrikaans – exists in South Africa. For such a significant historic empire, the global imprint of the Dutch language was relatively small.[14]

French colonisers had no such hesitance. To say the French are proud of their language – its poetry, its expressiveness, its artistry – is understatement par excellence. Breaking out in French was once a sign of culture and worldliness (recall Russian writer Leo Tolstoy's frequent use of French phrases in *War and Peace*). From the seventeenth until the twentieth century, French was the language of diplomacy but today, French does not numerically dominate the EU, where German has the more native speakers when Austria, Switzerland, Liechtenstein, Luxembourg and the regions of Alsace-Lorraine and Tyrol are included.[15]

The future global heft of the French language is now reliant on French-speaking Africa. Its past assimilation of its colonised peoples involved spreading the French language, where it remains in use in numerous ex-French colonies.[16] The Organisation Internationale de la Francophonie (OIF) promotes comity in the Francophone world.[17] Of the big four European-origin languages with global usage, France is the only country not yet outranked numerically for its native speakers by a single former colony (Brazil dwarfs Portugal; Mexico dwarfs Spain; and the US dwarfs Britain). However, France's purported leadership of Francophone countries remains controversial.[17]

'All colonised people,' wrote Frantz Fanon in *Black Skin, White Masks*, 'position themselves in relation to the language of the civilising nation: i.e. the metropolitan culture.'[18] Global networks of culture, business and education as afforded by Europe's languages live on after colonisation. To the extent these benefits wane, we may see changes in the global uptake of the European languages – but this does not appear imminent for English, Spanish, Portuguese and French. Conversely, due to unfavourable demographics, the usage of Italian, Russian and Japanese has trended downwards.

Italy's populace has shrunk in the 2000s, while Italian native speakers in the US, Argentina and elsewhere in Europe are not numerous enough to cover the gap. Japanese has dropped out of the world top ten of usage and will shrink to closer to 120 million native speakers as the decade progresses, and the cataclysmic end of Japan's empire meant it never embedded as a language of mass usage in other parts of Asia.[19] Whereas Russian spread through its Tsarist and Soviet empires, fertility rates in Russia and Belarus are now below replacement level, and the Central Asian states are becoming prey to China's economic influence. Moreover, Russia has clearly ended its language's growth potential in Ukraine.

The prevalence of Arabic across many centuries as the language of Islam, and through its many dialects, has provided a strong cultural protection against Westernisation.[20] The Chinese language also provided insulation in the era of Western dominance to its native speakers, which number over 1.2 billion in China, Singapore and Taiwan (with some 45 million people using Cantonese, another Chinese language). The Sanskritic languages of South Asia (Hindi, Bengali, Urdu, Marathi, Gujarati, etc.) and those with Dravidian roots (Telugu and Tamil) have huge communities of speakers too, and even if it is difficult to predict the future of language usage in fifty or a hundred years from now, these are all growing populations.[21]

English, by far the language champion of Westernisation, seems to have an assured future, but its usage has very likely already peaked as a first language – which means future expansions in its usage depends on continual uptake among non-native speakers as a second language.

Many people have adopted English and made it local with pidgins, hybrids and creoles. Singapore has its own pidgin, Singlish, replete with exclamations like 'Lah', which others must learn. There are also Spanglish and Hinglish, both of them hybrids. Rather than unsuccessful attempts to speak English, they are simplified and truncated versions of English for non-native speakers to become partially conversant. By contrast, *creole* languages (adapted from a French word for 'indigenous') are distinct from the languages they derived some of their words from. For instance, languages in the British West Indies are creoles, like Jamaican patois. Languages evolve and fuse, and European-origin languages can sometimes lose their European connection over time.[22]

In India, English retains official recognition alongside Hindi. A certain Indian upper class has picked up where the Raj left off by remaining attached to English, even at the expense of Hindi in some cases. However, Modi's nationalist BJP government has tended to spurn English as part of its nationalist leaning. It was telling that in 2023, Prime Minister Modi started insisting that the very name 'India' should be replaced with the Hindi name of the country 'Bharat', even when mentioning it in English.

There are those who still interpret the spread of the English language as a bellwether for human progress. A curious publication entitled the 'English Proficiency Index' correlates English language mastery in every country to governance, social and political trends. It tries to prove that the most English-proficient countries are more successful. Maybe there is some causation via the global linkages fostered by countries in which English is spoken with wealthy Western countries and influential global institutions that use English. But categorising the world according to English language proficiency ('very high' to 'very low') and linking this to a whole set of other outcomes seems like a presumptuous proxy indicator for Westernisation.[23] It confuses causation and correlation between language usage and other complex outcomes that are contingent on far more than speaking English.

In a less Western-centric world, paying tribute to the West in its own tongues and accessing Western networks may not be the same exclusive spur to development as it once was. As Ostler gleaned from his study of the history of languages, 'no language spread is ultimately secure: even the largest languages in the 21st century will be subject to either the old determinants of language succession or some new ones'. Just as in the past, 'migrations, population growth, changing techniques of education and communication – all shift the balance of language identities across the world, while the focus of prestige and aspiration varies as the world's economies adjust to the rise of new centres of wealth'.[24] For now, there does not seem much chance of this happening. By long imposing European languages on others, Westerners have made economic advancement contingent on these languages and especially English. Whether it remains true several decades hence is uncertain.

* * *

The global appeal of the Anglophone universities, English-language tuition and school examination boards have created powerful tools of Western influence, helping to produce a global English-speaking elite. In 2023, over a quarter of all world leaders (fifty-eight of them) who studied in countries other than their own were educated at a UK university, second only to US universities, which educated sixty-five serving world leaders. French universities accounted for thirty world leaders. The only other countries that had educated more than five serving world leaders were Russia (ten), Switzerland (seven), Australia (six), Italy (six) and Spain (six). Aside from Russia's old USSR links to various parts of the world, an astonishingly high percentage of heads of government and of state were educated in Western universities – itself 'a good proxy for the amount of soft power held by different countries', wrote the Higher Education Policy Institute, who compiled the data.[25]

No one part of the world owns education, of course, and examination was famous in imperial China to develop an educated and competent class of administrators, dating back to the first Qin dynasty, which existed well before the Common Era. Standardised exams were crucial to ancient China long before they became a regular feature in the Western states. Given this pedigree in education, why are only four mainland Chinese universities – Tsinghua, Peking, Zhejiang and Fudan – in the 2024 top fifty QS World University Rankings? In fact, there are only ten non-Western universities in this list, the others being the University of Hong Kong (HKU); Japan's universities of Tokyo and Kyoto; South Korea's Seoul National University; and Singapore's Nanyang Technical University (NTU) and

National University (NUS). In the QS top one hundred, there are still only sixteen non-Western universities.[26]

Another league table, the Times Higher Education World University Rankings, had eight non-Western universities in its top fifty for 2024 (Tsinghua, Peking, NUS, Tokyo, NTU, HKU, Shanghai Jiao Tong and Fudan). There are nineteen in its top one hundred.[27] A reliance on impactful academic research papers published in English has skewed the rankings. Even French universities have struggled to rise in these tables. Moreover, universities in countries like Germany and Sweden have begun offering more English language courses to attract foreign students to Western universities.

League tables play a big role in persuading foreign students to compete for paid scholarships and their families to part with the funds to pay for plane tickets, student accommodation and fees. But these rankings are driven not by the quality of teaching but by the impact of research. As such they rely on academic research paper databases like the Web of Science and Scopus that skew towards giving English language papers prominence. Producing non-English-language-centric league tables may become less prohibitive as time goes on, especially as open-source publishing of academic papers becomes more common (most academic work sits behind cost-prohibitive paywalls).

Recruiting foreign students for Western universities is a huge business. Anyone who has attended a Western university will recall the institutions that are awash with high-fee-paying foreign students and always busy in the race to attract more of them. In places like Singapore, I have seen all kinds of recruitment offices, joint ventures and in-country campuses for British, American and Australian universities, all tapping into the golden age for teaching courses in the English language.

Into a Westless world, some of these patterns in university rankings and international student flows will likely change. As Professor Jonathan Grant, a former Vice-Principal at King's College London, explained to me, 'The research performance of Chinese universities in citations and papers is equalling the US and could soon overtake it. When it comes to the Nigerian student market, I can easily see a lot of that market moving to China, as long as they teach in English.' Moreover, China may see additional economic benefits in attracting millions of extra students very soon given its population's own ageing demographics. Chinese higher education could adopt a parallel strategy to universities in the Gulf, which routinely buy in foreign academics to live in places like Abu Dhabi and to receive far better salaries than they received at home in Western universities.

In many countries, educating the workforce is the main undertaking, not research impact. This needs to be scaled up for an expanding population. Western countries have also been through this. Not too long ago, in the UK, barely 10% of people were university-educated and earning a degree was considered an elite undertaking. Now, a third of Brits earn degrees, reflecting changing social trends, the needs of a service-based economy, and social policies to remove obstacles to higher education for marginalised parts of the populace. In South Korea, some 80% of people are university educated. How will this manifest in countries like India and Nigeria? In Nigeria, those with university qualifications may have made up as little as 1% of the populace in 2018.[28] As and when this expands, there is little chance that the increase in demand could be tapped only by Western universities.

For Chinese universities to capture more student demand in the 2030s, China's government also looks to young foreign students augmenting its ageing population, especially from parts of Asia where Mandarin is common. For this to happen, Chinese universities have to increase their presence in the university rankings to change perceptions that the elite universities are only in Western countries. An opening salvo in challenging the hold of the Western universities could involve launching new league tables that reflect universities in Asia and elsewhere becoming better-known academic centres.[29] Another step will involve cooperation between non-Western universities. To take one example, there is a cooperative framework between China's Fudan University and leading universities in Latin America to foster 'academic conferences, faculty exchange, research cooperation, and annual leadership meetings' with the aim being 'to strengthen mutual understanding, inspire thoughts, spread ideas, and build up reputation'.[30] These kinds of partnerships will only grow.

It is still hard to imagine a world in which most of its leaders and many of its elites have not had some form of a Western education. The global influence of Western higher education is not yet overly challenged by alternatives – but it would be a big assumption to think this will not change in the long term. Not least since the capacity for universities to upscale and tap new student demand in growing populations cannot solely be met by Western universities.

The outlook for now is of Westlessness held at bay. The global ubiquity of the English language is not yet endangered, but if its leading lingua franca and its elite education advantages ever slip, the West will lose some of its most powerful tools of global influence. However, it won't be through universities that most of us sense changes in cultural appeal but in how we unwind.

8

Entertainment

> Every film that goes from America abroad, wherever it shall be sent, shall correctly portray to the world the purpose, the ideals, the accomplishments, the opportunities, and the life of America . . . We are going to sell America to the world with American motion pictures.
>
> William Harrison Hays, Republican politician and US Postmaster General, 1923[1]

HOW TIMES CHANGE. A full century after this quote on the export power of American entertainment was uttered, a Chinese-made entertainment platform was sweeping the USA, capturing the attentions of its youth and spurring their creative instincts. Even if most of the content on this platform was home-grown and user-generated, the masters of its distribution and the arbiters of its data were Chinese. The unease for American politicians was palpable.

On 23 March 2023, the chief executive of short-video smartphone app TikTok, Shou Zi Chew, walked into the US Congress to defend his company. He would be interrogated for five hours by irate politicians. Republican Cathy McMorris Rodgers kicked things off, complaining that allowing TikTok to be used by young Americans was 'like allowing the Soviet

Union to produce Saturday morning cartoons during the Cold War – but much more dangerous.'

Facing characterisations that he was an agent of the Chinese security state, Shou had to remind his Congressional interrogators that he was in fact Singaporean and not Chinese. He struggled to allay their fears that TikTok was inseparable from its Chinese parent company ByteDance and that the data of TikTok's users could thereby be accessed in mainland China. Shou confirmed that TikTok has 150 million users in the USA, and tried to reassure Congress with TikTok's 'Project Texas', a plan developed by his company to ring-fence the private data of its American users on US soil. No one in the room seemed reassured; Texan representatives even asked for TikTok's project to be renamed. Shou had been the CEO of TikTok since April 2021; its previous CEO, Kevin Mayer (a former Disney executive), had quit when then-President Trump had tried to force TikTok's sale to American investors.

Chinese netizens praised the young and telegenic Shou for his calmness under pressure in the televised hearing while mocking elderly members of Congress who displayed their technology illiteracy by asking odd things (Republican Buddy Carter's question, 'Can you say with 100% certainty that TikTok does not use the phone's camera to determine whether the content that elicits a pupil dilation should be amplified by the algorithm? Can you tell me that?' was a particular target for mockery by the netizens). The bigger point was that America saw TikTok as a national security threat and banning the app was a cause with political backing.

The fact that TikTok is a Chinese invention has been a rare win for China's soft power reach. Launched in 2018, it became one of the fastest-growing digital media platforms in history, with close to a billion users worldwide in 2023, while its sister platform Douyin registered 700 million users in its main market of China. Its success accelerated during the Covid-19 pandemic. Accessing user-generated meme and reality culture from the confines of wherever you might be stuck due to lockdowns became more appealing, offering windows to the outside world and to online communities. The confluence of the virus from Wuhan and the app from ByteDance has certainly rattled America. TikTok's triumph came down to its cost-free endless feed of untitled videos, algorithmically selected for users, rather than selecting content from a homepage (the way platforms like Facebook and YouTube were designed). The Chinese version, Douyin, was already well established, giving TikTok a head start in the viral short video market. US versions like Instagram Reels and YouTube Shorts were effectively attempts to catch up.[2]

The triumph of short video content, coming in the wake of super-fast internet (5G) and the visual turn in social media involving GIFs and Vlogs (video blogs), has shaped Generation Z, harnessing its need for immediacy and for creating its own visual grammar. This was a domain that US firms dominated in the infancy of the broadband and smartphone age but it has since become much more globally diverse. In the social media platform rankings for 2023, WeChat, TikTok, Douyin and Kuaishou all ride high. These Chinese-designed apps are used widely in countries like Indonesia while Chinese tech companies like Alibaba Cloud, TenCent Cloud and ByteDance have headquarters in Singapore. It now seems a very long time ago that Facebook CEO Mark Zuckerberg began learning Mandarin to try to crack the Chinese market, back in 2014.[3] Facebook no longer exists in China.

It takes some getting used to when 'Made in China' ceases being the butt of jokes around cheap plastic tat and for mass-manufacturing other people's designs. Chris Stokel-Walker reflects on this in his book about TikTok, writing that 'For a long time, China was just a factory for American technology companies, a place where cheap components were manufactured and assembled and then loaded into shipping containers for sale to Western consumers half a world away. In recent years that's shifted. Not just content with making the world's hardware, China has started exporting software'.[4] This change has prompted security concerns in Western countries that TikTok was a Trojan horse using its harmless attractions to develop a picture of the data habits of its users, and to feed them targeted propaganda.

This will not be the last scare around a foreign-designed social media app. Whereas the early era of the World Wide Web was dominated by America and uniquely favoured the English-speaking world, social media platforms and entertainment content will now reflect wider ranges of cultural and social norms, much of it made for local audiences but some intended for export.

'Soft power' is a term that refers to a country's powers of attraction, as expounded by American academic Joseph Nye, who regarded it as an essential adjunct to hard military and economic power. Cultural attraction has been crucial to America's modern success. European countries' soft power, in their globally popular football leagues, musicians, TV series and suchlike, has further contributed to the West's allure. But as Eric Li, a Chinese public intellectual, points out, 'There is no illusion, not least in Beijing, that any kind of soft power can exist and succeed without hard power.'[5] At a time of shifting world power, whose products, platforms and content will be entertaining future audiences?

The US has long been the biggest cultural exporter, offering the whole world a proxy vision of Western life, often subsuming European settings and characters in its films, games and music. Even if the overall balance of the popular cultural trade has overwhelmingly been in the US's favour, it cannot be assumed its soft power will reign in this century as it did in the last.

The global entertainment arena has transformed itself beyond all recognition from just a couple of decades ago. Streaming services and mobile devices allow entertainment produced in one place to be consumed across borders like never before, creating new avenues for the entertainment industry. This is happening as Western and particularly American entertainment products lose some of their prior uniqueness to foreign audiences. There is no sudden collapse in Western soft power appeal but emergent trend lines that suggest important changes are afoot.

* * *

Culturally enriching benefits await those whose sources of entertainment originate from diverse places. If what is broadcast or downloaded comes from friendly countries then it merely expands consumer choice. But if it originates from places with cultural or political principles opposed to our own, we should be concerned – at least, that is what governments in the West have concluded. Long before TikTok, back in the 1980s, a very different East Asian tech entertainment company made massive inroads into the lives and imaginations of American and Western youth. That company was Japan's Nintendo.

Video gaming in the West was initially dominated by US companies. California-founded Atari was the Western market leader in the late 1970s. Nintendo was founded in Kyoto in the 1890s and originally manufactured handmade playing cards. Nearly a century later, Nintendo expanded into the domestic Japanese toy market and used its existing distribution channels to sell its video games. Plenty of other Japanese firms such as Namco and Konami were selling arcade games like Pacman and Bomberman but Nintendo cut past the competition with its Donkey Kong arcade game starring a plumber called Mario. This character became the star of Super Mario Bros., a game adapted from arcades to the home console market and sold with the Nintendo Entertainment System (NES). Tens of millions of sales later, Mario and the NES had triumphantly captured the US's home video game market and soon afterwards broke through in Europe.

Super Mario himself, now a global icon, was an Italian plumber conceived by Japanese games designers, and the original Donkey Kong was set in New York. Hence, its character and the setting were primed for export to Western countries. There was still commercial resistance in the US to a Japanese upstart company swinging in to the entertainment industry, and in 1983, Universal Studios launched – and lost – a copyright lawsuit that alleged Nintendo's Donkey Kong had ripped off King Kong. Nintendo knew it needed a local base and set up a US imprint called Nintendo of America Inc. to manage its market entry there, which helped overcome another hurdle.[6]

In the 1980s, there was angst in the US against Japan's rising industrial competitiveness. This was despite Japan being a geopolitical US ally, humbled by its defeat in World War Two. The Nintendo company's success was part of a wider story of poverty-stricken post-war Japan's recovery. The parallels between US angst towards Japan in the 1980s and today's US–China economic rivalry are instructive. In the 1980s, Americans were shocked to see their iconic Firestone Tire & Rubber Company purchased by Japanese investors, and feared the US was becoming a Japanese economic colony, even as the USSR remained its main military and ideological rival.[7] Today, China presents all of these challenges to the US and its allies in one package. Even Nintendo, still headquartered in Kyoto and a proud Japanese brand, has kept its manufacturing costs down by using the huge Foxconn plant in Shenzhen, China, which also manufactures the products of global electronics brands such as Apple.

The video gaming industry has now mushroomed into becoming an incredibly profitable branch of the entertainment industry. Whereas in the 1980s it was the preserve of children and geeky teenage boys, it has since become an everyday pursuit, more gender-neutral and cross-generational to boot. Some people carry the habit into adulthood, and the advent of downloadable smartphone games has further widened the catchment. Sneak a glimpse at the time-passing activities of smartphone users on a typical daily commute to register this, even if you kicked the habit long ago.

Market shares in the modern games industry embody what we expect to see in the Westless era. East Asian proficiency in computing technology, software and hardware has competed healthily with US and European firms for decades. China has a big stake in producing games played all over the world. In 2022, three of the world's top profit-generating mobile games came from Chinese companies (Honor of Kings by Tencent; Genshin Impact by miHoYo; and Three Kingdoms Tactics by Qookka, which is owned by Alibaba). The latter is a homage to a famed work of Chinese literature, the Ming Dynasty-era book *The Romance of the Three Kingdoms*, which recounted epic battles in ancient China. A fourth top-grossing game, PUBG Mobile, was made by a South Korean company but distributed by Tencent in China, where much of its profit was made.[8] The remainder of the top ten featured games from the US, Israel and Japan.

The question is whether exotic and culturally distinct products influence the minds of foreign users. Cultural proclivities seep into video games, such as in the case of the ancient Chinese history example. In another example, although popular in South Korea, E-sport events are yet to make the jump to big Western audiences, in which arenas fill with crowds who watch gamers play on big screens (a live extension of watching online play-through videos).

'Historically, when it comes to entertainment and the export of culture, it's been generally one-way; it's been Western cultures, mainly the US, exporting around the world, especially here in Asia,' said the moderator of a panel about the gaming industry at a conference in Singapore. His co-panellist, who had worked in China on gaming and entertainment, answered: 'Interestingly, I think it is gaming that is the biggest area that is being exported in terms of Asian culture, more so than film/television or music . . . predominantly through mobile.'[9] Not all storytelling is culturally specific, but Korean, Japanese and Chinese influences on a pastime favoured by so many people around the world are noteworthy.

On the demand side, the US was still the biggest single gaming market, in 2022 generating $54.9 billion, and China was in second place with $44 billion in annual revenue. Japan ranked third with $39.9 billion and South Korea was fourth with $12 billion. In fact, the top ten revenue-generating markets for gaming comprised the G7 nations, plus Australia, China and South Korea.[10] The demand for mobile gaming markets is expected to grow in Africa, the Middle East and Latin America, and they will inevitably imbibe hefty doses of non-Western gaming material. Geopolitical tensions are shaping gaming as this industry study has explained:

> Toward the end of 2017, it seemed the games market was globalising in a huge way . . . Gaming's borders were blurring, so to speak. It seemed that gamers across East and West alike would be playing many of the same top titles. However, due to regulatory changes in the Chinese market, the prospect for Western games to make a splash in China was gated off [and] the game market's globalisation hit an undeniable roadblock. These regulatory changes had a second-order effect of incentivising Chinese developers to

> globalise into other markets ... and game content from across the world has begun to globalise – albeit in slightly different ways than we first expected.[11]

The trend lines for an industry that reaches into the lives of billions of people worldwide, and that is yet to expand into more regions, are important for the future of soft power. Plurality of influence seems in-built into gaming. Moreover, gaming increasingly influences many things, for instance through the gamification of other internet services to make them more interactive; with the creation of online social spaces that are second nature to Generation Z and Alpha; and the overlaps between gaming, animation and films, as the stories and characters from computer games become the inspiration.[12]

Back in the 1980s, Nintendo's Super Mario was an ingenious global brand, designed in Japan and angled at the West. Picture the Marios of tomorrow, when gaming reflects not only Western and East Asian proclivities, but captures expanding markets elsewhere too.

* * *

Everyone likes to kick back and relax with a movie or a series, and more often than not for many of us, it has arrived from Hollywood. The global appeal of its films and actors are a staple reason as to why Americans have become so accustomed to playing the role of the influencer rather than the influenced. A popular American film even has the power to take some of the sting out of simmering scepticism against

America and the wider West (with the exception of fanatical anti-US advocates; those exhibiting Taliban-levels of hatred towards the West condemn Hollywood as culturally degenerate).

For the rest of us, the British author of the book *Hollywood Abroad* explains the magic at work: 'What "Americanisation" has represented abroad is not necessarily what any individual or official ideology has privileged, supposed or assumed, since what circulates beyond the boundaries of the US is not a full-blown mythology but rather its icons, its random fragments,' which are consumed all over the world and interpreted in ways that are meaningful to each individual. 'These lessons were learned as an American discourse or, perhaps more exactly, in American accents [and] my imagination was Americanised because the iconography and plots of my childhood play were those of the lore of American exceptionalism.'[13] Versions of this are true for many of us who were raised on these films.

Ever since the American motion picture industry moved from the East Coast to the West Coast in the 1910s, the 'Hollywood' moniker has grown to represent much more than the place on the hill with the white letters, since it encompasses the whole industry of film production and financing and serves as a magnet for attracting plenty of non-American actors and directors. How Hollywood tells its stories is an ingrained part of many people's consciousness, and it is no exaggeration to say that chunks of the post-war world were partly raised by Hollywood films.

Whether this is generational and subject to change is well worth pondering. Hollywood's appeal cannot be separated from America's overall rise and the gravitational pull this has exerted on others who want to look at things through US eyes. There are the obvious Pentagon-funded war movies that crop up from time to time depicting Americans who struggle to do their best in foreign wars. More tellingly, sci-fi movies like 1996's *Independence Day* (directed by a German, Roland Emmerich) placed Americans front and centre in humanity's response to a global crisis. Much of this is amiably entertaining nonsense, depending on one's tastes, but it comes from a slickly run machine. Hollywood has been at the cutting edge of special effects and moviemaking techniques, attracting global talent to its productions while tying all this into promoting the pro-US and pro-Western messages.[14]

As with much surrounding Westlessness, Hollywood movies are not vanishing in appeal or being beaten by a single competitor. So much change is coming in the wider world that even this aspect of America's world-leading dominance cannot be considered immune to its effects. First, changing sources of profit based on growing cinema-going audiences elsewhere mean that American films have to appeal to wider international audiences to guarantee the greatest box office revenues. Second, there is a closing quality gap in production values between Hollywood and other large film industries; whereas not too long ago, non-US movies usually represented technically inferior and amateurish-looking alternatives, the gap is narrowing. Third, the advent of streaming and on-demand video has changed how local and global audiences can be reached with likely impacts on how films will be produced and which stories will be told in the future.

Where are the movies originating from that people watch in droves? The top ten highest grossing movies in the US, UK and BRICS countries reveal the following. All ten films in the annual US lists tend to be made in the US. This was often the same in the UK (it takes the occasional James Bond film to propel a British film into US box office top tens). So far, no surprises, but in the BRICS countries, things vary. Even if Brazil's and South Africa's leaders offer paeans to a post-American-led world, their publics still prefer mass-marketed Hollywood movies, and there is no substantive local film industry to rival this at the blockbuster end of the spectrum. Conversely, in India, China and Russia, it is home-grown films that dominate.

Bollywood, India's film industry, has its own pedigree almost as old as Hollywood's; whereas in Russia and China, it is the outcome of more recent efforts to avert the gazes of domestic movie-going publics away from Hollywood. In Russia, this effort has since 2005 been bolstered by a local imprint of the Disney company, which helped to produce high-quality films for domestic markets of the former Soviet republics starring Russian casts backed by high-grade special effects – but in 2022, Disney was under pressure to withdraw from Russian as part of the exodus of Western firms following Russia's war in Ukraine, leaving the domestic Russian blockbuster film industry to its own devices.

India is famed for producing more films than any other country, covering different sub-markets for its specific language groups. The industry began in the 1930s and was originally controlled by a handful of powerful producers, actors, their family mafias and by business tycoons. In 2001,

Bollywood was given 'industry status' by the Indian government, which allowed film producers to secure finance for their projects with bank loans. Bollywood has since become more professional and increasingly profitable as satellite TV spread in India in the 2000s, and as foreign revenues from its films have grown.[15]

Quality in art is clearly subjective, but something that can objectively be seen as having improved are the production values, special effects and overall presentation of top-end Indian films. Bollywood had a classic golden era that its appreciators place on its own pedestal. Young generations want slick entertainment products that do not look embarrassingly inferior to the average American movies. I must confess, on a personal note, after watching copious amounts of 1980s and early 1990s Bollywood with my parents, I developed a personal distaste towards the typical Indian film due to its corny theatrics, musical interludes and cheap-looking special effects. To my eyes, the quality gap with Western films was unbridgeable. Then, a decade ago, on a flight to India, I watched *Ek Tha Tiger* (2012) starring Salman Kahn. Corny it undeniably was, but having not watched an Indian film for so long, it was immediately apparent that the blockbuster end of India's film oeuvre had rebooted itself: dance routines no longer continuously derailed the film's pacing and the film felt angled to wider export markets. Amplifying this point, in 2022, the film *R.R.R.* (*Rise, Roar, Revolt*) became India's first film to win an Oscar, for 'best movie song'. A Telugu-language film that was set in India's colonial era, its plot not insignificantly depicted local heroes rebelling against British Empire rule.

There is still a huge gap in budgets: the biggest Hollywood films cost hundreds of millions of dollars while the biggest Indian and Chinese films cost tens of millions of dollars. Nevertheless, this is still a huge budget. It is also a success for the globalisation of the film industry that production values and special effects have improved dramatically in recent years in Indian and Chinese cinema, more in line with Hollywood standards. Part of the reason is that Hollywood has itself outsourced much of its animation work to studios in India, with the Philippines and South Korea also destinations relied on for this work. Even if Hollywood's creative processes have remained in the US, the overwhelming shift to animation work in Asia has had its own wider impacts.[16]

Important trends are afoot in Chinese cinema. Unlike India, there was no pedigree of film production, since film-making was curtailed during China's Cultural Revolution between 1966 and 1972. More recently, China's nationalist turn towards greater patriotism in public life has been mirrored in its film industry. In the early 2010s, many of the highest grossing films in China were still American. Since then, China has invested in its own film-making apparatus and drawn on technical expertise gleaned from films co-produced with American studios to learn the tricks of the blockbuster trade.[17] This has now paid off with an increase in its home-grown blockbusters including patriotic historical war movies; contemporary action movies showing Chinese soldiers saving the day; and elaborate science fiction films showing Chinese characters leading the way in the cosmos to save humanity.

At the same time Hollywood studios want to tap China's increasingly profitable audience market for their own films, especially after 2012, when China's box office overtook Japan's to become the second most profitable behind the US's, reflecting the fruits of China's cinema building spree, increasing its capacity to attract huge domestic audiences.[18] But China protects this market. It banned screening new Marvel films between 2019 and 2023; the reason for the ban was not explained but the state-controlled China Film Administration approves the domestic release of a foreign film, creating a mechanism for censorship that restricts the number of foreign films released in China to an annual quota of a few dozen. This approval process is akin to a cinematic version of the historic port city of Canton, used by the Qing dynasty in the nineteenth century to pen eager foreign traders into one tiny beachhead. Prising open the profits of Middle Kingdom is still not an easy task for Westerners.

Films allow us to dream. Over time, cultural products arising from American imaginations may no longer enter dreams across the world in quite the same ways as they once did. For now, Hollywood's global soft power seems assured, but US films must increasingly speak to global audiences. Much of the world had long ago noticed the lack of diversity of casting in typical American films' leading roles and joked about the old habit of compensating for this with token characters from other communities and nations. Now, American movies must become more diverse in their casting to reap the profits from appealing globally. At the same time, blockbuster Indian and Chinese films have ceased looking dramatically inferior, and even if their wider appeal varies, the future of the global film industry will not be the same as its past.

***

Streaming entertainment is the way of the future, forcing cinemas to compete by offering worthwhile spectacles that tempt audiences to leave their homes, while broadcast television and the physical media of DVDs and CDs have been rendered obsolete for younger generations in a few short years.

Streaming creates enormous opportunities for the localisation of content, which means that Western entertainment distributors can readily co-commission and supply local-language material, reflecting local tastes in expanding markets. Streaming companies clearly do not follow the logic of borders but of audience demand. Netflix operates in 190 countries but has struggled to penetrate the Indian market and has postponed entering China. Westerners familiar with Netflix, Disney and Amazon Prime would find it instructive to glance at a list of the streaming services worldwide that have crossed the 10 million-plus subscriber mark. The aforementioned sit in the top three followed by Baidu's iQIYI (which broadcasts worldwide) and Tencent Video (which serves several Asian countries). Beyond this, the list goes global with US streaming services like YouTube Premium and Paramount rubbing shoulders with India's ZEE5 and SonyLIV in subscriber numbers, while other platforms exist to serve large growing local markets in countries such as the Philippines and Nigeria.

Once upon a time and not all that long ago, more people around the world would consume a certain quotient of cultural products in common. It is likelier that they will now consume more localised content. The cultural and commercial implications arising from this vary depending on where one looks. China seems set to consume more self-generated entertainment than other countries. There are new incentives for countries to carve out their own market share in entertainment production. Saudi Arabia, for instance, invested in 'Saudiwood', building a desert hub for producing Middle Eastern media to meet the burgeoning demand for Arabic language content, and to attract film-making and music production to the country. It also launched the Red Sea Film Festival in Jeddah in 2021, attended by Hollywood, Bollywood and Arab stars.[19] Whether Saudi Arabia's bid to attract entertainment production to its shores works or not, the incentives for doing so are clear.

In the soft power of entertainment, fragmentation is the driving trend. A report produced by PricewaterhouseCoopers on trends in the entertainment sector in 2022–2026 summarised this:

> As recently as two decades ago, entertainment and media industry – and therefore consumers' attention – in each market was dominated by a handful of easily identifiable players that had changed little in many years: broadcasters, film studios, record labels, news organisations, large social media platforms. That previously established order has been decisively ripped apart, as consumers' attention has migrated elsewhere in rapid and unpredictable ways. Today, apps can come and go very quickly.[20]

The swift collapse of the old-style music industry reflected this, as the giant record labels and their business models quickly lost viability in the 2000s. In their wake, investment companies have purchased the lucrative legacy back catalogues of legendary artists like Fleetwood Mac for future streaming profits. Newer artists struggle for different reasons to their forebears by now hoping to make a viral online music video. In 2021, 175 songs that trended on TikTok charted in the US Billboard Hot 100 chart, and thirty songs gained a billion TikTok views.[21] The music industry is ripe for yet more localisation as opposed to further Westernisation. The International Federation of the Phonographic Industry reported that its most popular artists and bestsellers in 2022 included two non-Western artists, BTS from South Korea and Jay Chou from Taiwan. With China having moved for the first time into the top five revenue-generating music markets in the world, further diversification in the music industry seems inevitable.[22]

Changing trends in where leading entertainment products are produced and where they are consumed is an important subset of the changing world. At least the US intelligence community was not taken by surprise, since back in 2004 it published the following observation in its survey of global trends:

> A new, more Asian cultural identity is likely to be rapidly packaged and distributed as incomes rise and communications networks spread. Korean pop singers are already the rage in Japan, Japanese anime have many fans in China, and Chinese kung-fu movies and Bollywood song-and-dance epics are viewed throughout Asia. Even Hollywood

> has begun to reflect these Asian influences – an effect that is likely to accelerate through 2020.[23]

This prediction has proven accurate and, in a few decades, we can expect yet more diversification. As globalisation blurs into Westlessness, being entertained by globally marketed Hollywood films like an *Avatar* or *Avengers* movie, or by a globally marketed music group like South Korea's BTS, will juxtapose with slickly produced localised entertainment. Young people around the world will *not* rely heavily on Western entertainment products and platforms. Higher quality non-Western options, and the potential for locally curated distribution networks, will further dilute whatever influence the West and especially the US entertainment industries held over global imaginations. Growing middle classes elsewhere will contribute to taste and content trends, as rich centres of influence try becoming entertainment suppliers, infusing productions with their own norms. There are still billions of people who cannot yet regularly access high-speed internet and some of these are captive markets yet to be entertained. The artefacts of popular culture will inevitably shift to reflect their growing voices in the less Western-dominated world.

9

Identity

> Everything my guidebook said was true and also meaningless. Yes, the East was vast, teeming, and infinitely complex, but wasn't the West also? Pointing out that the East was an inexhaustible source of riches and wonder only implied that it was peculiarly the case, and not so for the West. The Westerner, of course, took his riches and wonder for granted, just as I had never noticed the enchantment of the East or its mystery . . . As with the Westerner, the Easterner was never so bored as he was when on his own shores.
>
> Viet Thanh Nguyen's novel *The Sympathizer*[1]

EACH OF US grapples with the question 'who am I?' at points in our lives. When it comes to how we have constructed our identities, it is sobering to consider just how Westernisation has impacted people all over the world, even if it has influenced rather than defined their identities.

The West has offered aspiration and prosperity while dangling the keys to modernity for those wishing to grasp them. The awkward acronym 'WEIRD', which stands for 'Western, educated, industrialised, rich, and democratic', reminds us that there is a package of identity markers that amount to the stereotypical Western identity. There are many versions of a Western or partially Western identity, and there have always been plenty of non-Western and non-WEIRD communities on the planet.[2] What it means to be Western has many forms, can be expressed according to individual tastes, and has changed over time. We cannot generalise about any of this, but there are some very specific questions that are now more pertinent than in previous decades.

The reference points for forging one's own sense of a well-recognised and prestigious cultural national identity are almost certainly going to diversify. The pressure and the incentive to Westernise one's identity even if only to limited extents may recede somewhat, at least relative to the recent past. The ingrained sense that non-Western identities comfortably sit in a 'traditional' realm, whereas Westernisation is the main route to being 'modern', will shift in line with further economic development. Even as these rising levels of development fail to touch every corner of the sprawling non-West, just a few standard-bearing examples will be enough to judder our past assumptions around identity formation and Westernisation.

On this matter, it is instructive to consult writers who considered the formation of post-colonial identities in the twentieth century. This was the last truly seismic inflection point when people's identities the world over faced big questions of balance and coexistence between Western and other influences. Back then, there were huge incentives to imitate the West.

The Indian academic Partha Chatterjee considered the tricky balance between copying Western models to modernise post-colonial nations while still wanting to stay true to your heritage. This process deeply impacted identity formulation, in effect by 'dividing the world of social institutions and practices into two domains – the material and the spiritual. The material is the domain of the "outside", of the economy and of statecraft, of science and technology, a domain where the West had proved its superiority and the East had succumbed.' Consequently, 'the greater one's success in imitating Western skills in the material domain . . . the greater the need to preserve the distinctiveness of one's spiritual culture.'[3] This idea, that to be modern is to identify with and imitate the West, while keeping one's heritage distinct, became deeply embedded.

While this was truer in the mid-twentieth century, it will be decreasingly true in the future. Some cultures in East Asia are so technologically modern and aspirational in their own right and yet more nations will follow, often looking more to each other for inspiration rather than to the West. As identity formation evolves, this does not mean other cultures will become automatically hostile or rejectionist of the West and its history – they might just become increasingly indifferent.

Having a mixed cultural, linguistic or ethnic background can make questions of identity more complex to answer. Identity is a perilously difficult concept to pin down, and I have long appreciated Amartya Sen's deft approach. Our sense of identity is complex and multilayered by design, Sen explains:

> In our normal lives, we see ourselves as members of a variety of groups – we belong to all of them. A person's citizenship, residence, geographic origin, gender, class, politics,

> profession, employment, food habits, sports interests, taste in music, social commitments, etc., make us members of a variety of groups. Each of these collectives, to all of which this person simultaneously belongs, gives her a particular identity.

Now to the ingenious part of Sen's conception of identity: different contexts and stimuli will bring to frontal prominence certain layers of our identity over others. 'It is not so much that a person has to deny one identity to give priority to another, but rather that a person with plural identities has to decide, in case of a conflict, on the relative importance of the different identities for the particular decision in question.'[4] We can probably all relate to instances when this has been the case.

When the juggling act involves different layers of inherited and adopted identity, interesting things happen. Some people with non-Western heritages may have mobilised an overtly Westernised sub-identity to tap into or intermingle with globalised Western norms and tastes, while retaining a more traditional identity for religiosity, to engage with elders, and to pass on to children. This will certainly be true of ethnic minorities living in Western countries. It is also true for some people living further afield who have bought into the 'West is best' idea, even if doing so partially or cynically.

* * *

If you could force yourself to experience a personal moment of reckoning with your national and cultural identity, would you dare to? There is an obvious way to do this. It involves travelling far from home, preferably out of your continent, and becoming the proverbial fish out of water, keeping your eyes and ears open to absorbing what is local. It's a big world out there, something we are reminded of if we are privileged enough to browse travel destinations abroad for holidays, study or work. Our choices are theoretically vast but we tend to be funnelled by such sensible practicalities as not wanting to spend a fortune, wanting to feel safe, or heading to where family members reside.

Degrees of familiarity influence our choices, which is why many Westerners stick to the West. If you are American, you could stay put in North America, a continent so large you could never explore it all in a lifetime. Famously, many Americans don't have passports, and with such an expanse at their doorsteps, who can blame them? If you are European, you can travel elsewhere in Europe to experience national diversity. There is the lure of transatlantic travel, for North Americans to see quaint old Europe, and for Europeans to see how the USA measures up to their Hollywood dreams. Westerners may favour visiting Britain's ancestral cousins in Australasia; speaking the same language makes things less taxing on the other side of the world. But to venture out of the West is where real cultural differences await, unless you maroon yourself on a resort and barely meet any locals, aside from the waiting staff.

Interactions involving travellers and émigrés tend to reflect prevailing power balances, not only due to relative wealth and spending power but through a sense of perceived prestige about where you come from. For some time now, the

West's gigantic global influence has given generations of people from its biggest countries the confidence that they will find others around the world who are keen to learn Western languages and habits, chat about Western sport teams and films, and who want to participate in the Westernised global commons. A Westerner abroad also becomes an inadvertent brand ambassador for some of the West's famous cultural products.

The West has been the cultural magnet. For some people of other heritages, looking up to or adopting Western ways continues to be aspirational; nothing short of embarking on a rite of passage into modern living as distinct from more familial, traditional or theological heritages. This has made obvious sense for people who arrive as minorities in Western countries; they are assimilating into the dominant cultures of the US, Britain, France or elsewhere, seeking the acceptance of the locals to get ahead in life for themselves and their children.

Versions of this story were also experienced by migrating Europeans, like the Italians who settled in the US a century ago, or the Irish who settled in the US or UK and who faced their own journeys of adaption and overcoming resistance to their arrival. Throughout history, cultural assimilation has involved adjusting one's personal identity to one's new surroundings. Without making a value judgement on this delicate matter, those from 'visible ethnic minorities' (those who are not white or Caucasian) still face some very specific hurdles in this journey. Notably, the process of assimilation can stimulate shame or neglect of their own non-Western cultures, as being backward, less interesting or less monetarily rewarding, to be shed for a more modern Westernised identity.

The inverse is not really true these days. How many Westerners are there who truly assimilate themselves into a non-Western country and culture? Some will do so for reasons of personal intellectual curiosity, religiosity, heritage, or after intermarriage, all of which are strong motives for people to leave the West to fully integrate in a non-Western place. There are also Westerners who move far from home and live as expats without expending too much effort to integrate, because they find they don't need to.

And when we think of Western countries, the only thing that has firmly embedded a plethora of non-Western influences into everyday mainstream life has been mass migration. Diaspora communities settling in the West have preserved cultural umbilical cords with their heritages, the earliest generations often livening up the local cuisine by popularising their foods with Westerners.

Cultural fusions abound. How differently will these journeys proceed in a less Western world? In some ways the balance has already tipped. 'For most of its history the West has been exporting its ideas, in the expectation that people will become Western in their own countries,' wrote Ben Ryan, bringing European colonial-era practices into mind as well as US-led globalisation of consumer habits. Change is already afoot. 'Now, more than ever, the West is trying to make Westerners of new arrivals within its own borders.'[5] This imperative has grown as migrant flows into the US from Central and South America and into Europe from Africa and Asia hardly let up, adding to population diversity and reinforcing a sense within rich Western countries of still being the 'city upon a hill' for the world's poor and dispossessed.

Economic migration into Western countries is a huge issue and will remain so given the wealth disparities between regions. But it cannot be the only dimension to consider since the appeal of coming to the West has also been marketed to foreign elites. It is distinctly possible that the cultural export power of Western influence will peak relative to other aspirational alternatives. Aspects of the West continue to gleam with unique appeal to onlooking eyes around the world, and the West will still feel the sensation of the world expectantly arriving at its doorstep – but this sensation could become illusory.

* * *

In the immediate future, things won't seem to be changing very much at all. People will continue to seek out the richest Western countries as favoured destinations for work, study and sometimes for a new life. But as they do so in the future, they will think differently about the wider world and where the West fits into other rising places. Over time, it is distinctly possible that the value and appeal of adopting a partially Westernised identity will fluctuate and reduce for others around the world. Some examples of this are already in an embryonic stage, suggesting that great changes are on their way this century.

As India gains greater standing in the world, will those of us who are of Indian extraction be proud of their heritage, just as they always were, but in different ways? It is one thing for India to be widely regarded for its cuisine, yoga, prowess in cricket and the seemingly exotic allure of its traditionalism – but quite another when it becomes one of a tiny group of countries to land a space probe on the lunar surface. This feat was achieved in July 2023 when the Chandrayaan-3 moon rover's success made India only the fourth country to achieve this feat after the US, USSR and China.

India clearly has a very long way to go in its rise to greater global stature. A cynic would argue that a successful space mission juxtaposes awkwardly with the air pollution that blights everyday life experiences of so many in India and the persistence of extreme poverty for parts of society. Then again, when the US dispatched the Apollo 11 mission in 1969 and astronaut Neil Armstrong stepped onto the moon's surface, the African American civil rights movement was still reeling from the assassination of Martin Luther King the preceding year and the social position of ethnic minorities remained poor, viscerally illustrated by their deaths in disproportionate numbers as Vietnam War conscripts. So, it would be quite wrong to assume uniform progress in how a major country develops during its rise. Or to expect that big steps forward to boost a country's national stock will benefit every citizen at home.

Having pride in certain layers of one's identity need not stand in contention to holding several identities at once. The 'Overseas Citizenship of India' (OCI) serves as an official way of recognising this, and it acts as a lifelong visa which you can claim if your parent, grandparent or great-grandparent was Indian. In other words, pretty much anyone with Indian heritage can apply, and it is similar to having 'Non-Resident Indian' (NRI) status. Two decades ago, the prospect would have filled me with utter indifference, steeped as I was in an assiduously Western, English and London life with the Americanised cultural supplements as was the norm, fulfilling my passage away from my Indian and African family heritages to scale Britain's meritocratic ladder. I cannot speak for anyone other than myself. Now, however, having visa-free entry into a rising country seems like placing a sensible bet on the future.

How might future generations feel when India becomes a greater global force? When India is flying spaceships and making movies that are watched by wider audiences while lifting more of its people out of poverty? So long as its developmental trajectory remains a positive one, what India is associated with will change. What about the Indian-American identity – how has it evolved as it produces a greater number of CEOs of major US companies, and indeed as former PepsiCo CEO Ajay Banga, a naturalised US citizen later in his life, was appointed head of the World Bank Group in 2023? There is absolutely no barrier between being British or American and having a heritage elsewhere, but our thoughts on this matter shouldn't stop at a complacent admiration of this laudable principle.

What happens in a world in which the West is not as uniquely aspirational as it once was? This is not to suggest that some kind of rebellion is brewing in the ranks of the diverse populations of Western countries, and not to cast aspersions on anybody's loyalties. My only suggestion is that, in the future, there will be different incentives for balancing the Western and non-Western components of some people's identities as the world changes.

For people of Chinese heritage, they are the targets of China's state-sponsored nationalism that tries to propagate greater national and cultural pride. Ham-fisted though such efforts are, how will overseas Chinese communities react to the country of their heritage summiting various indicators of success? To offer an example, Singapore's former Foreign Minister George Yeo explained the meaning of his heritage: 'I'm Chinese which means I have affection and emotional connection to a civilisation of which China is a large part. When China was downtrodden, when it was being ravaged by imperial powers, all Chinese in the world were stepped upon. And when China revived, all Chinese will feel their coinage has been revalued.'[6] Other people will reject this kind of collectivist rationalisation, finding it irrelevant to their individualism or repulsive because they are appalled by the Chinese Communist Party and they live away from China to avoid its grasp – but it is unwise to discount the wider point as an irrelevance.

Much depends on how China itself evolves. If – hypothetically – China overtakes the US to become the world's largest economy, runs a major space exploration programme and begins to excel in a number of other areas, retaining a revulsion towards the Chinese Communist Party from abroad will require different rationalisations. The scholar Wang Gungwu reflected on what it means to be of Chinese heritage while the motherland has changed beyond all recognition: 'There are something like 50 to 60 million Chinese, or people of Chinese descent around the world.' But, 'How are they

"Chinese"? Who is Chinese? What does it mean to be Chinese?' Being a citizen of the People's Republic of China is quite different to enjoying a cultural affinity with China. As Wang reflected, 'there are multiple ways of identifying with China as Chinese. And they're all legitimate, each in their own way.' Balancing these different layers of identity is the real question because 'much of it depends on self-identification, how you identify yourself, but also depends on how other people identify you.'[7]

What about Indonesia, another large and rising country? Here is a simple example from the 1980s regarding the part-Javanese origins of US guitar supremo Eddie Van Halen. (If you have no idea who he is, bear with me – he was so famous in the 1980s that he played guitar on Michael Jackson's song 'Beat It'.) Van Halen's music was marketed at young people in America and Europe with no mention made of his mixed Javanese-Dutch parentage. After all, why should it have been? His family moved from Java to Amsterdam in the 1950s, and after experiencing racism in the Netherlands for their ethnicity, relocated to the US, where Eddie became famous. It was perfectly reasonable to market Eddie and his band-mate brother Alex Van Halen as 'all American kids' rather than mention they were progenies of a Dutch empire-era family in Asia.

After Eddie Van Halen's death in 2020, a Tweet caught my eye from a fan of his music: 'I was today years old when I found out that Eddie Van Halen was of Asian descent. His mother Eugenia was Indonesian Dutch. I can only imagine how impactful knowing this would've been growing up as a half-Asian metalhead.'[8] There will be other stories like this around artists who were marketed in particular ways to appeal to either majority or minority communities in Western countries.

In Western countries, it has been down to national policy and social preferences as to how ethnic diversity is managed. In some countries, to counteract past racisms, people were guided that being fair-minded involved being 'race blind', judging each person as they are. This sensible advice had an inadvertent effect, as Ben Ryan explained: 'The effect of this colour blindness is actually to write people's identity out of the story. To be British-Ghanian, or an American-Vietnamese, or a Dutch-Surinamese is special to people, they do not want that aspect of their identity discounted or dismissed.' I have come to concur with this view, not because every sub-group needs special recognition. We need a central 'British' or 'French' or 'Dutch' or 'American' national identity, no matter how generalised, loose and open to interpretation it is. National identities cannot fixate on infinitely accommodating endless distinctions; some consensus-culture is needed to foster civic harmony.

But it will have been easier to write off the non-Western components of a person's identity and place it behind the Westernised part when the West dominated the world. In the future, managing blended Western/non-Western identities in societies will inevitably evolve to reflect new realities.

In the way that some dominant Western heritages have had a seemingly built-in prestige, to what extent will heritages from countries like India, China and Indonesia gain greater standing than they previously enjoyed? In the future, the immediate associations with some Eastern and Southern countries will no longer be poverty and exoticism, or the extents to which they have been Westernised,

Once, it might have been 'cool' to recite well-known film punchlines in an American accent when chatting with school friends (as I recall from my childhood, which was lived within the Anglosphere but far from the US). In the more distant past, it was a sign of authority to speak with British 'received pronunciation' diction. In an even earlier age, to master French was a marker of culture and learning. Let us wait and see what positive markers of identity association catch on in the future, as other places adjust their schooling, national narratives and cultural products to supplement or to shed the accumulated markers of historical Westernisation. And, just maybe, as Westerners see other parts of the world in a different light.

* * *

The voice over the loudspeaker caught my attention and the words stuck in my mind: 'British, American, European, Australian, Canadian, New Zealand passports walk to your left, all other passports to your right,' announced the staff member at London's Heathrow Airport. I dutifully filed left with the rest of the Western passport holders. The West is the West after all and 'all other passports' simply meant the rest of the world. There were a few exceptions and, as of 2023, if you held a passport from Japan, South Korea or Singapore, you too could also follow the exalted line of Western passport holders to the automated immigration barriers. Circles of trust and all that – the UK trusts the rest of the West first of all, followed by its like-minded rich Asian partners, and why not?

In the less Western world, it is hardly a stretch of the imagination to see the Western countries banding together ever more tightly while picking out a carefully curated list of other trusted partners. There are shared bonds in history and there are modern practicalities too. To be Western and to respect the West may become an interesting marker of kinship. Especially if the conversion rate for others to adopt fully or partially Westernised identifies plateaus and tails off for the reasons we have discussed, and as Western countries become relatively less populated due to their demographic trends. What then? Will Westerners finally be forced to learn more about the non-Western world in more systematic ways? Or will they reject this and stick to travelling most comfortably within the Western world?

The need to learn about others is going to grow for Westerners by necessity. The inverse was already true. As Viet Thanh Nguyen wrote in his novel *The Sympathizer*, set during the Vietnam War, from the perspective of one of his Vietnamese characters: 'We probably did know white people better than they ever knew themselves, and we certainly knew white people better than they ever knew us.'[9] Excusing the characterisation of 'white', which better suited its 1960s setting, this is merely a biting line from a fiction novel, but one that I fear conveys rather more truth than may be comfortable for some of us to admit. After all, it was not only the Vietnamese who may have felt this, having been colonised by the French and then embroiled in a war with Americans. Quite a number of non-Western people simply *had* to learn about the Euro-American hub of the world that was influencing the globe through fair means or foul. Now, as the meaning of being Western has evolved beyond its old exclusive association with being white, and as other parts of the world rise on their own terms, the West cannot automatically expect the same levels of convergence with its ways. As the balance of prestige between cultures and regions changes, so too will individual stories of identity formulation shift, especially for generations to come.

10

Politics

> When people argue that Democracy is obviously better than Autocracy, I think they missed the key point: Leadership. In the history of mankind, there were good Kings and good Emperors. There were renaissances and famines. There were bad Kings and incompetent rulers. What matters is Leadership and competencies in the system. Instead of grooming generations of better leaders, the world seems to be lacking them. Elected leaders tend to be populists and short-term because their term of office is also short-term. I don't think changing prime ministers every few years in UK, Australia and Japan is good for any form of government. Our ruling party could plan for long-term because they are confident that they'll be around to deliver the promises. They've been the same ruling party since 1959. So let's look for Leadership and forget about the obsession on Democracy vs Autocracy. It doesn't make a difference if all promises are broken after the election.
>
> Anonymous post from a Singaporean citizen[1]

TO MY EYES, this comment posted in response to a news article is deeply disagreeable – but it makes me think. I disagreed because I have been raised to respect the British parliamentary system of first-past-the-post elections that offer the electorate a real choice between rival parties and manifestos. An American, accustomed to two big parties oscillating in power, would be similarly aghast at not being able to kick out an incumbent through the ballot box. As would the European Parliament, which encourages democracy and democratic values in its member states and beyond the EU's borders, 'because elections build democracies and raise public trust in institutions', it dutifully explains.[2] Australians, Canadians, South Koreans, Taiwanese, Ukrainians and many more extol the virtues of democratic choice in their own political systems. The Japanese, who have been governed almost continuously since 1955 by the same Liberal Democratic Party, and have seen their democracy turn into a gerontocracy based on a 'dominant party' model, might better empathise with Singapore's experience of elections generating predictable results. Political systems are intensely local and are shaped by their own cultural and historical forces. Democracies come in unique forms, each adapted to its locality and evolving according to its own national conditions.

Since contemporary Westernisation has come to be closely associated with the global spread of democracy, an important question beckons: why is democracy no longer catching on elsewhere as it did before? Ravi Agrawal, the editor of America's *Foreign Policy* magazine, summarised the state of play:

> After the fall of the Berlin Wall in 1989, it seemed like democracy had won a grand battle of ideas. Countries

> around the world began to democratize. Democracy just seemed . . . cool. Right? But we now know it didn't quite last. Over the last fifteen years, several important data points suggest that democracy has weakened around the world. Elections don't always produce democrats; we now know they can produce strongmen and leaders with dictatorial instincts too. And many of the pillars that usually support democracy – an independent judiciary; a fearless press; checks and balances – have been weakened for a majority of the world's population.[3]

How perilous is it for the West's global standing if liberal democracy cast in its mould ceases its spread? Must Western countries get their own democratic houses in order to project this aspect of their influence in the wider world? The tribulations of Western democracies have correlated with an erosion of democratic norms and practices in other parts of the world. Which begs the next question.

Are chunks of the world becoming autocracies as cast in the Chinese and Russian moulds – or, if the 'democracy versus autocracy' formula is too basic to grasp the variety of political systems that are out there, how can we describe prevailing political trends in other regions? It is now looking distinctly possible that the sentiment quoted at the start of this chapter gains traction in parts of the world where benign one-party rule and government efficiency is prioritised over the electoral circus of expensive political campaigning featuring politicians of varying seriousness.

* * *

In the West, we are raised to treat autocracy with disdain by considering how absolute power corrupts. In Britain, we consider it to be a vital stage in political maturation to have long ago replaced absolute with ceremonial monarchy. We keep the modern parables of Hitlerian Germany and Stalinist Russia firmly in mind as to the brutality unleashed by these deplorable authoritarian regimes against their own people and on others. How we organise ourselves politically is core to our sense of self. It is informed by our reading of historical progress, and it reflects our expectations of how social stability is balanced with the rights of individual self-expression.

For some people, liberal democracy is more than just a political system of parties and elections – it is an article of faith, a creed by which to judge oneself and others around the world depending on whether they are striving for democracy or rejecting it outright. These debates end in predictable ways, with some vocal Westerners telling others they need to adopt liberal democracy to better themselves and to – dare one say it – progress more along Western lines. So fervent and earnest are some believers in the superiority of their democracy over other systems that in parts of the West it has arguably replaced a void left by religion as a system of communitarian belief for fostering more virtuous lives. If you are raised in the West, you will be well accustomed to the argument that your style of democracy is not only the least-bad political system out there, but that it is infinitely superior both morally and practically to its bête noire, authoritarianism.

I cast myself in this category. Raised in the UK, an original beacon of parliamentary democracy, and with my family heritage in Commonwealth countries (Kenya and India) that inherited democracy after they were denied self-governance as colonies, I have associated the adoption of democracy with the striving for human progress. Feeling strongly about these principles, I volunteered as an international election observer at the start of my career. This led me to monitor elections in Kenya for an EU mission, and in Ukraine for the Organization for Security and Co-operation in Europe (OSCE), to report on how free and fair they were. I witnessed the onset of Kenya's 2007 post-election violence after a dispute over the outcome between the leading candidates, and the mobilisation of violent militias associated with their rival interests. I also saw Ukraine's 2004 Orange Revolution, another dispute between candidates this time over voter fraud, leading to peaceful protests and a political stand-off. These episodes provided a visceral education on troubled elections in radically different contexts.

Looking back, as well as being out for adventure, I clearly thought it worthwhile to contribute to safeguarding democracy in places where it was still taking root. It was inspiring to see democracy thrive against the odds. Look at what has happened since in these examples. Following the debacle of its 2007 election, Kenyans have since managed their presidential elections far more peacefully. While Ukrainians have been forced to shed their blood in defence of their democracy and sovereignty against the brutal Russian invasion. Alas, these stories are not the current global norm.

Taking a bird's-eye view of the trend should alarm those who were schooled in the virtuous ways of democratic transitions as progressive advancements. When aggregated at a global level, things are not trending in favour of Western-approved democracy. Washington DC-based organisation Freedom House, which tracks the prevalence of democratic political systems and values, is concerned. In 2023, it marked the fiftieth year of compiling its annual report by warning of 'the stakes of the struggle for democracy' as avoiding 'the devastating costs that authoritarian rule can impose on entire populations'. The Freedom House Index rates 210 countries and territories based on whether people can access political rights and civil liberties 'ranging from the right to vote to freedom of expression and equality before the law'. Its 2023 report solemnly reported '17 years of democratic decline', meaning 'countries with aggregate score declines in Freedom in the world have outnumbered those with gains every year for the past 17 years'.[4] Hence the term 'democratic backsliding', used by Western political commentariats for a country where the democratic system and values have eroded.

The US academic Larry Diamond has also tracked this trend, adding nobility to the cause by entitling his 2008 book *The Spirit of Democracy: The Struggle to Build Free Societies Throughout the World*. He wrote of 'a world partially transformed' in adopting the values and attributes that a democracy ought to have.[5] Returning to the subject several years later, he was now much more concerned:

> Democracy had a remarkable global run, as the number of democracies essentially held steady or expanded every year from 1975 until 2007 . . . And then, around 2006, the expansion of freedom and democracy in the world came to a prolonged halt. Since 2006, there has been no net

> expansion in the number of electoral democracies, which has oscillated between 114 and 119 (about 60 per cent of the world's states).

The end of the Cold War and the uptake of democracy in parts of the former USSR, as enshrined by the expansion of the EU, certainly gave these stats a boost in the 1990s and 2000s. Since then:

> . . . there has been a significant and, in fact, accelerating rate of democratic breakdown. Second, the quality or stability of democracy has been declining in a number of large and strategically important emerging-market countries, which I call 'swing states'. Third, authoritarianism has been deepening, including in big and strategically important countries. And fourth, the established democracies, beginning with the United States, increasingly seem to be performing poorly and to lack the will and self-confidence to promote democracy effectively abroad . . . Democracy has been in a global recession for most of the last decade, and there is a growing danger that the recession could deepen and tip over into something much worse.[6]

This has worsened as Russia and China consolidated their axis of partnership to create a world that is far safer for other autocracies such as Iran and North Korea; Türkiye has kept the same person in power for two decades and counting at the time of writing; coups in West Africa have displaced elected governments in Mali, Niger and Gabon; and more examples abound.

In the Middle East, recall the promise of the Arab Spring back in 2011 as ushering in a wave of democracy, heralding a genuinely new chapter for the Middle East and North Africa. Some in the US and its Western allies, scarred by the difficulties of forcing democracy onto Iraq, thought that the levee had burst and the wider Arab world was about to experience what Eastern Europe had two decades prior. It was not to be, despite heroic pro-democracy protest movements around the region. Military rulerships reasserted themselves violently in Egypt and Syria. Libya fell into civil war. Tunisia was the sole success story for democracy but soon ran into trouble. Monarchies elsewhere in the region stayed put. Expectations of a regional outbreak of real multi-party democracy were dashed.

Democracy has remained patchy in Asia. When the young reformist politician Pita Limjaroenrat won elections in Thailand in 2023, he was prevented from becoming prime minister by a deeply vested elite comprising the Thai military and monarchy. Other South East Asian countries have drawn the line at adopting human-rights-led democratic systems, even if they otherwise like the West. The scholar Kanti Bajpai studied this phenomena country by country, concluding that 'virtually all the Western-led- liberal international order's regulatory norms find support in Asia, except the idea of a progressive march towards liberal democracy'. While all Asian states were elected democracies of some kind, except for China and Vietnam where communist parties ruled in perpetuity, democracy rarely looked like its Western version, except in Japan and South Korea. In India and Indonesia, while Modi and Jokowi 'certainly supported electoral democracy, they avoided the term *liberal*', Bajpai observed.[7]

The mere fact of holding elections cannot alone equate to a liberal democracy. Liberalism is the vital ingredient in why Western democracies aspire to be more than just election machines. Liberalism confers rights on individual citizens to make up their own minds about things; it confers protections on individuals and it suggests checks and balances on those in power; and it encourages airing competing political opinions in the media.

As a volunteer election observer in the 2000s, I felt as if the winds of history were blowing in favour of spreading real systems of multi-party democracy. In the 2020s, it is worth asking: have we reached peak democratisation as cast in the Western mould? Was the global spread of liberal democracy across the globe always a Western-centric pipe dream? And is it fair to lump the global practice of democracy with Westernisation anyway? Surely the rights and basic dignities associated with liberal democracies should be everyone's rights – or was even this framing just the West talking? To get a better sense of what is happening, we first need to inspect the lighthouses of democracy themselves, the Western countries that were supposed to be providing the guiding light to others.

* * *

The nadir of Donald Trump's controversy-wracked presidency came at its end with the Capitol Riot on 6 January 2021, when his supporters marched angrily and violently to protest his electoral loss to Biden. The incident tarnished the lustre of US democracy for those looking in from abroad. There was genuine concern the US could descend into a new civil war. Law enforcement, and even respected US academics who studied terrorism and insurgency abroad, turned their attentions to home in case Trump's supporters pursued their deep-state conspiracy theory grievances with systematic violence.

Trump's political career has revealed ugly authoritarian tendencies sitting at the heart of US democracy. He saw the checks and balances for regulating the power of the executive branch as hurdles to vault to preserve his power. Just as the dust settled from the Capitol Riot, in 2023, Trump promised to run again, despite facing various criminal proceedings. As Biden turned eighty, he also decided to run again. No matter what you thought of either candidate, it would be a struggle to associate their electoral contest with any notion of dynamism, only with the ageing demography of Western electorates.

In a different kind of controversy, the UK witnessed the spectacle of Boris Johnson's shoot-from-the-hip governing style. Johnson's 'Partygate' scandal, in which his staff partied in Number 10 Downing Street while the British public were told to stay put during the pandemic, caused a great deal of popular bitterness. Even more consequential is the possibility of the UK simply falling apart after politicians like the charismatic Johnson encouraged the British public to vote to leave the EU. It turned out that many of Brexit's consequences were never properly thought through by its advocates, like Johnson, who in 2019 also advised the Queen to suspend

Parliament (prorogation, to use its technical term) during the UK's political crisis around implementing Brexit – a move that was later deemed unlawful by the UK's Supreme Court.

With Brexit now implemented, the coherence of the UK's four-nation union is under renewed threat as active discussions continue around the prospects for Scotland's independence and the island of Ireland's unity. The 'Better Together' slogan used successfully in the Scottish independence referendum of 2014, when the Scots voted to remain in the UK, contrasted with the pro-Brexit campaign sentiment of 'better off on our own' regarding the EU. Some Scots and Northern Irish found membership of the UK more palatable if it also came with EU membership – without it, and with the resurgence of English nationalism surrounding Brexit, Scottish nationalists and Northern Irish republicans alike have new arguments to mount to their supporters.

Elsewhere, France's cities were paralysed by strikes after Emmanuel Macron tried to force several top-down policy changes, showing an unflattering side to freedoms to protest. In 2024, facing further challenges to his rule, Macron appointed a thirty-four-year-old acolyte, Gabriel Attal, to become Frances's prime minister – who promptly appointed his thirty-eight-year-old former partner Stéphane Séjourné, a politician with little foreign policy experience, to become foreign minister. What does this convey to the outside world?

These episodes generate easy propaganda fodder for anti-democratic Russia and China, who can play protest footage on repeat to demean the decadence of the West and extol the virtues of iron discipline at home. This is clearly unfair: in the real world there is no Platonic ideal of a democracy, only messy accumulations of political traditions layered on top of each other, topped off with the enduring vanities of presidents and prime ministers. Nevertheless, when leading Western states have practised an increasingly clownish version of democracy, we cannot rule out the reputational damage being done.

What about liberal democracy's great virtue, that it can reset the system with electoral change? After all, a questionable leader can always be replaced by the electorate. For those who place more stress on the liberal end of democracy, they might look to Jacinda Ardern in New Zealand to remind us of how transformative democracy can be, by electing fresh and committed female politicians, and only the third woman to lead New Zealand's government. And then there is ethnic diversity in Western politics.

'Rashid Sanook', said Biden, as he mangled his pronunciation of Rishi Sunak, the newly installed UK prime minister at a press conference in October 2022. 'A ground-breaking milestone and it matters, it matters,' said Biden, as he rescued the point he was making. Biden had a ringside seat for America's path-breaking moment in which Barack Obama became president in 2009, although Obama won office via an election rather than through party chaos, which was Sunak's path to power. Sunak was not chosen by the electorate in 2022, becoming prime minister by internal Conservative Party succession after four predecessors had fallen by the wayside since 2016 (David Cameron, Theresa May, Boris Johnson and Liz Truss).

Given their inbuilt powers of course-correction and self-improvement, why are major Western democracies suddenly malfunctioning? An unsung and vital ingredient appears to be missing – namely *civility* in political discourse. Civility is essential for a liberal democracy to function smoothly with its associated free speech and freedom-to-protest clauses. It only works if people, politicians and the electorate can disagree well. Oxford academic Teresa Bejan studied the importance of civility by going back to the philosophies at the origins of Western democracy:

> Plato, a source of many Stoic and early Christian ideas of *concordia*, [observed] the true art of *politikos* was the weaving together of diverse souls through the 'divine bonds of true opinion' – that is, through education oriented towards a kind of consensus of 'like mindedness' . . . In *The Republic*, Socrates compares this agreement to a 'kind of harmony' in which all citizens 'sing the same song together'. And while Aristotle accused Plato of 'turning harmony into a mere unison', he too believed certain kinds of disagreement posed a problem for community.[8]

Absent of consensus reached through civil debate, the nature of political disagreements in some democracies has become toxic. In the West, the populism of angry political tribalism has many causes. Globalisation negatively affected some communities in the West. Local traditions and industrial jobs were snuffed out by the pressures of standardisation and (as the populists argued) by immigration. With some Westerners feeling that their customs were under threat, they turned to politicians like Trump.

Perhaps, in another age, these problems would seem cyclical, a tricky phase that will pass as so many passed before.

Just as Watergate and angst against the US government's conduct in Vietnam became acute but eventually subsided in America. This time, there are convincing reasons to believe the challenges to Western democracy are in fact *structural* and will not so readily pass. The reason for this pessimism is how technology has impacted Western politics by exacerbating tribalism like never before.

Social media has been a boon for capitalism, boosting the marketing potential for products and for generating advertising revenues, but it has been a disaster for liberal democracy. Selling political messages online requires techniques that are similar to other social media marketing campaigns, and this has irrevocably transformed democracy. Online tribes form around certain political views in ways that deepen pre-existing polarisations. There are no easy ways to insulate the old practices of democracy against the novel possibility that banks of voters can be suddenly provoked into holding more extreme views by agitating forces online, whether these provocateurs are within their own electorate or abroad.

Online 'misinformation' is also known as 'fake news', whereas 'disinformation' is intentionally biased content. All of this propagates online and is consumed by countless people unknowingly because as we whizz through our feeds, nothing visually distinguishes this fake or misleading content from trusted sources. Writer Siva Vaidhyanathan explained that 'Facebook is explicitly engineered to promote ideas that generate strong reactions, whether joy or indignation' since the most polarising messages and images generate the most engagements, whether supportive or in disgust. To be successful, other social media platforms followed Facebook's example.

Echo chambers are stoked by social media platforms as people more typically see content that plays to their existing biases. As Vaidhyanathan sums up pithily, 'Facebook is great for motivation. It is terrible for deliberation.'[9]

Social media has amplified the potential for toxic and tribal societal disagreement; it has turned free speech into the routinised lambasting of politicians; and it has made assembling street protests easier than ever before. Anyone with an internet connection can anonymously stir arguments in front of potentially huge online audiences. Enemies of liberal democracy are empowered once again to characterise freedom of speech and the freedom to peacefully protest as resulting in nothing more than shouting and mobs.

Social media is only the tip of the iceberg. Will liberal democracy survive, in its current form, the unstoppable march of technology? Imagine AI-generated industrial-scale quantities of fake news swaying voter sentiments. Liberal democracies are worried. The G7 issued a joint statement during its 2023 summit in Hiroshima promising to 'advance international discussions on inclusive AI governance and interoperability to achieve our common vision and goal of trustworthy AI, in line with our shared democratic values.' Sure, there have been technological disruptions to democracy before, like twenty-four-hour news in the 1990s forcing professional spin doctors to take over political message control in newer ways, rather than waiting for the next day's print newspapers. Now, the electorate instantly reacts to breaking events. And with mass communications, even the idea of representative politics based on *local* constituencies makes different sense today compared to when regions were more isolated from their capital city. 'Sending' your locally elected politician to Washington or London is a different matter in the age of video calling.

Western societies may yet get to grips with all of this through the regulation of emerging tech and with greater voter education. 'Freedom of speech depends further on norms of civility and respect for other people's zones of privacy,' wrote Fukuyama as he grappled with the disruptive impact of the internet on democracy. Where did the problem originate: 'Do the platforms simply reflect existing political and social conflicts, or are they actually the cause of such conflicts?' Both are true since modern technology 'bypasses the once-authoritative institutions that used to structure democratic discourse and provide citizens with a common base of factual knowledge over which they could deliberate'.[10] This is not going away and Western liberal democracies now face a set of tech-infused structural challenges.

* * *

In Europe, on average, an astonishingly short amount of time – sometimes as little as one or two years – elapses before governments fall apart as coalitions fracture due to snap or scheduled elections. The post-1945 median in Italy, Belgium and Finland of a government term was especially short at only one year. Even in Germany, when Chancellor Angela Merkel looked like a towering figure of continuity to the outside world, her era comprised three different governments lasting four years; a short caretaker government; and a final truncated term after she struggled to build a working coalition.[11] At least the continuity afforded by the EU helped to offset the regular turnover of Europe's governments.

It can never be taken for granted that far-flung parts of the world see the European or North American versions of democracy as anything other than parochially suited to these places rather than representing a universally aspirational norm. This brings to mind an amiable conversation I had at a Commonwealth Secretariat conference on countering extremism in 2019. Sitting next to a community-conscious Ugandan civil society activist, I was surprised to hear her personal view on democracy: that elections were a waste of time, and the resource expended on running them distracted from the needs of running a country. Merely an anecdote, but it forced me to think about the kinds of quasi-democratic models that will be seen in the future combining different political traditions.

Other political systems should not solely be judged as failed transitions to liberal democracy, but as political systems in their own right evolving according to their own logics. In just a couple of decades since the West scaled the peak of its global standing, the export potential of liberal democracy has hit major obstacles. We should start taking the alternatives seriously, even if they bring us distaste, because they are here to stay in parts of the world.

Lampooning any alternative to Western-style liberal democracy as jack-booted fascism is just not enough. While a spread of Russian-style or Chinese-style authoritarianism is a scary thought, these are far from the only alternative political systems out there. All manner of hybrid systems have hidden in plain sight, which do not sit fully in either the democracy or autocracy camps. The missing ingredient in many other political systems is not 'democracy' but 'liberalism'.

The West has both political liberalism and economic liberalism, even if they sit in tension with each other. Plenty of the other parts of the world think that you can have economic and market liberalism to get rich along with 'managed' elections and without political liberalism. Moreover, some people living in non-liberal political systems or in full-blown autocracies genuinely believe they have better political systems and may not be open to persuasion otherwise.

China's political system is a very particular type of all-powerful one-party rule. As the investor Ray Dalio noted, China's 'system of governance is more like what is typical in big companies, especially multigenerational companies, so they wonder why it is hard for Americans and other Westerners to understand the rationale for the Chinese system following this approach.'[12] Power is passed from one generation to the next in an opaque way, and no one gets to choose their boss – like it or lump it and if you protest against it, then you disappear into prison. China's political culture has evolved to prioritise stability delivered by top-down rule over individual self-expression and minority rights. Given the civil wars and invasions China has experienced into its modern history, stability is prized above all else. The prospects of China changing its political system appear close to nil.

All kinds of regimes seem to be running Potemkin elections, or gaming the field so that a ruler or ruling family never leaves office. Whether this involves 'strongman' presidents in Türkiye or managed leadership transitions in Singapore, these are political systems that rely on the appeal of consumerism, as well as on patronage networks and media management to secure legitimacy.

As Australian political scientist John Keane explained, it is wrong to assume that anything not modelled after the Western political systems is authoritarian and 'devoid of democracy'. In fact, 'rulers may claim they are shining examples of "managed democracy" or "people's democracy".' In these countries 'elections function as weapons for periodically cheering up disappointed citizens' and citizens 'can be taught to understand elections as a device for rewarding those who rule their subjects well'.[13] The outcome of the voting is a forgone conclusion, so it is about ritual and the illusion of participation in endorsing the ruler. Some call this 'electoral autocracy'. Fareed Zakaria called it 'illiberal democracy' and has explained how in Türkiye, Hungary and elsewhere, 'elected presidents and prime ministers use their majorities to pass laws that give them sustained and structural advantages over their opponents', for instance by filing court cases against rival politicians, journalists and NGOs to disempower any source of challenge before they win elections.[14] In exchange, for not complaining, the people – at least they are told – will be looked after. Often, this backfires, and spectacularly so when mass protests have gripped countries that have denied their people the power to reject a disliked leader.

Swathes of the world's populace live in such systems involving managed leadership transitions and no real choice at the ballot box. Such arrangements are understandably off-putting to Americans, Australians, British, French and others who thrive on the irreverence, individualism and identity-affirming social norms served up in their countries. But right now, Westerners will have to reconcile with a wider global reality in which their vaunted and in many senses laudable political ideals have no hope of carrying global influence in many other places.[15]

If all politics is indeed local, the long-term outcomes will surely not be the arrival of Westminster- or Capitol Hill-style democracy in the four corners of the globe – just as it will not only involve caricatures of autocracy. As if the world was headed to adopting a single political system anyway. 'Universalism, which dominated opinion in the US and in much of the EU, was taken to be the essence of the West,' wrote David Gress in 1998, '[b]ut the illusion that the modern West had escaped from history was precisely that.' Indeed, 'Liberty grew because it served the interests of power. This apparent paradox was the core of Western identity.'[16] We are now seeing the limits of Western influence on other political systems. The Western mould of politics has many unmatched virtues, but it is also parochial and idiosyncratic to specific Western countries, just like the politics of other places. For now, its export potential has peaked alongside other aspects of Western power.

The Westernisation of political systems around the world has had an incredible run so far. The initial burst of democracies spreading around the world came during decolonisation from Western rule, and another burst followed the defeat of the USSR by the West. These historical conditions will not repeat. It is not impossible that liberal democracy has another heyday but it is harder to envisage why that would be the case in a less Western-dominated world, where other political traditions can flourish.

We are moving towards greater *entrenchment* in the diversity of political systems around the world. Rather than paying tribute to the West and its preference for free and fair elections, the protection of individual rights and media freedoms, other governments and monarchies around the world will feel the pressure of keeping up these appearances lifting. Their politics can be practised with fewer hoops to jump through to secure Western approval for their democratic political systems.

This is part of moving away from the era of peak Western power. Even well-established democracies like India and Indonesia are putting their own spin on their political systems, symbolically differentiating their modern politics from the systems they operated after independence. Both Modi and Jokowi have been accused of engaging in grand political vanity projects: Modi by abandoning the old Edwin Lutyens-designed government buildings of the Raj and commissioning a new parliament building, which opened in Delhi in 2023. This closed a chapter on 'Lutyens' Delhi', evocative of its colonial past. For his part, Jokowi wanted to abandon his capital city, which had turned into a car-filled and polluted conurbation built on the Dutch colonial city of Old Jakarta. So, Jokowi announced that a brand-new capital city called Nusantara would be built in southern Borneo.

In 2024, the popular Jokowi respected his term limit and agreed to step down that October after two election wins and a decade in office. One of his former trade ministers, the Harvard-educated Thomas Lembong, spoke candidly after leaving his own post: 'The vast majority of Indonesian elites admire China. They think Western democracies are decadent, in decline, messy, slow.'[17] How many other political elites in the countries of Asia, Africa, the Middle East and Latin America share versions of this sentiment? How many will do far more than close up old colonial-era buildings or abandon an old capital to differentiate their systems in the future?

At this point, the more crusading parts of the West would do well to question if their democratic aspirations for other parts of the world were genuinely inspired by the desire for the betterment of others, or how much was inspired by the vanity of encouraging imitations in their own likeness, the ultimate act of flattery. Both can be true at the same time, even as the West's influence over how politics is practised in the four corners of the world fades.

Part Three

POWER

11

World Economies

> The world's centre of economic gravity has been shifting eastward for decades – causing trade patterns to shift as it moves. This eastward shift is due to rapid growth in the Indo-Pacific. Between 2000 and 2019, the Indo-Pacific accounted for 50% of global economic growth in real terms. By contrast, the EU contributed only 10% of growth over the same period . . . Economic power is expected to continue to shift from the G7 to the largest emerging economies in the 'E7 group' of 7 largest emerging economies – China, India, Brazil, Russia, Indonesia, Mexico and Turkey [and they] are expected to overtake the G7 in economic size during the 2030s.
>
> UK Department for International Trade, *Global Trade Outlook* (September 2021)[1]

IF YOU PICTURE the world economy as a pie, the slice that accounts for the combined economies of Western countries is becoming thinner. When the wealth of the world rebalances, so do the attentions of powerful people – this is an ironclad rule of life. Companies and countries instinctively head to where the money is, perhaps doing so warily when the wealth sits in places that they do not consider close to home, but they rarely resist the temptation outright.

The rebalancing world economy is the appropriate theme to begin Part Three, which covers the different forms of power. Economic strength is the cornerstone for achieving other forms of hard power like military, diplomatic and financial influence. It is necessary for fostering technological innovation and also for developing the tools of soft power. There is no point having big ideas for projecting influence if you cannot pay for them, and if you will be comprehensively outspent by your rivals.

Several stories are at play here. There is the changing balance of economic power within the West. There are the emerging economies of the rest of the world that at some point will presumably be considered fully emerged, thus requiring a new name. Amid all of this, there is the unfolding sense of saying goodbye to the world as it once was, when the West was fully economically dominant.

Western economic dominance has passed through successive eras. It was initially the Europe-centred world order that exploited steam technology, its military prowess and its favourable demographics to outpace other parts of the world – conditions that have long since vanished. Maritime colonialism played a role in Europe's economic growth, since expansionist countries that owned the capital, labour and raw materials of other countries reaped larger profits.[2] Even without annexing other places, this basic principle still applies. The richest countries achieve lofty levels of wealth via strong domestic production and by investing abroad to secure additional streams of profit, while the poorest countries see their natural endowments and part of their wealth flowing out of their borders.

The extent of Western economic success was astonishing. As explained by Piketty, 'from 1900 to 1980, 70–80 per cent of the global production of goods and services was concentrated in Europe and America, which incontestably dominated the rest of the world'. This situation arose because 'the lead that Europe and America achieved during the Industrial Revolution allowed these two regions to claim a share of global output that was two to three times as large as the global average.' He caveats the presentation of a singular 'Western bloc' by explaining that their economic peaks were scaled at different times: Europe's combined economic strength peaking before the Great War when it accounted for half of global output, while the US reached its peak of almost 40 per cent in the 1950s.[3]

The US was most dominant after the world wars because the other major economies had been devastated. The path opened for the US to assist in Europe's recovery and to dominate the world economy. The US fully harnessed its continent of riches by becoming a leading centre of technological innovation and a magnet for attracting foreign talent. It also benefitted from a lack of serious competitors. The Axis powers of Germany, Italy and Japan had been utterly defeated, and while Britain and France initially clung on to their colonies, they soon divested themselves of empire due to their bankrupted economies. Asia was in no position to compete: India only became independent in 1947 while China was mired in civil war until 1949, which had devastated its still largely agrarian expanse. While the USSR rose to challenge the US ideologically and militarily in the Cold War, by the 1980s, the weakness of Russia's economy signalled its own spiral of demise.

The US presented its economic system as the archetype for others to emulate – a claim that became more plausible after the implosion of the USSR in 1991 and the fall from grace of its Marxist ideology. Russia and Eastern Europe was opened to 'capitalist penetration' in the words of US historian Gary Gerstle, who explained 'it also dramatically widened the willingness of China (still nominally a communist state) to experiment with capitalist economics'. On top of this, the USSR's collapse also 'removed what had been an imperative in America (and in Europe and elsewhere) for class compromise between capitalist elites and the working classes', whereas previously the 'fear of communism made possible the class compromises between capital and labour that underwrote the New Deal order'.[4] Not only had capitalism gone global in the 1990s, but it had also entered a newly unfettered phase in the West.

* * *

Taking stock of the last century, it is possible to interpret the sheer extent of Western economic power to have been a historical aberration and one that couldn't last forever.[5] What is now happening is a far cry from the 1990s. A paradoxical situation has been emerging for the West in which the US economy is expected to retain its own large slice of the global economic pie, but its closest allies are not. Western Europe's economies do not share such healthy prognoses and nor does the economy of their sole Asian G7 partner, Japan, in terms of expected future growth.

These trends are clear when their economies are measured according to Gross Domestic Product (GDP, the total value of goods and services produced in an economy) based on Purchasing Power Parity (PPP, which compares countries' GDP by adjusting for their different currencies, thus calculating how much each country spends to afford the same amounts of goods and services).[6] In 1980, the US's economy accounted for 21% of world GDP; by 2000, it was 20%; and by 2023, it had shrunk to 15%, due to the rise of China and the other emerging economies eating away its share. In comparison, Western Europe's collective share of global GDP had shrunk more dramatically, from 28% in 1980 to 22% in 2000 and falling to 15% in 2023. Japan's shrinkage has been acute, from 8% in 1980 to 7% by 2000 and to just 3.7% by 2023.[7]

Economists also use another yardstick measurement: nominal GDP (which uses the exchange rates set by markets to compare economies). This measurement favours the US, showing it to have enjoyed a roughly consistent 25% share of the global economy between 1990 and 2022. Because of Western Europe's and Japan's falling shares, the US has accounted for a *rising share* of the G7's collective heft. In 1990, the US accounted for 40% of the G7's nominal GDP; and by 2022 this had grown to 58%. When using the PPP measurement of GDP, the US's economic dominance of the G7 is again evident, having risen from 43% in 1990 to 51% in 2022.[8]

The implication is clear: the US is inadvertently creating for itself an island built on its strong economic performance that floats in a sea filled with major allies that grow less impressively. A key reason for these uneven economic performances is that Europe and Japan face more acutely unfavourable demographic situations than the US. This returns us to a question posed earlier. What global significance can the US claim to have if it is *not* leading a bloc of several powerful Western and Western-allied democratic countries that *collectively* have the power to shape the world? Even if the idea of a 'collective West' cannot be taken at face value, the US cannot indefinitely go it alone on behalf of the West. Nor would it have the political will to do so.

You can forget about burden-sharing if the US has to pick up a bigger tab for hugely expensive global engagements on behalf of the wider West. There will always be US politicians who complain about free-riding friends who underpay their share of the costs in a supposedly collective endeavour, like funding Ukraine's military to defend itself against Russia's invasion after 2022. Even if the US remains resplendent atop a pedestal of its own continuing economic success, the overall economic clout of the Western world and the G7 is declining in relation to other groupings.

* * *

At the turn of the millennium there was much anticipation around the rise of the emerging economies. Memorably, Lord Jim O'Neill, then at investment bank Goldman Sachs, coined the term 'BRIC' to refer to Brazil, Russia, India and China, which he identified as holding at that time 23% of world GDP based on PPP at the end of 2000 (it was a little later that

South Africa joined the grouping, making it the BRICS). The acronym clearly stuck. At the time, O'Neill surmised that globalisation would no longer be US-led in the future since the benefits of international trade and the diffusion of modern standards and technologies would lift other economies. He grouped the BRIC countries together as the larger emerging market economies that were projected to experience faster economic growth than in the G7. He argued that 'In line with these prospects, world policymaking forums should be re-organised and in particular, the G7 should be adjusted to incorporate BRIC representatives.'[9]

Initially, this suggestion was heeded. It was a happier time back then, geopolitically speaking. For a number of years, Russia was incorporated into what became the G8, until it was expelled in 2014 for its invasion of Ukraine involving the annexation of Crimea. Russia and the other emerging economies had to settle for being in the G20, a body that cannot agree to take decisive actions on major issues given the diversity of its membership. While Russia and China sat at the UN Security Council as two of its five permanent members, India and Brazil remained outside this symbolic top table of world affairs. The World Bank and the IMF remained Western-dominated, and it was not lost on anyone that both these bodies were headquartered in Washington DC, while the UN was headquartered in New York – so US government officials always had the greatest ease of access. These arrangements for global governance began to look incongruous as the pecking order of world economies started to shift.

In the mid-2010s, China overtook the US in terms of GDP according to PPP. The significance of this needs to be caveated by pointing out that China's GDP per capita has remained much lower than that of the US and most European countries, meaning that the Chinese have on average less individual wealth. In addition, when measured according to nominal GDP, the US remains king with a far larger economy than China.[10] For China to close the gap with the US on nominal GDP, let alone GDP per capita, could take decades or indeed may never happen. Nevertheless, the world took note that, after 2015, according to the widely recognised comparative measure of GDP by PPP, China had dethroned the US as world number one.[11] The symbolism of this dethroning by PPP partly reflected the cheaper costs of things in China compared to the US – but it was a dethroning, nonetheless.

China's economic rise has given hope to emerging economies that they can grow faster than mature economies since they are still exploring their growth potential. Just compare these past growth rates as summarised by economic historian and energy expert Daniel Yergin: 'Between 2003 and 2013, China's economy grew more than two and a half times over; India's more than doubled. The world economy grew by just 30%, the US by 17%, Europe by 11%, and Japan just 8%.'[12] Economies with the potential to productively harness their huge populations such as India and Indonesia are expected to grow significantly in the future, since labour productivity in these emerging economies can improve faster than in mature economies. Emerging economies can also rapidly raise productivity by adopting tried and tested techniques from overseas, creating 'second mover' advantages – but despite their catch-up potential, they also face huge challenges around fostering their own innovation, avoiding indebtedness and lifting people out of poverty (the so-called middle-income trap, where higher incomes are never realised for much of the population).

Another perspective on whether an emerging economy can realise its growth potential is offered by a different metric: its sovereign debt rating, which conveys its ability to attract investment and to borrow money. The most influential sovereign debt ratings agencies are predictably enough US-based (Standard & Poor, Moody's and Fitch Ratings). The Western-centred nature of the global financial system again rears its head. These ratings agencies score each country's economy by assessing the strength of its institutions and governance, its ability to afford its existing debt, and the external risks to the stability of its currency. A higher sovereign debt rating indicates a greater ability of a government to pay its debts, and hence to raise capital by borrowing money.

This is where we see unevenness between regions. When looking across the sovereign debt rating score from across these three ratings agencies, the highest scores belong to the economies of the Anglosphere, the EU, East Asia and the Gulf. The lower sovereign ratings of countries like Brazil, India, Indonesia and South Africa convey some of the hurdles they are yet to vault to realise their potential. While the conventional thinking is that since they are already in the G20, and their large and young populations mean they are expected to grow in the future, there is more to it than this. To fully explore their growth potential, emerging economies may need further domestic institutional reforms and to reduce some of the sources of risk to their economies.[13]

Nothing is guaranteed in the forward passage of emerging economies, but the broad trend lines do suggest a very different future featuring the rise of *several* non-Western economies. From where we are poised today, the world is experiencing a decentralisation of economic power away from the West. The world economic outlook to 2050 is expected to involve a continuing eastward shift, with Indo-Pacific countries altogether accounting for 56% of global economic growth in this time, while the EU and North America will collectively produce 25% of growth.[14] Even if China's annual GDP growth slows to 4% or 5%, rather than its previously heady double-digit annual rises, the economic balance of the world will still de-Westernise. The question is how much more this will slide away from the West.

When on 1 January 2024 the BRICS expanded to BRICS+, one of the most striking implications was the combined size of their economies. Lord Jim O'Neill, now an advisor at Chatham House, reflected on this. 'Clearly, the BRICS' symbolic power will grow. The group has been able to tap into the broader Global South's suspicion that post-World War Two global-governance organizations are too Western.' However, there was number-crunching scepticism also voiced by O'Neill (and others in the West) that this was not as terrifying as it seemed. The figures said different things based on which measure of GDP (by PPP or nominal) was used: 'It is true that in terms of purchasing power parity, the BRICS are slightly larger than the G7. But, because their currencies trade at prices far below their PPP-implied levels, the group remains significantly smaller than its advanced-economy counterpart, when measured in current nominal US dollars.'[15] While this is true for now there is potential for the gap to close significantly in the coming decades. The great economic catch-up with the West is well underway.

* * *

The G7 was once described by a senior Biden Administration official as the 'steering group of the free world', indicating that the US, Western Europe and Japan were still the guardians of decision-making on crucial matters.[16] The US found the G7 especially useful for coordinating sanctions against Russia, for leading efforts to support embattled Ukraine, and for organising a collective stance against China's rising clout. The West had other forums to use as well, but it would be more painstaking or impossible to arrive swiftly at a consensus and engage in coordinated action through the NATO alliance or the EU, given the greater number of member states and formal decision-making structures of these bodies. The G7 was smaller and more informal, since it is literally a gathering of leaders, not an institution in its own right. The term 'forum shopping' is diplomat-speak for choosing from all your active club memberships the one that is suited to the specific task at hand, and the G7 had become the go-to choice for expressing 'the will of the West' in the 2020s.

The rise of the G7 as a control centre for Western decision-making on global issues must be juxtaposed with the relative fall of the G7 as a singularly dominant economic bloc. When you tally up the G7's collective economic clout relative to the rest of the world, it represents a declining proposition. One of the main rationales for originally assembling the G7 in 1975 was that these 'advanced economies' accounted for a dominant share of the world economy back then.

Like a downward arrow on a graph, the extent of the G7's share of the world economy has since dwindled. In the 1980s, the G7 collectively amounted to around 65% of the world economy based on nominal GDP, a share it still held into the 2000s. But by 2020 this had dropped to 46%. It is projected to drop to 36% by 2040. The 'steering committee of the free world' is not quite in free fall but its collective economic power has markedly declined. Conversely, the illustrative grouping of the E7 (China, India, Brazil, Russia, Indonesia, Mexico and Türkiye) has a share of the world economy that has risen from a paltry 11% in 2000 to 28% in 2020, and it is likely to keep increasing.[17]

Moreover, when using the PPP measure of GDP, which favours developing economies more than the nominal GDP measurement, the G7's share is just 30% while the five core BRICS member countries have already overtaken it by claiming a 31.5% share of the world economy. When this is broadened to the BRICS+ members, they have almost half the world's population and 37% of world GDP by PPP.[18] Theirs is an upward arrow on the graph, a very visible representation of the changing world.

For so long, Western leaders have had the economic clout to deliver messages that the rest of the world had little choice but to heed, or to disobey and suffer through exclusion. This is still true to a big extent: defying the G7 countries and losing access to their markets remains a risky gambit. If the EU is corralled to act in concert with the G7, as it did when sanctioning Russia in 2022, this magnifies the impact of Western economic clout. But the calculations for defying the West are continually shifting.

Take the example of Russia's economic survival in the face of withering Western-led sanctions imposed in 2022. Not only could Russia buttress itself against Western sanctions by trading with China, which accounted for 15.4% of the world economy according to the IMF's PPP calculations; Russia also traded with India, Indonesia, South Africa, Türkiye and Brazil; these countries altogether now accounted for 14.34% of the world economy in PPP terms.

The multipolarisation of the world economy is well underway. Some people argue that calling it multipolarisation is going too far, since it is only the two horses, the US and China, that really matter in the race, with their economies head and shoulders above everybody else. However, it is a misnomer to think that a multipolar system requires *many powers of equal size*; all it requires is at least three or more countries to have significant power. Multipolar systems tend to include a few huge powers and several middle-sized powers, all with varying amounts of independent power and influence. Academic uses of multipolarity to describe past historical eras also referred to unequally sized but independently powerful nations and empires, so why can't the same principle apply again?[19]

Moreover, this is a continually shifting picture. The West can hardly stop emerging economies from emerging, and nor can the West stop them from trading with each other to greater extents than before. A priority of US foreign and commercial policy in the 2020s has been to tempt other emerging economies away from the authoritarian clasps of China and Russia, notably by trying to draw India's attention away from the BRICS. Debating whether a country does or does not trade extensively with China seems like everything today. But the long-term trends suggest a diversification in trade options and a widening of successful models of economic growth that are not exclusively guided by the West.

Rather than wondering how the rest of the world comports itself in relation to the West's greater economic strength, the more pertinent question of the future might ask how the Western countries will slot into the wider world of these emerging economies.

***

The impressive power of the US's economy cannot stem Westlessness alone; conversely, the growth of China's economy is but one part of the wider emerging economic landscape. Which countries are expected to shoot up the rankings later this century? Nothing is inevitable: when projecting tomorrow's top-ranked economies, big assumptions are being made around the faster global growth potential of the emerging economies over the established ones.

The current membership of the G20 already conveys the diversity of the global economy. It comprises nineteen countries (Argentina, Australia, Brazil, Canada, China, France, Germany, India, Indonesia, Italy, Japan, Mexico, Russia, Saudi Arabia, South Africa, South Korea, Türkiye, UK and US) plus the EU. In September 2023, thanks to a push by that year's G20 host India, the African Union became a new permanent member of the G20. Collectively, the G20 countries represent a large percentage of global GDP, trade and of humanity. But the G20 annual gatherings of world leaders often don't achieve much more than photoshoots of world leaders, while also allowing them to discuss their own country's concerns on the sidelines of the conference. The grand finale of G20 summits tend to produce lowest-common-denominator final statements covering the big issues of the day.

Tomorrow's top-ranked economies are likely to be even more diverse. A radical projection was offered by investment bank Goldman Sachs: according to nominal GDP, which is the measure that currently still places the US in pole position, China overtakes the US around 2035, and India catches up by 2075, moving ahead of the US to second place and creating a three-horse race near the top. The Euro area would lag far behind and Japan even further behind than that by 2075. Indonesia, Nigeria, Pakistan, Egypt and Brazil would be in the top 10. These projections were based on assumptions that 'the prospect of rapid population growth in countries such as Nigeria, Pakistan and Egypt imply that – with the appropriate policies and institutions – these economies could become some of the largest in the world.'[20] In other words, for these projections to come true depends on these countries making the necessary structural reforms that would allow them to harness their growing populations into productive workforces. Today, such prospects seem highly speculative, but 2075 is a long way away.

There is something abstract and almost fantastical about gazing at an entirely hypothetical table of future world economies. It turns on its head our assumptions about economic success. Far too much could happen between now and 2050, let alone 2075, for these rankings to come to pass so precisely. But they do fire up the imagination about just how transformed the world could be in terms of the balance of economic power between the regions of the world.

The speed at which China has urbanised and modernised its once heavily agrarian economy, and having done so under a strong and oftentimes tyrannical one-party rule system, has been inspirational for some others looking on to make similar leaps – not because they want to copy China's model wholesale but because China has reinterpreted methods advocated by the West for economic development in its own ways. Any nation's economic rise is a unique outcome of its circumstances and its political culture (which, in China, has been a top-heavy and repressive one-party rule that is very specific to its own political evolution). Other countries may not want to carbon-copy China's rise, but they can still learn and benefit from it.

Nothing like China's accession into the World Trade Organization in 2002 will happen again; this gave it uninhibited access to 163 new markets, while injecting its huge manufacturing base and its millions of workers into the world trading system.[21] This is why some Western geopolitical thinkers feel ripped off, arguing that after its entry into the WTO, the 'CCP exploited its 20 year grace period to the fullest. China sucked up Western technology and capital, dumped its products in foreign markets while keeping its own market relatively closed, installed Chinese officials atop international organisations, and proclaimed a peaceful rise.'[22]

As we have already seen, however, protecting domestic markets (albeit in different ways to China and in certain circumstances) was also a tactic employed by Western countries years before to grow their own economies.

There is a tendency in some Western circles to consider the rise of others as being mainly thanks to the West, with the US in particular having created opportunities for others to benefit from participating in the global economy. This is not entirely without justification given the US's leading role in propagating globalisation, and in providing security to some of the world's major trade routes and chokepoints with its military deployments. Be that as it may, it hardly means West-worshipping gratitude will follow. Hammering China's rise only mentally displaces the fact that we have no modern precedent for managing more balanced economic relations between a plethora of Western and non-Western countries. The rejoinder – that China's own industriousness and its market reforms, which began in 1978, should be given more credit for this outcome – is also being argued in other quarters.[23]

Regardless of the never-ending debate over whether and to what extent China's rise depended on the West, the outcome is clear. The era of singular Western dominance of global economies is ending. Piketty estimated a steep decline: '[B]y 2010, the European-American share had declined to roughly 50 per cent, or approximately the same level as in 1860. In all probability, it will continue to fall and may go as low as 20–30 per cent at some point in the 21st century.'[24] As the world economy ceases orbiting the Western sun, breaking out into its own solar systems, things are rebalancing to resemble what they once were. There is a closing of the historical circle when, 250 years ago, China and India accounted for nearly 60% of the world economy, before the West's dramatic industrialisation, imperial propulsion and population exportation propelled it to a commanding global position.

The US will need to pursue its own strategy of diversity, moving far beyond the other Western countries and Japan to solidify its economic relations with newly emerging economies. There is also the possibility that, having looked at the declining graph of the G7's collective economic heft, there are active minds in the West wondering how and who to recruit to expand this grouping of the US-led leading liberal democratic economies. Looking at the current top economies, it is hard to see other viable candidates (Australia is not large enough to arrest the decline; India is too independently minded, and its liberal credentials have been called into question during Modi's more personalised and majoritarian style of leadership). Geopolitical allegiances may well be rewired several decades from now on the basis of the changing patterns in the world economy.

Consequently, will the diffusion of economic heft across the non-Western world further fragment the West itself? For instance, if the EU decides in the future to trade more enthusiastically with a still-authoritarian China, while the US snubs some European countries for doing so. One might readily predict a further loosening of the 'collective West', in which bonds that will still be shared in culture and in political ideologies end up threatened by a continental drift across the Atlantic Ocean, as different economic paths are pursued by individual Western countries to profit from the emerging economies. Even if the BRICS+ grouping does not expand further, or even fragments in years or decades from now, there will be new alignments of economic relations that we cannot yet foresee, but that will look completely different to those of the last century.

12

World Policing

> 'The end is inevitable, Maverick. Your kind is headed for extinction.'
>
> 'Maybe so, sir, but not today.'
>
> Tom Cruise's fictional navy pilot in *Top Gun: Maverick* responds to a superior telling him that his piloted warplane will be replaced by unmanned drones.

THE SIGHT OF US and British aircraft carriers sailing past your high-rise office is one way to be reminded of who rules the waves. Tipped off by a ship-spotting colleague, I watched through binoculars as the USS *Ronald Reagan* weaved its way at pace through the densely packed container ships that permanently throng the waters off Singapore's coastline. On her maiden voyage to the Pacific, the aircraft carrier HMS *Queen Elizabeth* headed like its US counterpart to the South China Sea, performing a 'freedom of navigation' voyage, in the jargon of naval specialists. Which meant that by dint of the very presence of these vessels, China would be reminded of who's really boss because everyone can sail in international waters. Its adjacent waters may be called the 'South China Sea' but China cannot claim to own it, since a country's territorial waters typically extend twelve nautical miles off its coastline, so says maritime law.

US Navy admirals would periodically head onshore to make the case for their country's military presence in the region. From their bases in Yokosuka, Japan (hosting the US Seventh Fleet), and Honolulu, Hawaii (hosting Indo-Pacific Command, which is responsible for US military forces in the Pacific and the Western Indian Oceans), they covered a huge geographic sweep. Their pressed white dress uniforms made them look like throwbacks to a different era as these US Navy delegations did the rounds in Singapore, the Philippines and Vietnam, shoring up basing rights for US ships and coordinating naval exercises with partner countries. All of this effort was intended to deter China's military from thinking it could do such things as harass Filipino patrol boats or Vietnamese fisherman, let alone invade Taiwan.

Unsurprisingly, China claimed that these Americans were turning the region against them. I saw this unfold when my employer in Singapore hosted US Defence Secretary Austin for a public lecture in July 2021, which he entitled 'The imperative of partnership', something he accused China of lacking due to its 'destabilising military activity and other forms of coercion against the people of Taiwan', while also declaring that 'Beijing's claim to the vast majority of the South China Sea has no basis in international law'. China's embassy in Singapore blew a gasket at Austin's talk: 'It is the interference and meddling of the US that have made many regional issues worse,' because 'China and its neighbours have the capability and wisdom to handle differences through friendly consultations, and surely do not need the US pointing fingers,' they wrote in a published complaint about Austin's lecture.[1]

A rhetorical struggle is preferable to a military one, but tension has risen partly because of China's attempts to change its balance of military power with the US. China is well underway in its ambitious warship construction programme. Its first aircraft carrier was built on an old Soviet-era hull that it purchased from Ukraine, but its later aircraft carriers were domestically built and are more advanced with every iteration (the third, *Fujian*, was launched in 2022). China's naval ship-building has sent shockwaves through the US Navy, resulting in the US redoubling efforts to modernise its fleet. Both sides have invested in the unmanned air and naval vehicles that feature in any modern war. Swarms of drones could render lumbering aircraft carriers like the USS *Ronald Reagan* or *Fujian* into sitting ducks. Russia's war in Ukraine has offered a glimpse into how drones have inflicted losses on tanks and ships.

Well aware that they cannot again fight yesterday's wars, the US Marine Corps has freshened up its combat doctrines for a future war in Asia, so that relatively small teams of marines can quickly disperse to commanding positions across the so-called 'first island chain' that stretches across Japan's Kuril and Ryukyu Islands, Taiwan, northern Philippines and Borneo. From here, the marines could launch and coordinate anti-ship missiles and drones to target passing Chinese vessels in the event of war. The US Marines have drilled for these island-hopping operations in northern Australia and in Papua New Guinea, which in 2023 signed a security partnership deal permitting the US military to use its bases. This deal was being sought with desperation by the US and Australia, as the nearby Solomon Islands went the other way in 2022 by signing its own security deal with China's government, creating the concern of Chinese naval bases one day popping up in Oceania.

Concern around future war in Asia has caught on in London and Canberra, when together with Washington DC, these capitals of the Anglosphere announced the 'AUKUS' submarine programme in 2021. It involves British and US defence companies building for Australia a fleet of nuclear-powered attack submarines, adding further naval capacity in years to come to deter or fight China. Japan was also brought into the fold after it made the historic move of modifying its pacifist post-1945 constitution, which had prohibited the types of offensive weapon systems Japan could procure and prevented it from exporting arms. As Japan loses its living link to World War Two, its fears of China's rising military power have reaffirmed its desire to band with the West. It was the late Japanese President Shinzo Abe who coined the term 'Free and Open Indo-Pacific', now used by Western officials as a unifying concept for making a collective stand over any forceful attempt by China to overturn the status quo in the region. Capping this off, in December 2022, Japan signed a deal with Britain and Italy to design and build a new stealth plane called 'Tempest'. As with the AUKUS subs, Tempest planes will take decades to develop, conveying a long-term commitment to deterring China, if these projects are finished.

Despite this burden-sharing between the US and its allies in policing the Indo-Pacific, it is hard to avoid the impression that the West's military power is really just US military power. The US defence budget is so much larger than any other nation and it is the only military with a truly global presence. The US remains the ultimate security guarantor for many countries in Europe, the Middle East and East Asia. Western military reach in Africa is more mixed, where the French retain a string of bases in some of their former colonies. The US military's 'Africa Command' failed to find an African country to sponsor its headquarters, and has hence remained based in Stuttgart, Germany, managing its operations from afar using planes in Djibouti, where it does have an airbase, and Italy, from where its aircraft swiftly cross the Mediterranean. It would be a misnomer (as I heard a US undersecretary of defence explain) to look at the static map of bases to grasp the US military's reach – much of it operates as a rapid reaction force capable of surging US military power to wherever on the globe the President deems necessary.[2]

Opponents of this global US role have fixated on the human and military disasters that followed its wars in Vietnam, Afghanistan and Iraq. For all the debate that still surrounds its ill-begotten wars there is also the humdrum business of America's constabulary role. The US military's standing missions involve safeguarding major trading chokepoints like the Malacca Strait alongside Malaysia, the Hormuz Strait in the Gulf, Bab-al-Mandab at the tip of the Red Sea and the Panama Canal closer to home. Supporters of the US global security role argue that it has helped to keep the peace by policing these trading routes and more often than not helping deter other would-be aggressors.

We may well miss this aspect of the USA's global security presence if it were to vanish. Its global military bases are a modern version of the legions posted at the frontiers of empire, odd capsules of Americana in far-flung places. Even their greatest sceptics must accept the US has chosen to exercise its imperial potential with relative restraint.

The world has no such thing as a mandated international policeman, which is lesson one in an international relations university degree. In domestic life, if the rule of law functions, you are locked up for committing a gross crime – but in international life, anarchy can reign since would-be transgressors can only be deterred by a superior force, not by international law. The UN is no world government. The International Criminal Court cannot enforce its writ when it comes to the transgressions of powerful countries, be it China or Russia or the US itself.

With memories of the devastation of World War Two still just in living memory, and with the shock of Russia's invasion of Ukraine fresh in our minds, there are parables aplenty showing the horrors of larger states gobbling up smaller ones. So, there are good reasons to want the US to retain its global constabulary role. Dominant views on this vary from country to country. In tiny Singapore, it is very much considered to be a good thing. Here was Prime Minister Lee's verdict at the 2023 'Asia Future Summit', which incidentally was presented as a bilingual event in English and Mandarin:

> The Americans have been a major force in Asia since at least the Second World War. It is now nearly coming on

> eighty years. And they remain welcomed. I mean there are times when people talk about the Ugly Americans. But given that it is eighty years – two and a half generations, three generations – actually the Americans have been dominant in this region, while giving countries space to grow, to develop, to compete with one another peacefully and not to be held down or squatted upon. And that is why they are still welcomed after so many years. And if the Chinese can achieve something like that, I think the region can prosper [because] it depends on how China plays its cards and how deftly it is able to grow its influence without making other countries feel that they have been squeezed, pressured or coerced.[3]

The US's critics would point to the absence of Vietnam's fate in this account of Asia's last eighty years. But the US's friends still hope it can help to keep the peace in their own backyards and to do so without blundering into war. Which line of argument around America's global military role will win out?

* * *

As the relative power of economies changes, so does their war-making capability. This is familiar to anyone who has read Paul Kennedy's classic book *The Rise and Fall of the Great Powers*. He explained how changes in a nation's wealth ultimately determined its place in the global pecking order. 'This does not mean, however, that a nation's relative economic and military power will rise and fall in parallel,' since the historical examples studied by Kennedy 'suggest that there is a noticeable "lag time" between the trajectory of a state's relative economic strength and the trajectory of its military/territorial influence'.[4] This theme is now increasingly pertinent.

For better or for worse, the world will change if the US military loses its qualitative advantages over its rivals. Or if enough other nations outside the West no longer want to partner with it and host its bases. Or if the US tires of its global military role. Eighty years after the US decided to leave its troops deployed in huge numbers in Asia and in Europe after World War Two, the financial burdens of imperial overstretch are routinely debated in its domestic politics. Can we expect another eighty years of America's world policing?

At present, there is little evidence of a qualitative risk to the US's military dominance. The US's military budget is so much larger than the next ten largest defence budgets combined. 'Overmatch' is what the US looks to maintain against its challengers so that its military and its alliances remain so far ahead of any putative opponents. The numbers so far still add up to this principle of keeping the gap wide. In 2022, the top three defence budgets were the US spending $766.6 billion; China spending $360 billion; and Russia spending $192 billion (with the Chinese and Russian figures estimated in PPP to account for their lower local costs).[5] According to data from the Stockholm International Peace Research Institute (SIPRI), which conducts defence budgetary analysis, the US accounted for 39% of world military spending in 2022 and China for 13%, with Russia at 3.9%, India at 3.6% and Saudi Arabia at 3.3%. This top five accounted for 63% of global military spending in 2022.[6] Overmatch indeed, since the US has a towering lead not only in total defence expenditure but also in the technological and tactical know-how that gives its military a further qualitative edge.

Notably, aside from the US, the remainder of the top five defence spenders are non-Western. This was not always the case and in 2009, SIPRI reported the top five as the US at 43%, China at 6.8%, France at 4.2%, Britain at 3.8% and Russia at 3.5%. European countries have slipped down these rankings over many years. With China's and India's economies having grown in size many times over, even if they spend the same percentage of their GDP on defence as they did before, their overall expenditure will be ever larger.[7] This is in line with the expected lag time between GDP growth and consequent increasing military power.

Another indicator of the Westless drift in defence comes in the terrifying shape of nuclear-weapon arsenals. Although Russia has the numerically largest nuclear weapon stockpile, the US is not far behind and is likely to have a higher percentage of well-maintained nuclear weapons and delivery systems, given that some of Russia's legacy weapons date back to the USSR. Worryingly, the US and Russia have pulled out of some of their mutual agreements to transparently communicate their military deployments and arsenals made at the end of the Cold War (a trend that has been accelerating ever since the collapse in US–Russia relations over Putin's war in Ukraine). If this was not worrying enough, then China is also making serious investments to expand and modernise its nuclear arsenal. Recognising this dual risk, in 2023, a Congressional Commission investigating the US's 'nuclear posture', meaning its ability to deter its opponents, warned that the US 'will soon encounter a fundamentally different global setting than it has ever experienced: we will face a world where two nations possess nuclear arsenals on par with our own.'[8] This is in addition to the smaller nuclear arsenals of India, Pakistan, Israel and North Korea, with the UK and France completing the list of nuclear-weapons-armed countries.

Western defence analysts tend to think China is hiding the true extent of its defence spending, especially around expanding its nuclear arsenal. China's government plays this down, saying things like 'China's annual defence budget will remain single-digit growth for the eighth year in a row, with an increase of 7.2 per cent in 2023', while pointing out that, by their calculations, China's defence budget is still just a quarter the size of the US's.[9] For now and in the foreseeable future, its nearest competitors cannot catch the US in defence spending. But fielding effective military capabilities is about more than massive expenditure. It is also about morale, quality of political leadership, being sent on achievable missions, with troops who have the will to fight. It depends on drones for remote surveillance, satellite guidance of weapons and other forms of modern and future warfare. For a military to operate ambitiously and globally it also needs foreign basing rights, formal alliances, informal partnerships and international legitimacy. All are vital parts of the equation, and some of it is showing signs of tilting against the US military's ability to police the Western-led world order.

* * *

One clear change is in how the US uses its military power. Over the last three decades, this has tipped from expansionist to defensive aims. By expansionist, I mean the era of the US military embarking on democracy crusades to rewrite the political destinies of far-flung places. Now the US military is being used more defensively, circling the wagons to better protect the West and its close democratic allies.

This transition has been stark. Back in the 1990s, the world view of the West and especially of the US was guided by an orthodoxy of 'the democratic peace thesis'. This theory posited that a world of democracies was a safer world for all. Historical data was produced to show that countries run as democracies did not tend to fight other democracies – although the US government thought this should not prohibit it from fighting in certain other places to turn them into democracies.

Others interpreted this with cynicism. Retired Chinese Colonel Liu Mingfu wrote that 'without the USSR to check its power, the US began to lose its restraint' by waging the Gulf War, Kosovo War, Afghanistan War, and invading Iraq 'to cement its hegemonic interests', while noting with some envy that the 'USA excels at occupying the international moral high ground' in attempting to justify these interventions.[10] In ideological terms the West placed itself at the vanguard of a world of democracies with the US military being the tip of the spear. For this mission's most fervent believers, the cause of spreading democracy periodically needed to be sanctified by spilling blood.

This rationale was one aspect of the wars the US launched after 9/11. In 2003, *Time* magazine placed US General Tommy Franks on its cover and wrote that 'the US mops up one war in Afghanistan and prepares to launch a second in Iraq'. The article summed up the essence of unchecked US power: '[President George W.] Bush would love as much support as possible against Iraq, but in the end he requires only his own resolve.' But the Iraq invasion went disastrously wrong. Iraq suffered a horrific civil war as occupying US, UK and other Western forces battled a brutal terrorist insurgency waged by jihadists while also fighting militias backed by neighbouring Iran. Those who devised the invasion in faraway Washington DC did not have the foggiest clue about Iraq, the diversity of its people, the region, and that their war of democratisation would be widely interpreted as an act of neo-colonialism.

Despite the disaster in Iraq, the US, UK and France tried it all over again in Libya in 2011 by helping to oust the regime of Libyan dictator Muammar Gaddafi, after a local rebellion erupted against his rule. Western warplanes bombed from up high while Libya's rebels did the bulk of fighting against Gaddafi's forces, killing the dictator in the process. Initially, advocates of forcefully spreading democracy felt validated. The US opened an embassy and posted Ambassador Chris Stevens to support oil-rich Libya's transition out of Gaddafi's dictatorship. But Stevens was murdered when a Libyan militia attacked his embassy compound. A decade later, Libya was still riven with civil war. Western countries again failed to foster a democracy transition in a complex and culturally distinct post-colonial country.

More chapters of Western overreach followed. Like in Libya, an uprising began against Syria's dictator Bashar al-Assad. The West declared Assad *persona non grata* due to his army's brutal repression of the protesters. Since the US,

France and Britain had just helped to end Gaddafi's rule in Libya, and had now used similar rhetoric to condemn Assad, there was widespread expectation that Western military action in Syria was coming. In the end, chastened and drained by its failure in Iraq, and still committed to its war in Afghanistan, the US only half-heartedly assisted Syria's rebels. In 2013, a vote in the British Parliament against taking military action in Syria further discouraged the West. President Barack Obama, never as committed to these wars as his predecessor Bush, decided not to attack Syria.

Russia, not believing its luck, correctly sensed the winds were changing in this era of energetic Western military action. So, Russia launched its own game-changing intervention in Syria in September 2015, which after years of bloody war succeeded in its mission of keeping the dictator Assad in power and reinforcing Syria's status as a Russian client state (as it had been of the USSR). Assad's rule was even rehabilitated by other Middle Eastern countries, leading also to an embarrassing situation for the West in which a decade after it had called for Assad's removal, the failure to achieve this was clear to see.

All of this unfolded *before* the pinnacle of Western military interventionist humiliation – when the US military and its close Western allies pulled out of Afghanistan in summer 2021. It was a striking moment of imperial retrenchment after another failed attempt to use Western military power to change political destinies in culturally remote and faraway places.

After an exhausting, costly and unsuccessful two decades of waging foreign wars, the domestic US political debate had turned against its military fighting far from home. The phrase 'forever wars', lifted from a science-fiction novel by Joe Haldeman, was invoked by Americans to warn of the perils of embroilment in wars with no good end in sight. The spectrum of support for this view has widened in the US. On the political right, Trump's 'Make America Great Again' movement argued that costly foreign wars distracted from needs at home. On the left, endeavours like the Quincy Institute think tank, co-founded by a retired army colonel whose son was killed in Iraq, advocate for 'restraint' in the wars the US wages. Badly burned by its costly failures, the US has seemingly ended its more expansionist phase to refocus on defending the world order that the US had a leading hand in building after 1945.

Parallel to twenty-plus years of US military misadventures abroad, another pattern has emerged – the prominence of military interventions by major non-Western states. Russia has been belligerent in Syria and Ukraine, and has been using its private military companies, which comprise Russian veterans, to carve out influence in war-torn countries like Libya, Mali, Central African Republic and Sudan. Russia is not alone. In 2015, Saudi Arabia assembled a coalition of Arab states to wage war in Yemen against Iranian interests – an intervention that went badly for the Saudis (and brought the US and UK supply of weapons to Saudi forces under scrutiny in their countries). Türkiye has also become extrovert in its military ambitions. It always had this tendency, having invaded Cyprus in 1974 and retaining thousands of troops in Northern Cyprus, a territory that only it recognises. Türkiye also mounted incursions into Iraq since the 1990s in pursuit of its enemies, the Kurdish rebels. In the 2020s its troops also fought in Syria and Libya, and supported Azerbaijan in its war against Armenia. Also, Türkiye deployed troops in a constabulary role to Qatar to help police the World Cup.

An era of more frequent unilateral *non-Western* military interventions by other G20 countries has begun. The data supports this finding: back in 2011, the only major countries staging these kinds of active military interventions were Western. Fast-forward a decade, in 2021, the range of interventionist countries had widened.[11] China and India are still absent from this list for now, but for how long? When the opportunity presents itself for an assertion of national pride, for a statement of strength, and to pursue strategic interests, it is possible that more countries will fill the void created by a more defensively minded West.

***

In a Westless world, the US will struggle to enforce its writ in every region at the same time. In 2023, the US military was pulled in three directions: arming Ukraine to fight Russia; supporting Israel to fight Hamas; while arming Taiwan at a more frantic pace to deter what it assessed to be a growing Chinese temptation to invade. It remained within the US military's ability to *support* all three of these partners – but shifting to *fighting* in any of these places would drain the US and its Western allies of their arsenals, while also trying their population's tolerances for sustaining yet another cycle of US-led foreign wars.

The US sees itself as an 'offshore balancer', strategic jargon meaning that its armed forces are situated within easy striking distance of unstable regions to keep a lid on things. Picture the two US aircraft carriers that sailed to the Eastern Mediterranean in the immediate wake of Israel's war against Hamas, which began in October 2023 – they were there to support Israel and to deter Iran and its proxy groups from wading into the conflicts. This strategy is akin to the British Empire before it, which relied on naval and later air power to enforce its writ all over the world.[12] Whether this approach works indefinitely for the US in every region seems unlikely. In 1995, President Bill Clinton ordered a pair of aircraft carriers to the South China Sea to support Taiwan and deter China from taking military action. China was angered by the US hosting Taiwan's president for a visit and by Taiwan's first ever democratic election. But this was when China was still weak. In the event of a major Taiwan Strait crisis a decade from now, the US Navy would struggle to assert itself in this way again as China's military gains strength with every passing year.

Being an offshore balancer has its limits, especially if venturing further inland. Beyond the coastal shores and islands of East and South East Asia, swathes of 'inner Asia' are more open to Russian and Chinese influence, especially after the US and NATO abandoned Afghanistan in 2021. Russia may be economically weaker than China, but it still has a stake in Central Asia due to its abundant energy trade and its old Soviet links. For China, establishing land-based networks into Europe and the Middle East bypasses its heavy reliance on using maritime routes for its trading needs. Having enlisted both Pakistan and Iran as economic partners, China is in a stronger position than before to guarantee the security of its energy imports and its manufactured exports.

China and Russia have consolidated these advantages by expanding a club that they set up back in the 1990s, called the Shanghai Cooperation Organisation (SCO). The SCO's original aim was to give China and Russia a forum to cooperate over security in Central Asia after the USSR's collapse. Its membership already had Kazakhstan, Kyrgyzstan, Tajikistan and Uzbekistan. In 2017, the SCO also admitted India and Pakistan; in 2023, Iran joined. The significance of the SCO's expansion needs some context, since it is hardly a non-Western NATO – it is not a formal military alliance.

The SCO charter instead reads like a non-contractual memorandum of understanding between its signatories, especially around not interfering unduly in each other's affairs, and for nipping in the bud any nascent separatist or terrorist movements. The SCO holds regular counterterrorism exercises for its members, but they seem more akin to military jamborees in the desert than real exercises in joint military training. Nevertheless, the SCO's regular summits further normalise cooperation between its members, offering them a deliberately non-Western forum at which to gather.[13] Clubs and initiatives of this nature are all about setting up the global chessboard for the Westless world.

The US has not been outmanoeuvred yet. It still leads the way in something the British and French empires also relied on: a global network of bases. The lynchpin of its garrisons in the Pacific are based in Japan and Korea, where the US fought in devastating wars in the 1940s and 1950s respectively. Its Middle East lynchpins are the airbases it uses in Qatar and the UAE plus the US Fifth Fleet moored in Bahrain (all former British colonies). Britain used its vestiges of empire to retain bases in the Falklands, Gibraltar and Cyprus, which gave its navy and air force South Atlantic and Mediterranean way stations. France kept its troops and bases in Chad, Djibouti, Gabon, Ivory Coast and Senegal after its empire, although in 2024 it began to downsize its presence in the latter three countries after meeting with greater local political discontent over its enduring military presence.

Non-Western militaries cannot compete with this spread of military bases – but there are signs of change. Russia exploited its role in the Syrian civil war to gain a base in Latakia, giving it Mediterranean access. Russia's own vast expanse gives it basing options from the Barents Sea in the Arctic Ocean to the Kuril Islands in the Pacific (which the USSR took possession of from Japan in the dying days of World War Two, and which Russia has retained to this day, to Japan's discontent).

China only operates a single foreign military base in Djibouti. There is strong expectation this number will rise. The RAND Corporation think tank studied the prospects of Chinese bases popping up all over the place; it concluded that Pakistan, Bangladesh, Myanmar and Cambodia were the top potential hosts based on how much China would want this access and how feasible it would be to establish the base. As China's need to safeguard its foreign economic investments grows, so will the desires of its military to operate far from home.[14] Although, since operating foreign military bases is so costly, China may cynically bide its time and benefit from the global security offered by the US.

This is unlikely to remain a static picture. Consider a future where China's military has at least a handful of independently operated foreign bases; where the Russian and Chinese navies jointly patrol the water near the Kuril Islands and along Russia's far east; where the navies of the BRICS countries hold joint exercises off South Africa's coast; and where the SCO runs the security affairs of Inner Asia. All of these are realistic possibilities and some are already happening. Yet another domain that could slip beyond Western military reach is the Indian Ocean, which is likely to become a greater centre of the world economy in the future – just as the Atlantic Ocean was in the twentieth century and the Pacific Ocean has become in the twenty-first century – but unlike these oceans, the US has no border with the Indian Ocean. Which leads to a tentative conclusion.

We are likely to see a future of *regional* rather than world policing, as no one group of countries will be able to call the shots everywhere. The US will find itself forced to make judicious choices as to where it can and cannot focus its deployments and alliance-building efforts. The US already badly needs more burden-sharing with its allies in Europe due to Russia's war in Ukraine. This is indicative not so much of US weakness but of the absence of its military omnipotence.

The outlook for Europe's security is bleak, barring a course-changing implosion in Putin's Russia. European governments are grappling with how to convey this stark reality to their publics after so many decades of the geopolitical good life, with no credible military threats to their countries. From afar, some non-Westerners shake their heads and utter words to the effect that 'Europe really messed up its own security,' which is why many in the Global South have had such divergent views over Russia.

Russia's sinister imperial motives for invading Ukraine are a given. Some non-Western audiences find it harder to also ignore how unwise it was for George W. Bush to push the open promise to Ukraine and Georgia that these countries would one day join NATO. Bush told NATO to make this promise in 2008 at the height of Western power. Fast-forward to 2022 and this promise still had not been acted on. Russia was angered by the Ukrainian government's determination to join NATO. For its part, Ukraine felt misled about the offer to join NATO and badly vulnerable with no treaty allies to fight to protect it. It remains to be seen if Ukraine will ever formally join the transatlantic alliance. A legacy of this mess is the imperative for European countries to pay for a greater share of their security needs rather than free-riding off US security commitments to Europe dating back to World War Two.

Ukraine's fate remains vitally important in its own right and a bellwether for the West's ability to defend its friends and its ideals. The war will also determine where the political boundaries of the West begin and end in Europe. It is Ukraine's tragedy to become the new version of Cold War Germany, the new divided land, with Western influence flowing to one part and Russian influence (likely bankrolled by Chinese money in the future) to the other. A trip to Kyiv is, for a Western politician or a tourist, a trip to the front lines of the free world. Although it never asked for this, Ukraine has become today's altar of sacrifice for defending the West.

* * *

With all this intensifying geopolitical rivalry, it is hard to recall that world policing was also supposed to be about the UN and its blue-helmeted peacekeepers. Recall the genteel authority of the Ghanian UN Secretary General Kofi Annan, who held this role between 1997 and 2006, and how optimism around the UN's authority in the twenty-first century was shattered when the Bush administration decided to unilaterally invade Iraq. Since then, the idea of the UN Secretary General being a decisive figure of authority in world affairs has faded. Moreover, the ability of the UN Security Council to decree on crucial matters of war and peace has collapsed because of irreparable disputes between its permanent five member states. Each of them (US, UK, France, Russia and China) can veto a UN resolution, and these vetoes have been played with increasing frequency. In the first decade of the 2000s, China only used its veto twice and Russia four times. Russia has since used its veto twenty-three times, often to block resolutions aimed at pressuring its Syrian client-state, while China has issued nine vetoes. The US has continued to wield its veto power to protect its ally Israel from pressure.

The prospects of reforming the UN Security Council appear slim. Its membership still reflects the power dynamics of 1945 and this distorts all manner of things. India has no seat at this table so it sometimes relies on persuading Russia to veto things on its behalf, which is another reason why India keeps its friendly relations with Russia. The UK has previously spoken about backing India's bid for a permanent seat at the Security Council, but Pakistan would be livid and could work with its close economic partner China to stymie this.

Japan has wanted a permanent seat but China would be resistant. Brazil and Germany have also queued up with requests to join. The fact that there are zero African or South American representations renders countries of these continents dependent on the lottery of having one of the ten rotating seats, which is a far lesser position of influence than being a permanent member. There is little chance of breaking the logjam on Security Council reform.

This is not to say the UN is redundant. UN agencies remain vital responders to refugee and other humanitarian emergencies. The trick to using the UN is to avoid the most geopolitically sensitive matters that ruffle the feathers of the US, China or Russia. The UN's blue-helmeted peacekeepers have deployed to countries like the Democratic Republic of Congo and Haiti. But wars in Iraq, Syria and Ukraine involved sky-high geopolitical stakes for the major world powers; in such wars, the UN's ability to stabilise these conflicts is non-existent.

Policing the Westless world is going to get tougher. There will still be Western leadership in select forums and with specific groups of allies. But in no way can Western politicians claim to speak on behalf of the 'international community' as they sometimes did (it was a phrase used repeatedly by former UK Prime Minister Tony Blair, for instance in his speeches on the Afghan War to the US Congress in 2003, and on the Kosovo War to an audience in Chicago in 1999).[15] Western military advantages may also slip in specific localities. Other powerful countries that build effective military capabilities and secure foreign basing rights will take on regional policing roles in partnerships with each other, sometimes assisting the West, sometimes ignoring the West outright. Transitioning to this world while avoiding Armageddon remains one of humanity's gravest undertakings.

13

World Currencies

There is a risk when we use financial sanctions linked to the role of the Dollar that over time it could undermine the hegemony of the Dollar. But this is an extremely important tool that we try to use judiciously in circumstances when we have support of the allies. Of course it does create a desire on the part of China, of Russia, of Iran to find an alternative. But the Dollar is used as a global currency for reasons that are not easy for other countries to find an alternative with the same properties.

Janet Yellen, US Treasury Secretary, speaking in 2023[1]

Every night I ask myself why all countries have to base their trade on the dollar . . . Why can't we trade in our own currencies?

Brazil's President Lula Da Silva in 2023 during a trip to Beijing[2]

IF YOU ARE American, you may have taken the global ubiquity of your currency for granted. To those of us elsewhere, the sheer reach of the US dollar likely hits us at an early moment in our lives. My moment of awareness came in a trivial teenage encounter at a port in Dar es Salaam in Tanzania, as my parents purchased a ferry ticket to the island of Zanzibar. With no credit card machine at the port, the ferry operators only accepted physical greenbacks from foreigners. Carrying some US banknotes can be a good idea when travelling but back then, I couldn't fathom why this would be so in East Africa. The ubiquity of the dollar further hits home when you see it cited in books and news articles as the currency used to compare all kinds of data between countries. Like no other, it seems like the world's currency.

The enduring global power of the dollar pushes back against Westlessness. The dollar still gives the US a material ability in its global leadership, one that is as important as its military power. Before we consider whether the dollar's power will fade, we should recap where it came from.

Currency primacy has passed through its European and North American stages in line with the successive stages of the West's global expansion. The Portuguese and Spanish came upon gold and silver in the Americas and used these metals to fund the first transoceanic empire. Silver 'real' coins became a currency of global trade that people wanted to save in. Over time it was displaced by the Dutch guilder, not because the Dutch empire was especially large but because its currency was backed by a more sophisticated financial machinery, including the Bank of Amsterdam, at a time when the concept of a central bank was yet to be established. Money and other units of exchange existed throughout history, but the internationalisation of a single currency, backed by a banking system that guaranteed its value in exchange and in lending, was new.

By the time of the British Empire and the Bank of England, which was established in 1694, and later on with the advent of steam power to mass-produce a paper currency that was hard to counterfeit, the financial machinery we recognise today started to take shape. Branches of banks were established in British colonial outposts all over the world as an adjunct to transoceanic maritime trade. In 1899, the year the pound was made legal tender in India, it accounted for around two-thirds of assets held in central banks the world over. The German mark and the French franc accounted for the remainder, while the dollar was not commonly used outside of North America.[3]

Dollarisation of the world economy started around a century ago. The US central bank was only created in 1913, when President Woodrow Wilson passed into law the Federal Reserve Act. Thereafter, New York became a global banking centre, and it became more important for European central banks to hold dollar reserves. In 1929, the Wall Street Crash and the ensuing Great Depression blighted Europe's economies because of the scale of dollar lending that was now taking place. This included the perilous scheme in which US banks financed the massive reparations Germany was ordered in 1919 to pay to the countries that had defeated it in the Great War. This US intervention was called the Dawes Plan, which is a lesser-known precursor to the famous Marshall Plan that followed World War Two.

The aftermaths of both world wars showed Europe to be increasingly dependent on the financial muscle of the US to reconstitute itself. The supremacy of the dollar was formally agreed in July 1944 in a hotel in Bretton Woods in New Hampshire, where alongside the decisions to create the World Bank and the IMF, the dollar was officially named as the international reserve currency in which a hefty slice of international trade would be settled. Writer Craig Karmin puts this into perspective:

> Never had the world's major nations signed a document that officially enshrined one currency as the leader; never before had the world's powers formally agreed that there would be just one currency among which all other currencies would be measured. It was a major coup for the US, among its greatest spoils of victory from World War Two . . . By the 1960s, dollars accounted for some 60 per cent of all central bank foreign reserves, an amount that was double that of its closest rival, the British pound. A decade later, nearly 85 per cent of all foreign reserves were held in dollars.[4]

As part of the Bretton Woods agreement, the dollar was fixed against the value of gold. This arrangement did not last since the US only held gold worth the equivalent of a fraction of the growing amount of dollars held by foreign countries. In 1971, President Richard Nixon made the decision to de-link the dollar from the value of gold, breaking this part of the Bretton Woods deal but increasing the flexibility and the volatility of its dollar. International trade drove more and more demand for dollars. As the US printed more money to meet this demand, the dollar's value began to fluctuate. Other countries habitually used the US dollar to trade with and to fill their central bank reserves. Dollars held outside the US are used in international transactions by other countries without the involvement of US banks, making the dollar a true world currency.

Despite the dollar remaining as the world's primary reserve currency, there are noticeable signs of decline from its previous dominance. The IMF has documented that the percentage of global central bank reserves around the world held in US dollars had fallen from 70% in 1999 to 60% in 2020. Central banks in other countries are now saving in a wider range of currencies than before, and the IMF expects the US dollar's share of global reserves will fall further still as the emerging and developing economies diversify further the currencies held in their reserves.[5]

The US dollar's lineage as the leading reserve currency in the world is only the latest phase in these successive eras of Western currency dominance. Just as the pound sterling, the guilder and the real shifted in line with the rise and fall of their respective empires, are we seeing a slow countdown to the inevitable end of US dollar dominance?

* * *

The primacy of the US dollar is part of America's prestige and its global power. By issuing a currency that other countries want to stock up on, this has allowed the US to fund its own debt through issuing Treasury bills. Other countries pay real money to the US government in exchange for these Treasury bills, which promise reliable and regular future returns. Another way to fund the national debt is for the Federal Reserve to increase the monetary supply as more 'greenback' banknotes are printed. Using these methods, the US government can live beyond its means to an extent that would risk a crisis of creditor confidence in other countries, paying for its huge defence budget and running up budget deficits because of the superpowers afforded to it by the dollar.[6]

This has been great for the US and is a key part of the Western-led world order. In foreign exchange (forex) markets, where currencies are bought and sold on a daily basis, the dollar is by far the most traded currency. In distant second place is the euro, which forms a significant slice of global commerce around the common market of the EU. The Japanese yen is third, followed by Britain's pound sterling, still significant thanks to the City of London's centrality in the global trading of goods and services.

Eight out of the ten most traded currencies on the forex market in 2023 were from Western or Western-allied countries (with the Australian dollar, Canadian dollar, Swiss franc and New Zealand dollar completing the list). These currencies collectively accounted for over 80% of trading on the world's largest financial market. Aside from the Hong Kong dollar, only China's renminbi, also called the yuan, was from an emerging market, sitting in fifth place and having risen in the forex rankings over the last two decades.[7]

This has given the West and the G7 dominance over the world's finances. If the US, EU, UK and Japan agree on concerted actions to cut another country off from their financial systems, this will truly hurt the targeted country. Russia experienced this in 2022 after it invaded Ukraine but the financial sanctions against Russia had an inadvertent effect: it panicked some other countries over their dollar dependencies. The catalyst was the Western countries' freezing of Russia's assets held abroad. Russia found that it could no longer access its foreign reserves, valued at 300 billion dollars, referring to assets held in the US and EU by Russia's central bank. By comparison, China's US-dollar-denominated reserves are worth many times as much. If China ever fought a war to seize Taiwan, the US could try to freeze some of China's foreign reserves as punishment, cutting out a part of its war chest.

Russia and China have driven efforts to loosen the dollar's hold over global commerce and to further separate their financial systems from Western countries. During the Russia–Ukraine War, when Xi Jinping visited Moscow in March 2023, Putin told him that two-thirds of Russia–China trade was already being paid for in yuan and rubles, and that Russia would also pay for some of its trade in Asia, Africa and Latin America in yuan.[8] For Russia and China, this has been a rapid transition, since much of their bilateral trade used to be paid in US dollars as recently as a decade ago.

This is the leading example of 'de-dollarisation', meaning the active efforts to reduce usage of the dollar. It is not the only one. Iran has unsurprisingly been receptive, since it has also had its dollar assets confiscated and been under US sanctions for its support of various Middle Eastern insurgent groups, and for its past forays into nuclear weapons research and development. Iran would be delighted with any erosion of US and Western dominance of global finance. But it is not just Russia, China and Iran. Rather than being limited to an axis of resistance against the West, a general trend is underway.

Even countries that are not bitterly anti-Western have taken notice of how comprehensively the US can cut another country off from the international financial system. De-dollarisation does not only mean switching over to yuan.

Countries can also use their own currencies to conduct trade. India for instance entered into an agreement with the UAE to conduct their trade in their own national currencies, the rupee and the dirham.

Holding stocks of rupees and dirhams is clearly less useful than hoarding US dollars, so why do it? Neither India nor the UAE are enemies of the US, after all. India wants to increase its freedom to manoeuvre outside the Western orbit and build the strength of its own currency. India also had in mind the incident when some US politicians in Congress threatened to sanction India when it decided to buy a Russian air defence weapon called the S-400. This episode was not significant in itself, as India bought the weapon from Russia and the US did not impose the sanctions. But there was a lesson: under America's watchful eye, India had not been able to trade with whoever it wanted to without US threats of economic reprisals. Diversifying currencies is a sensible risk management strategy for any country that worries it will not be in America's good books on every matter.

Similar discussions are taking place elsewhere outside of the West. Consider South East Asia, where the ten countries of the region belong to their own intergovernmental club, the Association of Southeast Asian Nations (ASEAN). The single largest economy in ASEAN is Indonesia, which in 2022 convened a meeting of the region's finance ministers and central bank governors, where they agreed to promote transactions between their countries in local currencies. Indonesia now uses local currencies in its trade with China, Japan, Malaysia and Thailand, while China grows the use of the yuan in ASEAN.

De-dollarising also better insulates your economy against future instability in the US, like the 2008 global financial crisis, which shocked countries the world over, or the advent of an erratic president like Trump. As with other Westless trends, there are both practical and emotional concerns driving countries to rethink and untether some of their past Western-centric dependencies.

Take Brazil, where Lula Da Silva has twice been president. A well-known Western sceptic, he even drew accusations of racism during his first term in office (2003–2011) by blaming the 2008 financial crisis as emanating from the machinations of 'white people with blue eyes', referring to Western bankers who left developing nations to suffer the aftereffects.[9] In his second time in office, his interest in de-dollarising has grown. As Lula explained, 'Some people get scared when I say that we need to create new currencies for trade. I don't know why Brazil and Argentina have to trade in dollars. Why can't we do this in our own currencies? . . . Why do I have to buy dollars?'[10]

This is far from the consensus view across Latin America. In December 2023, Argentina elected a populist president Javier Milei who declared he would ditch the peso and adopt the US dollar as legal tender to reinvigorate his country's moribund and inflation-wracked economy. If Argentina dollarised, it would join a handful of countries that fully adopted the US dollar as legal tender including Ecuador and Panama, which do not issue currencies of their own. Or it could follow Zimbabwe's path, introducing the US dollar alongside its own currency. One thing Milei decided on right away in his presidency was to pull Argentina out of the

BRICS+ expansion, reversing his predecessor's decision to join the club.

At the BRICS summits, de-dollarisation conversations happen with gusto. The idea was even mooted of the BRICS launching their own currency, which sounds fantastical. The more everyday incentive has been the pull of China's economy. For instance, South Africa, which became the 'S' in the BRICS in 2010 when it joined this club, had a year earlier seen China become its biggest trading partner, giving it new incentives to rely less on the dollar when trading with China in yuan. Brazil has wanted to conduct more of its trade with China in yuan and Saudi Arabia has also explored the possibility of doing so.

This appetite to find pathways around the US dollar is in keeping with the overall diversification of the world economy. In the long run, de-dollarisation *could* become a crucial part of the distancing of the world from the West. Some, like Argentina, aren't interested. For others, even if they use local currencies or the yuan to greater extents than before, this might cover only a fraction of their trading volumes, the rest being in dollars. But the trend cannot be discounted wholesale – if it carries on and more countries get involved, it could spell death by a thousand cuts to the previously unchallenged dominance of the US dollar.

* * *

Those who deal in the global financial markets on a daily basis tend to think the demise of the dollar has been greatly exaggerated. As an experienced banker who has managed financial risk in European and Asian markets explained:

> On the topic of dollarisation and de-dollarisation – as someone who has worked in commodities trading and now for a fairly long time in banking, let me just say that the US dollar is not going anywhere. De-dollarisation sounds like an interesting buzzword but it's more hype than substance. There will be some changes like greater renminbi internationalisation and certain countries using their own national currencies rather than the USD for some portion of their trade (such as India encouraging Bangladesh to use the Indian rupee for Bangladeshi exports rather than USD), but the central role of the USD in the global trading and financial system is set to stay for a long time.

There is scant chance of the yuan replacing the dollar outright as the world's reserve currency. It is one thing for the yuan to feature in bilateral trade invoicing with China and quite another for it to become a new safe-haven currency in the way the dollar has been for many countries.

According to the BIS Triennial Central Bank Survey released in 2022, which documented the leading currencies in foreign exchanges, the gap between the yuan and the dollar remains huge. The dollar was on one side of 88% of all trades, while the next three most traded currencies, euro, yen and pound sterling, featured in 30.5%, 17% and 13% of trading respectively (more than one currency can feature in a trade). This had not changed very much since their last survey in 2019.

It is true that the yuan has risen up the rankings from eighth place in 2019 (when it was on one side of 4% of trades) to the fifth most actively traded currency in 2022 (accounting for 7% of trades). In 2001, it was ranked thirty-fifth.[11] So the yuan has enjoyed rising international usage in the last two decades of China's massive economic growth, but it is still nowhere near being able to challenge the US dollar, let alone the combined heft of the leading G7 and Western currencies.

The attractiveness of the yuan has been dented by the capital controls attached to it by China's government. Strict rules govern the ability of companies and individuals to move money in and out of China. Then there are the poor optics of China presenting Hong Kong as a centre for international yuan trading and then brutally cracking down on pro-democracy protests in 2020, curtailing Hong Kong's autonomy from Beijing. Given the possibility that China could be punished economically by the West in the event of it waging a future war over Taiwan, saving money in yuan has its own risks.

The liquidity and reliability of the US global debt market remains peerless. It is why, at the peak of globalisation in the early 2000s, the Chinese built up their savings in dollars by effectively loaning the money for Americans to buy Chinese-manufactured consumer goods. China bought plenty of US Treasury bills at this time and remains the second largest holder of US government debt behind Japan and ahead of the UK.[12] Even if the Chinese government sells some of this US government debt it cannot rapidly reduce its global dollar dependency.

More generally, there is considerable inertia in international finance to move away from the dollar. According to the Global Financial Centres Index 2023 and its evaluations of the competitiveness of the major financial centres of the world, the most important cities are New York, London, Singapore, Hong Kong, San Francisco, Los Angeles, Shanghai, Chicago, Boston and Seoul.[13] In other words, the cities judged as 'global leaders' in international finance are with only two exceptions in the West or in countries closely partnered with the West. Other cities in the world tend to be marked as 'evolving centres', 'international contenders' and 'local specialists'. One might deride such an index as biased to favour the existing nervous system of international finance, but there are also objective reasons for these rankings. The criteria in the index include the quality of the infrastructure and the financial regulations in place.

For so long, transforming your city into a leading financial centre has meant aligning with the West. Singapore's story of doing this is instructive, when it became a hub in trading 'Eurodollars' (which are US dollars deposited outside of the USA). As Singapore's founding president Lee Kuan Yew wrote, 'Anyone who predicted in 1965 when we separated from Malaysia that Singapore would become a financial center would have been thought mad.' Lee engaged the services of a Dutch adviser, Dr Albert Winsemius, who suggested that Singapore's time zone meant that it was well suited to global trading when Europeans and Americans were still asleep. Between the close of the US markets and start of the European working day, Singapore filled a gap with the establishment of the Asian Dollar Market in 1968 to create an offshore hub for trading dollars in Asia.[14] Singapore has grown its financial services industry into a major part of its own economy and the world financial system. As with so much in the Westfull era, aligning with the dominant Western structures was the ticket to success.

* * *

It will take some time for things to change. Chipping away at the dollar's dominance is not going to transform things overnight, but some chinks in the dollar's armour have emerged. Central bank reserves around the world are diversifying the currencies they hold. More cross-border exchanges take place in local currencies than before. Oil, one of the most important export products, is being traded more and more in currencies other than the dollar.

The current wave of de-dollarisation efforts really kicked off at the 2015 BRICS summit, which was held in the Russian city of Ufa, where the BRICS countries agreed to consider new measures for their own financial cooperation separate from their reliance on Western currencies and structures.[15] Since then the BRICS countries have begun to diversify their reserve assets away from US dollars.

De-dollarisation comprises numerous initiatives. SWIFT, which stands for the Society for Worldwide Interbank Financial Telecommunications, is one of the main ways in which cross-border payments are processed. SWIFT allows different banks around the world to transfer money. In 2022, as part of the financial sanctions for invading Ukraine, Russia was thrown off the SWIFT system, cutting its banks off from sending and receiving global payments. SWIFT itself is privately owned and has an international board of directors, but the location of its headquarters, in Belgium, has made its operations subject to European law. For instance, when the US strongly pushed the EU to sanction Iran, SWIFT had little choice but to comply and cut Iran off from some SWIFT services. It was yet another illustration of how the nervous system of global finance has remained Western-centric.[16] Thousands of banks the world over use SWIFT, so a country being thrown off it equates to financial isolation.

Some countries have been building their own global payments system to settle transactions. China has been trying to encourage countries it trades heavily with, such as those in the Gulf, to use its Cross-Border Interbank Payment System (CIPS), which it launched in 2015. Russia has created its own international ruble payment system called the System for Transfer of Financial Messages (SPFS), which it started using in 2017. Russia also introduced its 'Mir' credit cards to reduce its dependency on the US-owned VISA and MasterCard. In China, the UnionPay bank card was launched in 2002 and has since become the country's most used debit and credit card.

China has founded alternatives to the Bretton Woods institutions. One of the most important is dubbed 'the BRICS bank', officially called the New Development Bank (NDB), which was founded in 2015 by the five BRICS countries. Based in Shanghai, in 2023 it appointed the former Brazilian president (and Lula's predecessor) Dilma Rousseff as its head. The NDB's membership has expanded to include Bangladesh, Egypt, the UAE and others, like Saudi Arabia, have been in talks to join. Eventually, the full set of BRICS+ countries may end up as members.

The NDB cannot suddenly ignore the US dollar, however. The NDB itself is still dependent on accessing US dollar funding. Tellingly, in the NDB's own 'General Strategy for 2022–2026', it still expressed its targets in terms of US dollars. So does the Asian Infrastructure Investment Bank (AIIB) annual report 2021, which similarly used US dollars in its reporting.[17] The AIIB was established in 2014 and has a much larger membership than the NDB. Even as they present themselves as alternatives to the World Bank and the IMF, they too still need to use US dollars to function.

De-dollarising the oil markets is another pathway around the US and the West, given that China has become the world's biggest energy importer, and Russia is among the largest energy exporters. At the 2018 BRICS summit, China launched 'yuan oil futures', also known as the 'Petroyuan', to be traded on the Shanghai Exchange, creating a non-dollar route to trading in a major commodity. In terms of volume, the larger share of oil trading still occurs in the London and New York, but the Shanghai-traded Petroyuan is now on the map.[18] If Saudi Arabia agreed to trade a large share of its oil in currencies other than the dollar, this would speed up de-dollarisation of oil trading.

There are limits to the de-dollarisation of oil and gas sales. There is a cautionary tale in the experience of Iran and Russia who, by settling their trade with India in rupees, ended up with large amounts of rupees in Indian bank accounts, which they struggled to spend because of low demand for Indian goods and services. Switching to trading in local currencies has a great deal of Westless symbolism, but in practice may not always be a good idea.

There is unlikely to ever be a currency so singularly dominant as the US dollar. It is now a long time since Bretton

Woods in 1944, and the structures dating to that era are naturally seeing new contenders arise. Diversifying away from the dollar is a sensible risk management strategy for many countries but there remain major limitations as to how far and how fast this can progress.

Chipping away at the dominance of the dollar and the Western-centric global financial system remains a work in progress. Many countries want to stay open to using overlapping financial platforms and currencies, some in the West and others outside it, to get the maximum benefits from a diversifying world. China, Russia and Iran have built on political momentum behind de-dollarisation after Russia was so witheringly sanctioned for invading Ukraine. Future geopolitical ruptures could accelerate these trends, but in some cases these could even lead some countries to flee *into* the US dollar camp.

This serves as an exemplar for just how hard it is to decisively erode the dominance of the West. No matter how powerful the forces are agitating against it, the West is far too rich and financially influential to be spurned entirely. Be that as it may, there is more to the great global rebalancing than controlling the flows of money.

14

Moral Force

I think that Iraq is going to go down in history as the greatest disaster in American foreign policy because we have lost the element of the goodness of American power and we have lost our moral authority.

Former US Secretary of State
Madeleine Albright in 2007[1]

Over ten months of this year, we helped everyone. We helped the West find itself again, to return to the global arena and feel how much the West prevails. No one in the West fears nor will they fear Russia.

Ukrainian President Zelensky in December 2022[2]

INTERNATIONAL REPUTATIONS ARE fragile, as this tale of two invasions shows. After Iraq, Western moral authority on matters of war and peace was depleted and in dire need of replenishment. Cast your mind back to the haze of hurt that followed the 9/11 terrorist attacks, and how it sent the US's moral compass spinning directionless, its government lashing out at both real and imaginary enemies. Tragedy in Iraq followed when the US led an invasion that involved British and Australian troops to depose a tyrannical dictator. The invasion was based on a false premise of threats posed by Iraq's apocryphal weapons of mass destruction. These weapons did not exist. Deposing the dictator created a vacuum that was filled by the murderous anarchy of civil war and terrorism. The world watched aghast – including many Westerners who opposed the invasion – as the US squandered its moral authority and betrayed some of the ideals upon which it based its leadership of the Western world.

Two decades later came the opportunity for repetitional redemption due to the murderous ills of Russia's invasion of Ukraine. By backing the good fight of the Ukrainians, the US and its Western partners were on the right side of this moral equation. That's what Zelensky sensibly emphasised to his benefactors in the aftermath of the invasion, to flatter them with moral affirmation while Western countries funded the substantial costs of Ukraine's war effort against the Russian invasion.

It is difficult to aggregate the moral reputation of the West as a whole since its countries speak with many voices. The West was hardly culpable in unison for invading Iraq in 2003 since France's and Germany's governments famously broke with the US and UK, trying in vain to argue against the weak case for invasion. When it came to helping Ukraine in 2022, France and Germany required some cajoling to supply weapons to Ukraine but they did so in the end. These examples highlight an important point: within the powerful countries of the West, the US has a greater tendency (and far greater resources) to view events and their solutions through a military lens. This remains true even when there are other pressing matters in the world to attend to, like climate change, poverty alleviation, economic development and the UN's Sustainable Development Goals.[3]

Much of the world fixates on these imbalances when weighing up the moral virtues of America's leadership of the West. If you throw into the list the occupation of Afghanistan run by the US that ended in ignominy in 2021, and two years later, the US's unflinching support of Israel's war against the Palestinian armed group Hamas, the US looks war-addicted. If it is not involved in the fighting itself, it is backing its allies to do so, drowning out other positive things Americans try to do around the world.

International reputations rise and fall cyclically. Recall the damage to its reputation caused by its war in Vietnam in the 1960s and 1970s, which degraded the US's self-proclamation that it was morally superior to the European colonial powers it was replacing on the world stage (directly so in Vietnam when American soldiers took over from the French). Almost two decades elapsed after the US withdrew from Vietnam before the 'free world' regained its sheen. In the early 1990s, the US presided over the end of the Cold War, democratisation in Eastern Europe, and it led an international military coalition in defence of Kuwaiti sovereignty after Iraq's invasion and annexation in 1990–1991. This was a less morally ambiguous war and one that ended in a clear victory in America's favour.

Will the West's reputation and moral clout rise once again like the phoenix from the ashes? Surely, one day, the stars will align and a dynamic and globally palatable US president will arrive to lead the free world to its old pedestal of being on the right side of history, rallying not only the US but the collective standing of the West, and fashioning this into what others around the world wish to emulate. Is this day coming?

On both sides of the Atlantic, in news shows and published commentaries, you can get the impression that the main problem comes from *within* the West. It is common to encounter bullish arguments around Westerners needing to take greater pride in the West's virtues, in its historic successes, and that the West's Judeo-Christian roots in Jerusalem and Athens need to be restated and defended. Being embarrassed by aspects of the West's chequered history and listening to naysayers is interpreted as defeatism. Is the West suffering from a crisis of confidence, these bullish commentators ask – is that why it struggles to rally itself to lead the way and to inspire the world?

Western conservatives also characterise 'woke' culture as a kind of late-stage civilisational decay from within. Importantly, some passionate defenders of the West's ways of doing things themselves have heritages from elsewhere, which leads them to point out that Western countries have been far more welcoming and pleasant places to live than the autocratic or poorer places their families originated from.[4] 'Be prouder of the West,' these voices contend, rather than succumbing to a self-criticism that borders on self-hate, which in turn begets less confidence and less respect abroad.

These debates within the Western world are a vital part of its democratic debate. When they descend into culture wars, they resemble a self-licking ice cream, perpetuated for its own sake as the conservatives continually take aim at those who are liberal and left-leaning for (among other things) their supposedly insufficient pride in being Western. The more interesting matter is how other parts of the world now view the West, even in its most bullishly confident guises.

Returning to the matter of international reputations, while in South East Asia I heard two senior government officials, one British and another American, sitting in different rooms on different days but answering the same question identically. Each was asked how prominently the Western values embodied by their governments and societies should feature in their engagements in Asia. 'We should not shy away from our values,' each said dutifully. These were boilerplate political answers, but the setting really gets one thinking about where the West's moral power resides in a world that no longer favours the Western countries in quite the ways it once did.

* * *

The important thing about moral power is that there is nothing necessarily *morality-based* about it, in the sense of saintly virtuousness or pure charity. It is not about a halo hovering over one's head. Instead, it refers to the perceived moral stature of an actor, and their ability to persuade others to take certain actions or to hold particular beliefs on issues at hand. For countries to be seen as having moral force, they must be perceived as having sufficient moral standing to speak on an issue and the legitimacy to talk others round. To wield moral power, believability and credibility are vital.[5]

Clearly, you cannot be believed by all the people all the time. The power to be perceived as trustworthy by *enough other people for it to matter* is the valuable commodity here, so that you can direct these people's attentions to the causes you think matter. At the very least, being given the benefit of the doubt by enough of those sitting on the fence, and not being seen to be crying wolf, adds to a country's power to persuade. The point is not to achieve unanimous consensus but to build a critical mass of support when and where it is needed.

You might scoff at calling this 'moral power' given the self-interests that guide attempts at talking us round to one set of opinions over others in the global commons. You would also agree that when moral power is defined in this way, it blurs with the age-old art of propaganda to which we are still subjected. Even the most inquiring and educated minds are susceptible to having their opinions swayed on major events. Young minds especially are open spaces for cultivation by forceful persuaders.

We regularly experience this whenever we see the issues of the day being debated online. Have you found yourself embroiled in a vicious dispute over a contentious political issue? Just visit Twitter (X) or Facebook or the comments sections under news articles where rival reactions and opinions about world affairs are debated. Observe how people rally behind certain messages over others and pile in to support the sentiments they agree with. And how this is rarely a fair fight since behind the scenes, the bots are busy augmenting certain messages. These online spaces are today's canvases for propaganda and for reputation-management, arenas in which competing narratives battle for our attention.

Moral power is not the same as soft power, even if it clearly benefits from and uses cultural appeals to draw attention to moral virtues. Moral power blurs with propaganda and is employed in the public sphere to make the case for a big issue. The power to shame and to blame is potent, as is the power to speak on behalf of the interests of others, purportedly uniting them to your cause. Sure, it might not be as direct as economic or military power. And even if you don't find it convincing, or you find it hypocritical even, it still works. The propaganda business is thriving as different voices in the world amplify their own interpretations of breaking events and of history to display their own virtuousness against their competitors.

Then there is the age-old principle of achieving virtuousness by comparison: standing next to someone shorter than you to make yourself look taller; or parking your car next to others that are less impressive. Making your part of the world look more appealing relative to the alternatives is a sensible guiding principle. The virtues of Western democracies are sometimes extolled along the lines that, for all of their faults, they are less hideous than the authoritarian alternatives.

In grand campaigns of persuasion, both the messenger and the message have always mattered. Now, user-generated content and user engagement also matters to affirm the credibility of official voices. The power to persuade flows from this reservoir of believability, and from having the money to spend on attractive and favourably disposed online platforms to make an impact. Increasingly, what also matters is how the West tells its stories through its non-Western friends to be better believed in a Westless world.

Only the truly naive would interpret Western voices as fonts of all moral authority. The West can be flawed and inconsistent like other places; its leading representatives can be right as often as they are wrong; they cannot be virtuous on all issues; and their countries inevitably act in their self-interest. Moreover, different voices within the West frequently contradict each other, which further confuses matters. Western voices have been so loud for so long that they have dominated the to-and-fro debates on numerous issues.

The West cannot mark its own homework indefinitely. The advent of an online global commons acts as something of a leveller for information flows from all over the world. There are now rival claims to moral legitimacy trying to convey the sense of being a force for right. Some of this is misinformation and disinformation peddled by actors maliciously trying to embarrass and confuse Western audiences. Some of it also simply reflects different perspectives on things. Take for instance the trend to revitalise stories about past Western colonialism: at once part of the West's own self-discovery about unsavoury aspects of its history; but also the emotional power behind rallying many Global South countries in solidarity around their shared modern historical experiences of colonialism and independence.

What happened to the good old stories of the US being a land of opportunity? And Europe as a land of culture and riches? These stories still have traction, but nothing lasts forever, and their power has to be continually renewed to maintain the globally aspirational allure around the West. Telling stories that have the power to inspire others far beyond our home shores is a vaunted skill. For the West's storytellers, it becomes harder to exercise the power of inspiration as the West becomes only one big global influence among several. In a more pick-and-choose world, how will its power to inspire others evolve? In which overall direction is the battle for moral power trending?

***

The West is naturally better able to persuade a critical mass of its own constituencies. Preaching to your own constituencies, and especially to the already-converted, is only one side of the challenge. To persuade and sell messages to others across the world is a different matter entirely.

The idea of framing this challenge as a 'new cold war' is a tempting analogy to some Western thinkers, and a comforting one because the West eventually won that struggle partly through the power of its ideologies and the lure of its cultural appeals. Back then, the world had coalesced into two rival ideological blocs involving the capitalist democratic US and Western Europe, who built supportive global coalitions, while the USSR led the rival Marxist communist coalition. The Cold War began due to events inside Europe after World War Two, events which then affected the whole world.

At the Cold War's start, much of the non-Western world was in a weak and pliable state. When Churchill, freshly out of office, delivered his 'Iron Curtain' speech in 1946, the British Empire still stood. The French were fighting to rebuild their empire in Indo-China, often using young, penniless Germans in the rank and file, plus French colonial troops to fight the Viet Minh. Even during the Cuban Missile Crisis in 1962, the Cold War's seminal mid-point event, much of Africa and Asia was still gaining its independence. Many non-Western countries tried to opt out of the need to choose a side.

Their Non-Aligned Movement was not only a rejection of superpower allegiance, but it was also a logical response of countries like India and Indonesia, which had only been independent for a few years, and were still consolidating their borders, populations and economies, to not wanting to be overwhelmed again by the problems of the Westerners.

Today, while some Westerners think they are involved in a new cold war, the prize being to tempt other countries to side with their democratic alliance and oppose a rival authoritarian bloc led by China and Russia, much of the rest of the world sees things as incomparably different this time round. The world is full of middle-ground emerging powers that see an increasingly diverse world ripe with fresh opportunities for them to get ahead. Unlike in the Cold War when many countries were in a vulnerable stage of early independence, things have moved on substantially since the 1950s, 1960s and 1970s, even if considerable development needs persist.[6] Today, it is lazy and misleading to say that 'the US leads the G7' and 'China leads the BRICS', thus creating two blocs that other countries choose to align with. Where does that leave Brazil, India, Indonesia, Türkiye, South Africa, the Gulf monarchies and so on? They can take independent stances on major issues, they can partner with both the G7 and the BRICS countries on different issues, and they do not want to be corralled one way or another.

We saw in the global response to the Russian invasion a fluidity entering international relations where concerns that were articulated by the leading Western countries as being existential were interpreted differently by other countries, notably as being of parochial Western interests. Few countries actively backed Russia's war effort (Iran, North Korea and Syria did so, but each was already a pariah in the court of Western opinion). Many Global South countries took an independent view as to why the war had begun in the first place and what the better remedies were for de-escalating it.

This matter of declining Western moral force comes into focus in a study of global public opinion conducted by researchers at Cambridge University. They examined data from opinion surveys in 137 countries and found striking contrasts. In Western countries, the opinion surveys conveyed growing allegiance to the US and NATO. Conversely, countries 'stretching from East Asia through the Middle East and out towards West Africa' have been characterised by rising support for Russia and/or China or by indifference to the cause of opposing them. The analysis of public opinion data from emerging and developing economies 'suggests this divide is not just economic or strategic but based in personal and political ideology'. As they concluded, 'we are seeing two trends: solidarity within the Western world and more free flowing autonomy in the rest of the world around other actors to choose the West or to choose others.'

Importantly, global divisions in opinions are not simply between democracies and autocracies. The data 'reveals a number of electoral democracies, such as Indonesia, India or Nigeria, in which the public remains sympathetic to Russian or Chinese influence' and 'thus it is not simply whether democratic institutions exist that counts' when forming opinions on issues of global significance.[7] It is true that China has bought some of this support by being a favoured development donor in parts of the world where it then fosters a more favourable opinion of itself. Russian propaganda also plays a role. But it would be wrong simply to understand people in the wider world as being empty vessels who are incapable of forming their own opinions of world events. There are inbuilt reasons as to why the West's words were not taken at face value by some global audiences, notably around how historical experiences of past Western domination have influenced the ways in which people think about the world today.[8]

This matter, of parts of the West persuading themselves of the virtues behind their own moral positioning but failing to persuade others, is vital. In another study, the European Council for Foreign Relations also observed 'The paradox of Western unity' in which Russia's full-scale invasion of Ukraine confirmed that Europe still depends on the US for its defence, while reinvigorating the G7 and NATO. However, in geopolitical terms, 'The West may be more consolidated now, but it is not necessarily more influential in global politics. The West has not disintegrated, but its consolidation has come at a moment when other powers will not simply do as it wishes. Are Western leaders and societies ready for this new world?' Using polling in eleven Western countries plus in China, India, Türkiye and Russia, it found that:

> . . . many people in the West see the coming international order as the return of a cold war-type bipolarity between West and East, between democracy and authoritarianism. In this context, decision-makers in the US and the EU may feel inclined to view countries such as India and Türkiye as swing states that can be cajoled into siding with the West. But people in those countries see themselves very differently: as

> emerging great powers that may side with the West on some issues but not on others. In contrast to the days of the cold war, today one's major trade partners are not usually one's security partners. Even when the emerging powers agree with the West, they will often maintain good relations with Russia and China . . . the West would be well advised to treat India, Türkiye, Brazil, and other comparable powers as new sovereign subjects of world history rather than as objects to be dragooned onto the right side of history.[9]

There are too many floating free radicals in the world to unite behind Western leadership. And there are now multifarious claims to moral legitimacy that are more nuanced and local. Old slogans like uniting behind the 'free world' have a waning power.

* * *

On 7 October 2023, Israel endured tragedy as well over a thousand of its people were killed, injured and kidnapped in a murderous spree by the Palestinian armed group Hamas. Israel's military retaliated. It battered Hamas and the inhabitants of the Gaza Strip, where Hamas had been the governing authority since 2007 and from where it had launched its latest assault on Israel. The Israeli Defence Force (IDF) went on the attack and caused immense destruction and loss of life in its campaign to rescue Israeli hostages and to eradicate the Hamas militants who were hiding in and underneath Gaza's densely packed urban areas. The IDF argued that it was acting in self-defence and that Hamas ultimately bore responsibility for the loss of many thousands of Palestinian lives. Hamas argued that it was the voice of Palestinian resistance against an Israeli occupation of Gaza that dated back to 1967. And to an earlier legacy of Palestinian suffering that began when the state of Israel was created at the end of the British Mandate in 1948.

Even when trying to write the above passage in neutral descriptive language, I expect different readers to take umbrage with some of my phrasing. There is simply no singular cause that so quickly inflames world opinion as the century-long dispute between Israel and the Palestinians. It immediately bifurcates moral arguments one way or the other. The 'who started it?' nature of it is truly invidious and the argument is waged most vocally by those whose allegiances and sympathies lie with one side over the other. Clearly, no one part of the world has sufficient moral force to adjudicate on this most vexed of issues, but the dividing lines in different responses were telling in the context of a less Western world.

The instinctive response in the US, as shared by the other Western governments, was to back Israel's military response to Hamas. The links between Western countries and Israel are deep and founded on strategic, cultural and emotional ties, including the ancestral people-to-people links between the Western countries and Israel. Prominent among Israel's backers was Germany, with its residual guilt over the Nazi Holocaust. President Biden urged Israel's President Benjamin Netanyahu to avoid America's lessons of overreacting to a terrorist atrocity with too much military force after 9/11; but the US Navy also deployed in force to the Eastern Mediterranean to deter Israel's other enemies from piling in to attack it during its moment of weakness. It looked as if Western governments, led by the US, were giving Israel the top-cover to retaliate militarily in Gaza however it liked, with little accountability from its backers.

The Western governments were at odds with the portions of their own populous calling for an immediate ceasefire and those in the Global South who saw a greater imperative to protect Palestinian civilians from Israel's retribution. More extreme anti-Israeli views claimed that, while Hamas's actions on 7 October were undeniably murderous, they were an inevitable reaction to Israel's past treatment of the Palestinians and, most notably, to Israel's lack of will over many decades to allow for the creation of a sovereign Palestinian state. Israel's Western backers were also partly blamed for Israel's harsh military offensive in Gaza. The *Financial Times* quoted a Western diplomat: 'We have definitely lost the battle in the Global South.' This diplomat's prognosis was bleak: 'Forget about rules, forget about world order. They won't ever listen to us again. What we said about Ukraine has to apply to Gaza. Otherwise we lose all our credibility. The Brazilians, the South Africans, the Indonesians: why should they ever believe us again?'[10] It was a fresh charge of hypocrisy against these Western governments. If you make such a stand against Russian re-colonisation of Ukraine, why don't you make a stand against Israel's war in Gaza and its settlers' annexations in the West Bank?

As with any complex issue, the divisions were not clear-cut. The Modi government in India for instance stood in solidarity with Israel, an allusion to India's own sense of being embattled in the past by Islamist terrorists sponsored by Pakistan. Plus, India was a keen buyer of Israel's defence exports.

Despite these exceptions, there was a dawning realisation that, as with the Ukraine–Russia war, governments in the West had ended up backing yet another war effort when the loudest and more widespread calls in the Global South countries were for ceasefires. For the US, UK, Germany and other Western governments, they felt they had good reasons to initially resist pushing for ceasefires in both wars. Backing Israel was a matter of counterterrorism and preventing another Holocaust. Backing Ukraine was about defending an innocent democracy against an authoritarian imperial evil, and Russia would likely renege on any ceasefire deal, it was believed. But the room to disagree in the court of global opinion was growing, especially over the Israel–Hamas war.

Those Western governments backing Israel's military offensive in Gaza and resisting calls for a ceasefire were increasingly isolated: in the UN General Assembly, 153 countries voted for an immediate humanitarian ceasefire, the unconditional release of all hostages and humanitarian access to assist the beleaguered Palestinians of the Gaza Strip. No mention was made of condemning Hamas in this resolution. The US was one of just ten countries that voted against this call, with twenty-three abstentions during this vote that took place in New York on 12 December 2023. The UN Secretary General also called for a ceasefire.

And then South Africa's government applied to begin legal proceedings against Israel's government at the International Court of Justice (ICJ) in the Hague. The allegation raised by

South Africa was that the IDF was committing acts that were 'genocidal in nature' against the Palestinians. Even if the case and this precise allegation went nowhere, it had immense symbolism: an African country had filed proceedings against a Western-backed state, Israel, at an international court based in the Netherlands. A plethora of non-Western governments expressed their support for South Africa's case at the ICJ, including Malaysia, Türkiye, Indonesia and Jordan. Also backing South Africa's move was the Organisation of Islamic Countries that included 57 countries and the Arab League of 22 countries.[11]

Imagine a world in which countries outside the West have better coordinated views on such a contentious issue, and use the very rules-based order advanced by the West to make their cases heard. This would be a very different world indeed. With global tensions bubbling up around topics such as how to end Russia's invasion of Ukraine, and around the morality of how Israel has waged its war in the Gaza Strip against Hamas, what other parts of the world think is becoming more important with every passing global crisis. Moral force – the power to be seen as taking a virtuous or at the very least a justifiable stand on a matter of major contention – is only going to become more contested in the less Western-dominated world.

15

Hemispheres of Influence

> The countries of the South are not properly equipped. They have become quite dependent intellectually on the North, its analyses, information, assessments and solutions, as concerns global issues and their domestic situations.'
>
> Boutros Boutros-Ghali, former UN Secretary General[1]

LIKE ANY SHORTHAND term being used for a big concept, 'Global South' has earned a mixed reception. It is useful for collectively referring to swathes of the world that had important shared experiences, for places that were formerly colonised, experienced modern independence struggles and have since gained their sovereignty and developed their economies. It is rather like 'the West', a catch-all term for a plethora of otherwise incomparable nations and peoples brought together by broadly shared historical experiences.

It is also cartographically ludicrous if considered in purely hemispheric terms. Much of Asia sits above where the equator passes through Indonesia's archipelago. Well over half of the African continent is above the equator, which runs through Kenya and Congo. Of all continents, Africa is the only one that straddles all four hemispheres. So, the 'Global South' cannot be located as south of the equator or even south of the Tropic of Cancer. The term only works if it refers to being located south of Europe and North America; which was always the point metaphorically, in terms of these countries being 'beneath' Europe and North America in terms of economic development.

There is symbolic power, rather than true unity, in the term 'Global South'. In several Asian and African nations, there is a simmering desire among some people for a reckoning for the historical sins committed against their forebears, although it does not define every inhabitant to the same extent. It exists more as an undercurrent of historical sentiment in many post-colonial societies. At times, this surfaces in specific disputes with Western countries. For instance, asking for the return of artefacts that were seized during the colonial era, such as Nigeria asking for the return of the Benin Bronzes housed in the British Museum. Or asking for apologies for colonial-era practices such as slavery and internment.

One of the tricks to pulling off an appeal to swathes of the non-Western world involves a moral appeal to anti-colonialism – but only against the past ills of *Western* colonialisms. Empires were clearly not only Western, but the maritime continent-hopping nature of the later European empires has created a very particular set of legacy circumstances in the Global South.

During the Ukraine–Russia war, Westerners tried to point out that experiences of colonialism are not unique to the Global South nations. Similar emotions are felt as strongly in Finland or Estonia or Ukraine about Russia, they pointed out with perfectly reasonable logic and evidence from history of

Russia's past imperial brutality. However, as I have found, despite intellectual appeals to a common revulsion against colonialism *in general and across time*, no such commonality exists for people in the real world. What people actually feel is a revulsion or unease with the *specific* colonialism that their ancestors suffered. This is what has real emotional traction – not some kind of adopted sympathy for the ancestral struggles of other people you have never met. Telling people in an African country once colonised by Europeans that they should feel equally fraught about the legacies of Russian colonialism in Ukraine is as absurd as telling Ukrainians to emotively engage with the bitter legacies of Kenya's Mau Mau struggle. Or with the causes of Subhas Chandra Bose and Mahatma Gandhi in India, merely on the basis of being generically anti-colonial. These arguments may work at an intellectual level but to widen their appeal at the popular and political levels, there needs to be some kind of emotional glue, not least since some favourable attitudes towards Russia have remained decades after the cold war, when the USSR assisted several independence movements in the Global South.

The burning question remains: who will lead the Global South? Can it even be led in this way – or does its coherence arise from the elusive and arguably superficial essence of simply being non-Western? After all, slowly developing economies rub shoulders with fast-emerging economies, making the Global South clearly too diverse and too loose a grouping to ever be commandeered wholesale. But the diversity of the Global South countries should not be the concluding thought on this matter. Is there a winning combination of material power, idealism and necessity that could inspire significant chunks of the non-Western world behind certain issues? These are vital questions to pose as networks across the Global South strengthen and the West sometimes struggles to get a look-in.

Every modern nation is the outcome of how its ancestors overcame their historical struggles. Nations in the West hardly had it easy: they have experienced a great deal during their modern histories of imperial rivalry, religious schisms, the world wars and during the Cold War. But at a certain general level, the Western nations just did not experience history in the broad ways that a large share of the Global South countries did. There are the shared memories and myths around having been colonised, often within living memory. And there can be the subsequent resentments at having been second-tier countries. Whether Westerners like it or not, these sentiments can still be germane to how some among the populations and politicians of the Global South countries perceive their place in the world.

* * *

Given the significance of the conference it hosted in 1955, the city of Bandung in Indonesia could be more famous than it is around the world. I suspect most people – and certainly many Westerners – would struggle to find it on the map. I certainly wouldn't have had a clue before living in the region and being able to visit it. Today, there is a high-speed Chinese-built railway connecting Jakarta and Bandung in less than one hour, a speedy way to cover the 150-mile distance between these cities on Indonesia's Java island. This train started running in

2023 as part of Indonesia's modernisation of its infrastructure, in which Chinese investment has played a significant role. There is another enduring reason as to why Bandung is iconic for people interested in the modern evolution of the Global South.

Sixty-eight years before this high-speed train line opened, delegations and representatives from twenty-nine Asian and African governments gathered in Bandung to discuss how the Third World should represent itself in the big matters of day, such as advocating for further decolonisation, and in trying to resist the competing superpower pressures of the Cold War. This was a really big deal: not since the 1927 League Against Imperialism meeting in Brussels had so many colonised nations convened to discuss their grievances, needs and hopes for the future. World War Two interrupted these efforts. By the time of the Bandung conference, ideas could be thrashed out to take to the UN and to strengthen the Non-Aligned Movement. These were peoples and nations that had been divided by colonialism and here they were, gathering in Bandung in April 1955, far away from the presence of the West.

There is a museum to the conference in modern-day Bandung. Its exhibits remind us of the heavy hitters of the formerly colonised world who attended: Nehru from India; Colonel Nasser from Egypt; and the host, President Sukarno from Indonesia. China's leader Mao Zedong did not personally attend and dispatched his deputy, Zhou Enlai, who was on a mission to reassure other developing-world leaders that China was not out to foment communist revolutions in all of their countries too. Some attendees were suspicious of China, which had only turned communist six years previously, and at the conference Nehru tried to smooth over the idea that communist China should be treated as part of the family of nations.

You may have heard of Pan-Asian movements or Pan-Arabism or Pan-Africanism, referring to the ideas circulating around the redrawing of regional maps around the time of independence to join together communities of people with overlapping or shared heritages. The magic of Bandung was its trans-continental component: it convened national leaders from all over the formerly Western-colonised world.

The host Sukarno welcomed all of these leaders to his country. He memorably called it 'the first intercontinental conference of coloured peoples in the history of mankind'.[2] The twenty-nine participating countries may have been incomparably diverse, but there were some principles which elicited a general agreement. The Philippines delegation was headed by Carlos Romulo, and he remarked that the participants at Bandung shared 'generally speaking, a common historical experience. We belong to the community of hurt, heartbreak, and deferred hopes.'[3]

The participants held a mixture of views towards Western countries. Some were pro-communist, others were pro-Western or trying to stay neutral. They did not present themselves as an anti-Western or an anti-white bloc (the racial line being far starker at that time). And it wasn't about picking a leading state from among their number. The British government was still worried about the conference and asked representatives from Ghana and Singapore not to attend. The

British exerted their influence over Sri Lanka, then known as Ceylon, as the US did over the Philippines, asking these countries' representatives to speak about 'communist colonialism'.[4] As the US State Department account of the conference concluded, 'in the end, Bandung did not lead to a general denunciation of the West as US observers had feared' since 'US allies in Asia were able to represent their shared interests with the United States in the conference meetings, and Chinese Premier Zhou Enlai took a moderate line in his speeches to the delegates.'[5]

What did it all achieve? Positive principles emerged from Bandung advocating for independence for the numerous peoples who remained colonised at the time (most of the European colonies in Africa were not wound down until the 1960s). The discussion at Bandung tried to counteract the sense of being ignored by the bigger and richer powers. For these nations, racism and colonialism was front and centre to these issues; 'we deplore forms of racial discrimination' was a line that made it into the Bandung principles in stronger wording than anything appearing in the UN Charter when it came to the specific matter of race. (The UN Charter, which was signed in San Francisco in 1945, mentions on four occasions rights that should apply 'without distinction as to race, sex, language, or religion'. So it is not absent of mentions of race. But at a time of persisting European colonialism, it is little surprise that the discussions at Bandung in 1955 opted for far stronger language on racial discrimination.)

During the Cold War, Westerners were not in the habit of taking seriously the idea of power and influence coming from the south. For instance, speaking in 1969 and caught off the cuff, the late US statesman Henry Kissinger happened to deliver an astonishing comment to a Chilean government minister. 'Mr Minister, you made a strange speech. You come here speaking of Latin America, but this is not important. Nothing important can come from the South. History has never been produced in the South. The axis of history starts in Moscow, goes to Bonn, crosses over to Washington, and then goes to Tokyo. What happens in the South is of no importance. You're wasting your time.'[6] The quote was recorded for posterity by journalist Seymour Hersh, and at the time Kissinger probably felt on the right side of history: as a German émigré to America, which now led the West and Japan in a stand-off with the USSR, itself the representative of a rival European political ideology, Marxism.

How history turns. When Kissinger died aged 100 in 2023, the world he left behind was heading in a very different direction. The Global South was coordinating among its nations like never before.

* * *

It is a long way from Bandung to the BRICS, which Indonesia demurred from joining in its tranche of expansion in January 2024. Argentina suddenly decided against joining but only at the last minute, after its new president took office a few weeks before Argentina was due to join. Even without Indonesia and Argentina, the BRICS+ is the most expansive and economically influential bloc of countries ever to emerge from the developing world. The lack of perfect harmony between the BRICS+ members is a given but it misses the point. It is one thing if Global South countries increasingly trade with each other; yet another if they release joint statements diverging from or opposing Western positions on global matters – and quite another still if they have regular forums to organise themselves politically and economically, and to bypass or to vault over Western gatekeeping.

The BRICS+ is in no way a non-Western bloc that could counter the G7 or NATO. There are vast differences among the BRICS members. Whereas Russia has been rabidly anti-Western, other members like India are simply non-Western. The two biggest BRICS economies, India and China, are implacable rivals in Asia. The members are a mixture of elected and illiberal democracies, totalitarian, theocratic and monarchical states. How could the BRICS ever amount to being greater than the sum of their parts, especially now that the number of members is on the rise?

There is disappointment in some circles that the BRICS does not actually present a coherent challenge to the West. The Marxist chronicler of the Global South Vijay Prashad has written of insurmountable limitations in what the BRICS can collectively achieve. His expectations of a new world order have been dashed because 'the BRICS alliance has not been able to create a new institutional foundation for its emergent authority. It continues to plead for a more democratic UN, and for more democracy at the IMF and World Bank.' So, reform of the existing system rather than calling for anything more ambitious, in other words. Moreover, 'the BRICS formation has not endorsed an ideological alternative to neoliberalism' and it 'has no ability to sequester the military dominance of the US and NATO'.[7] Given these limitations, then what is its significance?

The very existence of the BRICS as an expanding group had added fresh momentum to the rebalancing of the world away from the West. It provides new avenues for those that are Western-ambivalent to gather and articulate their arguments for more global representation, making it harder for Western-dominated bodies to ignore them. It is clearly a haven for those countries that end up as anti-Western. Most of all, it is about normalising platforms of power from which the West is excluded, diluting Western influences where once they dominated. Rather than tangibly achieving things in the ways that the task-focused and instrumentally minded West considers vital to success, it is about getting everyone – the West included – in the frame of mind for the very differently balanced decades to come.[8]

Thinking again in hemispheres, the trend underway is for more networks and greater convergences between countries in the East and South. The West has struggled to grasp the political and ideological significance of the BRICS, initially seeing it as a group of emerging markets. As the analyst Sarang Shidore astutely noted, the US military in particular is likely to have had to think in novel ways to grasp the BRICS' geopolitical significance. The US military has tended to view the world according to its combatant commands (Centcom, Southcom, Indopacom, Africom, Northcom and Eucom), each with its own commander who responds to scenarios and specific challenger states in their domain.[9] But the BRICS project is about building non-Western networks between regions and continents.

The point about geographic dispersal has another important dimension: apart from the rivalry between India and China, the five long-standing BRICS countries are all too far apart to have any beef with each other. Presumably, if there were disputes between newer BRICS members, it could become a forum for dialogue and mediation.

There has been a preview of this: in advance of Iran and Saudi Arabia both being invited to join the BRICS, China brokered the restoration of diplomatic relations between these bitter rivals. Their rapprochement was announced in March 2023 in a joint statement from China, Iran and Saudi Arabia. The BRICS was not used as the vehicle to achieve this outcome; instead, it was Beijing's economic relations with Tehran and Riyadh that gave China's foreign ministry its leverage and credibility as a convener. Tensions will clearly persist between Iran and Saudi Arabia, but China thinks it can help to manage these tensions through the strength of its economic relations with both countries.

Another coming trend is for countries in Africa, Asia and Latin America to form fresh opinions about each other more generally, and to learn more about each other through their own exchanges, rather than often refracting this knowledge and awareness through Western-produced histories and Western-dominated institutions.

The Brazil-based political scientist Oliver Stuenkel reflected on this, picking out a few examples. In the West, we have become more habituated to perceiving China as a threat. But whereas 'Western analysts often warn China's rise will "eclipse" the sun of Western Enlightenment, which will be blotted out by China's economic dominance and a shadow that would cover the Western world', it is far from clear that other places will forever come to this same conclusion because voices in the West urge them to.[10] Whether or not you and your countryfolk see China as a threat and are provoked into disgust by its one-party authoritarian political system is one matter. What will really make the world turn is how others come to their own conclusions about not only China's rise, but any number of other contentious matters of global concern.

* * *

China has been making moral claims to leadership of the Global South. The tactics it has used have evolved. Once, China used to emphasise the greatness of its civilisation to its East and South East Asian audiences when exerting regional influence over them, but it now focuses on awing them with its economic power. Over time, its military power will become a greater part of its claim to influence in Asia. But to Global South audiences, China's message is a different one.

There are already well-established ways to address the Global South collectively. One of the legacies of the Bandung conference was the creation at the UN of the 'G77', the informal grouping of Global South countries with a dedicated mandate of South–South cooperation and an annual summit, which was first held in Algiers in 1967. Now, the G77 has even more members and renewed significance.

In 2023, the G77 summit was held in Havana. Xi Jinping did not attend but he dispatched his senior official Li Xi, who made the following pitch to the attendees: 'The G77 was born nearly sixty years ago in the struggles of its members for national independence and against exploitation and oppression. Developing countries have since advocated the Five Principles of Peaceful Coexistence and the Bandung Spirit, won national independence, and endeavoured to safeguard world peace and promote global development.' Li reassured them that 'No matter what stage of development it reaches, China will always be part of the developing world and a member of the Global South.'[11] China's foreign ministry had also published a sweeping document on the 'Reform and Development of Global Governance'. To redress 'historical injustices', China argued for the UN to give Africa a seat on an expanded UN Security Council and for developing countries to have a greater global voice.[12]

India is also getting in on the act of rallying the Global South. When it hosted the G20 summit in 2023, it made its own pitch when Modi called India 'the voice of the Global South'. India had a big win at its G20 when it succeeded in its campaign to have the G20 induct the African Union as a full member. Xi Jinping skipped this G20 in India, as rival claims to leading the Global South have become a feature of India's and China's respective claims for moral power.[13]

India also used its hosting of the G20 to push for tangible benefits to other developing-world countries. India seems to be very well aware that non-alignment and Cold War analogies cannot produce diplomatic outcomes. So, it has engaged such ideas as encouraging its approach to the digitisation of consumer services to Africa, for instance advertising India's UPI system for cashless transfers. India has also pushed hard for reform of the World Bank on offering green financing (see Part Four). In 2024, the G20 heads to Brazil, and one can expect more claims to represent the interests of the Global South from a different perspective. There is no one country that can 'lead' the Global South, but this does not negate its importance.

All of this should be balanced with the reality that Japan finances heavily in Asia, and South Korea is a leading arms seller around the world. So, these Western-aligned Asian countries matter too and it is impossible to imagine Japan or South Korea ever spurning their alliances with the US to join the BRICS. But balances of power are clearly tipping away from the West and its closest partners.

The US retains a preponderance of military force and the world's reserve currency – but others are catching up with it. The singular standing of the G7 in terms of its overall share of the world economy is not what it once was. The US and EU have also struggled to assert their moral power globally, with the EU now primarily asserting its global influence through regulatory standards. We will return to the potential tipping points in the conclusion, but sticking with the theme of power for now, it is vital not to draw the wrong conclusion: of a West that is absent from the world or powerless.

Just as Putin misjudged the forces that would oppose Russia when it invaded Ukraine, one must hope that other misconstrued assessments of Western weakness do not play a role in other wars. A great deal of responsible conduct in foreign policy for influential governments big and small now involves discouraging these misperceptions, while managing Western countries' own changing sensibilities.

World power in an age less dominated by the West is in

constant evolution. The blocs and clubs we are talking about today will be subject to change at some future point. Partnerships between Western and non-Western countries will coexist with clubs that exclude the West until one day, the very idea of what the West is and what it stands for starts to change, if for no reason than to keep pace with the changes surrounding it elsewhere.

Part Four

PLANET

16

Fossils

We are on the way to consigning coal to history. This is an agreement we can build on. But in the case of China and India, they will have to explain to climate-vulnerable countries why they did what they did.

Alok Sharma, British politician and President of COP26 (the UN Conference of Parties on Climate Change) held in Glasgow in 2021[1]

You cannot stop using coal overnight. It will be done gradually as we reach 2070. Even today, the US and UK have not stopped coal production though they are among the most developed countries. If they are to achieve their net zero target by 2050, then they should achieve their goal of doing away with coal by 2030.

Bhupender Yadav, India's Environment and Climate Change Minister[2]

MANY POWER TRANSITIONS are taking place all at once: the shift to a Westless world; and from reliance on our overused fossil fuels to less polluting alternatives. 'Net zero' is the aim of cutting greenhouse gas emissions to as close to zero as possible, with the remaining emissions reabsorbed by the oceans and forests, assisted by carbon capture technologies that are being developed. Making meaningful progress towards this goal involves dramatically cutting down on using carbon-emitting fossil fuels to generate energy that our economies are reliant on.

This is a fascinating context in which to think about the future. We now most routinely hear '2050' and '2060' and '2070' mentioned in relation to pledges made by different governments to cut the harmful emissions produced by their countries. A growing number of companies have been setting their own targets for reducing carbon emissions in their commercial activities. These responses to climate change have made some of us more future-focused than before. It is unusual for such seemingly distant target dates to become prominent political and business realities.

This future-gazing aspect is noteworthy in itself. We have not been an especially future-focused species, living predominantly through our sensory experiences of the moment and sometimes considering even five or ten years from now as 'medium-term' or 'long-term' when setting targets. The debate around climate change and changing our energy-consumption habits is unique in this regard. Perhaps only the vague targets for space exploration can match it. By way of illustration, it is not as if the nations of the world have ever set a target date like '2060' for taking steps to ban nuclear weapons; not that these are comparable issues.

Considering the energy transition through the prism of Westlessness is instructive. By the time we reach the mid-century mark, around the time these net-zero targets start coming into focus, we can expect the overall transition away from a Western-dominated world to have matured much more significantly. Today, the less Western world is still somewhat embryonic in many ways. But it is evident enough to affect climate change negotiations. Already, a huge and gaping chasm has opened on this topic. I am not referring to visualising the implosion of Planet Earth but to differing perspectives over rights and responsibilities for taking action to reduce climate change.

The motivations for curbing greenhouse gas emissions understandably differ from place to place and so do the official target dates set by governments. The EU, UK, USA, Australia, Canada, New Zealand, Japan, South Korea and some others have set 2050 as their target for net zero. China agreed to 2060 and India to 2070 to achieve the narrower target of 'carbon neutrality', which refers specifically to zero carbon emissions. It does not include other greenhouse gases being emitted into the atmosphere, such as methane. There are also disputes as to where responsibility ought to sit.

The Western world industrialised first and long before the emerging and developing economies elsewhere. Ergo, the West should pay to clean up the mess it has disproportionately created. This is precisely the argument that has been voiced most notably in the Global South. Take for instance the countries in Africa and Asia, which barely contributed to historical greenhouse gas emissions, but that are oftentimes bearing the brunt of the negative effects of climate change. For the fastest economic risers, China and India consider it to be a very convenient truth that, just as their economies catch up with the West, they are told the very fossil fuels that powered Western industrial successes are no longer morally and environmentally admissible sources of energy. Other Global South countries may feel they are not even being allowed out of the starting blocks on their economic development journeys.

The ill feeling around this matter spilled into the open at the 2021 edition of the annual UN COP climate action conference held in Glasgow, where a classic diplomatic 'fudge' was used to smooth over a disagreement and reach an apparent compromise through clever wording in its final statement.

The UK, as the summit's host, had pushed for decisive global action to be taken to end the use of coal with a clear target to be agreed between countries. The UK's ambition was sound in principle. Coal is the most carbon-emitting fossil fuel still in heavy usage, something that dates back to the transition away from widespread wood-burning, when the switch to burning coal boosted the West's leading economies. To the British, who began their coal-powered and soot-stained industrial revolution in the nineteenth century, and introduced a Clean Air Act in 1956 to limit the impact of air pollution, these were experiences lodged in historical memory with useful lessons for others. In 2017, Britain even had its own first coal-free day of energy production since the nineteenth century.

Other nations still in the midst of rapid industrialisation did not see eye to eye with the British. 'Let's not forget, we have to provide electricity to our villages,' said India's Environment and Climate Change Minister. 'We are not dependent only on one source but will push increasingly for renewables. India has already done it in some sectors. The use of coal in railways has long been done away with and the railways has almost completed electrification,' he added. Coal is often used to generate electricity, and as Victorian as this sounds, India's industrialisation was unfolding at its own pace. After all, Victorian Britain, powered by its own smoke-stacks, had colonised India back in the day. What sounded like a modern British lecture on the energy transition could well sound churlish to some.

Still, no one in India today could ignore the problem of poor air quality. Smog around cities like Mumbai can be intense. I recall in recent years leaving Colaba on Mumbai's southern tip and not being able to see the rest of the city around the arcing bend of the waterfront because of smog. Anyone who has experienced this smog for themselves or heard from well-to-do Indians that they currently live abroad to avoid the bad air at home, will take this seriously. Nevertheless, India's Environment and Climate Change Minister did not want to be cajoled at COP26. 'India has set its own targets and we are achieving them,' he said, at a time when three-quarters of India's electricity was still generated by burning coal.[3]

To take another example, nor could problems of poor air be ignored in Indonesia, which was in the process of moving its capital city from Jakarta to a brand-new site being cleared for construction in the lush jungle of southern Borneo, to be called Nusantara. Jakarta was once named the most polluted city in the world with its famously clogged roads caused by vehicular pollution and by rising levels of industrial activity. Some Jakarta residents wouldn't leave home without a mask and complaints around pollution-induced colds had grown.[4] Indonesia remained a major coal user and showed no signs of being able to stop dead in a short space of time.

At COP26, President Jokowi pledged Indonesia's support to the world's net-zero emissions goal. 'The question is then, how sizeable are developed countries' contributions for us? What kind of transfers of technology can be provided?'[5] This was the other side of the coin, as emerging economies asked the developed countries to cover the costs of switching away from the fossil fuels that had been used for the last 150 or so years of industrial development.

These gaps in perspectives left the COP26 negotiators in a fix over wording the summit's closing statement. Diplomatic negotiation is the art of smoothing over disputes and closing gaps in different national positions. At Glasgow, the classic fudge of changing the words to achieve consensus was used. The Glasgow Climate Pact's wording 'calls upon Parties to . . . transition towards low-emission energy systems . . . including accelerating efforts towards the *phase-down* of unabated coal power and *phase-out* of inefficient fossil fuel subsidies.' The controversial term was 'phase-out', which Britain wanted applied to coal, but which was replaced by 'phase-down' in the final statement.

The emerging economies had a point about their nations not being overly responsible for historical emissions of greenhouse gases. Even so, since they are now so dependent on fossil fuel usage, their policy choices are critical to the global response, raising a novel set of conundrums for how the Western countries should respond.

* * *

The rise of the West would not have been possible without hefty fossil fuel use and through innovating new ways to extract energy resources from below the earth. How the Europeans and the Americans fuelled their ambitions for global influence is a key feature of how the world evolved both geopolitically and ecologically. In pre-industrial societies, people laboured in ways that had not fundamentally changed for centuries, using their own physical strength and employing draught horses, water power, windmills, rudimentary machinery and by burning wood. The Western economic take-off relied on innovating different ways of energy usage and securing the requisite natural resources.

Vaclav Smil, an authority in environmental sciences, explained how being at the forefront of previous energy transitions gave these countries advantages over others. Steam engines were invented in the eighteenth century and burning coal to create steam power became key to the industrial revolution. 'An abundance of high-energy-density coal ideal for fuelling steam engines was clearly a major factor contributing to the British dominance of 19th century maritime transport, as neither France nor Germany has large coal resources of comparable quality', he wrote. Navies that replaced their sailing ships with faster coal-powered steamships gained a huge competitive edge. Building coaling stations at strategically located ports was a vital enabler of the Royal Navy's power at the British Empire's apex.

During the Westfull era, the prevailing energy mix (meaning the combination of energy sources relied on by countries) changed with successive innovations. As Smil explained, 'We have been generating electricity by burning fossil fuels, as well by harnessing the kinetic energy of water, since 1882, and by fissioning a uranium isotope since 1956,' which also referred to the power sources harnessed in the successive eras of European and US dominance. In other words, the most energy-guzzling societies were the ones that had advanced the quickest. Smil cited the US anthropologist Leslie White, who explained in 1943 that 'Other things being equal, the degree of cultural development varies directly as the amount of energy per capita per year harnessed and put to work' – also called 'White's law'.[6]

These past energy transitions took their toll on the environment. The levels of carbon dioxide in the atmosphere had not changed for millennia until the mid-nineteenth century when it began to rise – just as the West achieved its global dominance. There can be little doubt it was humankind that brought about changes in the atmosphere by burning fossil fuels and by converting on a larger scale than before forests and other natural terrain into farmland to feed rapidly growing populations.[7] This has stimulated a sub-field of research into the links between colonialism and carbon emissions, which calculates the cumulative emissions of greenhouse gases of specific nations and sometimes gives them historical responsibility for the emissions that emerged in their former colonies. Just a handful of countries are disproportionately culpable for the state of the environment as it has degenerated since around 1850.[8]

Be that as it may, China is now the leading annual emitter of greenhouse gases, an inevitable by-product of its rapid industrialisation over recent decades, even if China contributed to a smaller share of historical emissions in its pre-industrial incarnation. Thinking beyond China, world population overall has roughly tripled since 1950 and standards of living will rise in many more places as their economies advance. As emerging economies grow, they consume more energy. Economic development has relied on fossil fuel usage for so long that old habits will die hard. Most of the world's energy is still sourced from coal, oil and natural gas.

Humanity's appetite for energy has grown in different ways. Just three decades ago a panoply of electricity-dependent devices like portable computers and smartphones were not widely owned or simply did not exit. Fossil fuels have remained the world's principal energy sources, counting for 83% of all primary energy in 2020. Fossil fuel usage will remain a lynchpin of how modern societies function.[9] There is a long journey ahead before the sources of energy we rely on diversify away from fossil fuels.

We are now heading towards peak oil demand, according to the International Energy Agency (IEA). The IEA, which is headquartered in Paris, was founded to help Western countries manage their energy demands without unduly undercutting each other after the oil shock of 1973–74. The cause of the oil shock was war in the Middle East. In 1973, a coalition of Arab militaries launched a surprise attack on Israel in what became known as the Yom Kippur War. As a result, Saudi Arabia led an oil embargo against the Western states that backed Israel in this war, causing a sudden drop in the supply of oil. The US and European countries found themselves competing with each other for favourable oil deals, and the IEA stepped in to keep an eye on the state of supply and demand in the market.

For the last 150 or so years, we have climbed the mountain of ever-greater oil consumption. Peak oil is the moment we descend the other side, not because the energy transition tells us to but because fossil fuels are a finite resource. Today, the IEA still includes the Western countries plus a select few others (Japan, South Korea and Türkiye) in its thirty-one-strong membership. In 2023, the IEA issued a stark piece of predictive analysis: 'Growth in world oil demand is set to slow markedly during the 2022–28 forecast period as the energy transition advances' and more specifically that 'growth is set to reverse after 2023 for gasoline and after 2026 for transport fuels'. There are a number of reasons for these trends including gathering efforts to use lower-emission sources of energy, the rise in electric vehicle sales, and also the successive impacts of the Covid pandemic and Russia's war with Ukraine adding to concerns around energy security.[10]

Whereas the West's global rise was powered by fossil fuels, the next energy transition is set to unfold in the maturing era of diminishing Western dominance, with wide-ranging implications for all parts of the world. Well-known cliches of the US and Europe only being interested in the Middle East and North Africa for its oil have been changing fast.

* * *

We are reaching peak oil demand at the dawn of the Westless era. Demand for fossil fuels has been de-Westernising for some time because of emerging economies. The Organisation for Economic Co-operation and Development (OECD) is another Paris-headquartered body, founded in 1961 to help the Western nations' economic growth. In recent years its membership has expanded to include a select few non-Western members and it offers up another anomaly for the

Westless age. Between 2022–28, almost 80% of global growth in GDP is projected to take place in *non-OECD nations.*[11] That is some slowdown for a club that was founded to represent the 'economically more advanced nations', as it called the West in its founding charter.

China's insatiable energy demands have transformed it into a massive consumer of fossil fuels. As Yergin recounted, 'the industrial countries were still using almost two-thirds of total oil as the new century began. But then came the shock – the demand shock – that hit the world oil market' that unfolded between 2000 and 2010, when 'world oil demand grew by 12%. But by then, the split between the developed and the developing world was approaching 50–50.'[12]

As recently as two decades ago, China barely made a dent in global energy demand. It was only in 1993 that China's petroleum production was outstripped by its rising domestic demand, transforming it from an exporter to an importer of oil. Since then, China's energy needs have grown. China overtook Germany's economy to become the third biggest in the world in 2007 and overtook Japan's economy in 2010 to take second place behind the USA. Around then, China overtook the US as the biggest overall energy consumer in the world, and it is still dependent on fossil fuels for around 85% of its energy.[13] For its part, although India was far behind, its demand for oil was also rising. The IEA has projected that in 2027, India will overtake China in terms of growth in year-on-year oil demand.[14] Moreover, both China and India were heavily reliant on coal for cheaply generating electricity.

China has become the biggest carbon emitter at the same time as it has become the world's largest factory manufacturer for goods that it exports globally, including to the West. After China entered the WTO in 2001, companies relocated more of their factory production to China, benefitting from China's low manufacturing costs and its fixed exchange rate, which made its exports relatively cheap.[15] It can be argued therefore that because the Western countries relied on Chinese factories to manufacture so many of the goods they consumed, the West had offset some of the emissions related to its own consumer economy to China. This adds a different perspective to the seminal moment in 2006, when China's carbon emissions outstripped the US's, and when angst in the US was growing over China 'stealing' US manufacturing jobs.

Over the last two decades, the US has become far less dependent on the Middle East's oil. The shale revolution has buttressed America's energy security. Achieving energy independence had become something of a political obsession in the US for decades. Energy independence means domestically producing the energy your country consumes rather than importing it.

In recent years the US has purchased more of its oil imports from Canada and Mexico than from Saudi Arabia or Iraq. The US still imports oil due to the specific types of crude and petroleum that its economy requires in certain amounts.[16] But the shale revolution has provided the US with a newfound flexibility in international affairs.

Shale oil was sourced by a drilling technique known as fracking to extract reserves buried below especially dense rocks that could not be penetrated by conventional drilling. The technique existed for some time but shale only began to decisively impact US fossil fuel supplies in the 2000s.[17] According to the US Energy Information Administration, 'Up to the early 1950s, the US produced most of the energy it consumed,' but this changed after 1958 when annual US energy consumption began exceeding its domestic energy production, requiring more and more energy imports, especially of crude oil and petroleum products. Total energy imports peaked in 2007 and latterly, as the US Energy Information Administration triumphantly assessed, 'The US has been a *net total energy exporter* – total energy exports have been higher than total energy imports – since 2019.'[18]

The US is now the world's largest oil-producing country followed by Saudi Arabia and Russia. The US has greatly prized its increasing self-sufficiency in fossil fuels. For European countries, however, the security of their fossil fuel supplies has become a vexing question and one that has worsened due to the overarching trends in geopolitics in which powerful non-Western countries forge closer ties.

* * *

The security of a country's energy supply is among its crucial national missions. Without energy, life shuts down. For well over a century, securing favourable and reliable fossil fuel supplies has been a huge driver of Western interests in other regions. It has bound the Western countries to the Middle East and North Africa, Russia, Brazil, Venezuela, Nigeria and other fossil fuel producers during the colonial and the globalisation eras. The extraction of fossil fuels and their transit from suppliers to purchasers continues to connect the world.

Regarding oil, the major non-Western producers have collaborated since the 1960s through the Organisation of the Petroleum Exporting Countries (OPEC), which brings together oil producers in the Middle East and North Africa plus Venezuela, Nigeria and a handful of others. OPEC has served as a non-Western cartel to manage these countries' collective oil supply. The OPEC countries produce well over a third of the world's oil and hold the dominant share of the world's proven oil reserves.[19] Saudi Arabia is OPEC's biggest oil producer and under its leadership, OPEC periodically limits its production to drive up the price of oil. It does not always work smoothly, such as when an OPEC member tries to defy Saudi leadership by not cutting its production. Overall, however, OPEC gives its members the solidarity to stand up to the demands of the largest oil consuming nations, many of which are Western.

In September 2016, a deal was struck by Saudi Arabia and Russia to create a new arrangement called 'OPEC+'. Saudi Arabia and Russia began to cooperate their production targets to forcefully drive up oil prices to a greater extent than before. Their cooperation was a reaction by Riyadh and Moscow to rising amounts of shale oil being produced by the USA. It was a way for Russia to resist Western-led efforts to try and drop the global price of oil in 2022, as part of the sanctions aimed at crippling Russia's economy after Putin launched the invasion of Ukraine. Saudi Arabia and Russia have periodically defied the West by controlling their huge collective share of global oil supply, keeping prices high. For these countries there is no incentive to stop selling oil since it is the source of their influence.

The advent of OPEC+ intensified geopolitical competition in world oil markets. As the IEA assessed, 'as China and the West grow apart' and 'with a China/Russia/Middle Eastern axis in the process of developing' this 'will affect energy supply, trade flows and outright prices'.[20] Most notably, the membership of OPEC+ overlaps with membership of BRICS+. Specifically, six of the world's top ten oil producers are now part of the BRICS arrangement (Saudi Arabia, Russia, China, the UAE, Iran and Brazil). This is bad news for the West and another big incentive for the energy transition.

Europe has been exposed to severe geopolitical shocks surrounding fossil fuels. Consider the overall situation: purchasing Russian energy is now largely closed to the West due to the sanctions imposed on Russia for invading Ukraine. European countries had relied on buying natural gas from Russia to cover around 35% of their gas needs and around 9% of their overall energy needs. Russia sold its gas to European countries on the basis of long-term contracts, arrangements that persisted even after it had annexed Crimea in 2014. The EU's largest economy, Germany, was particularly reliant on buying cheap Russian gas. These arrangements were shattered by the sanctions imposed on Russia after 2022. Even then, it has been impossible for European countries to fully cease buying some Russian gas to meet their energy needs. Russia was their largest proximate natural gas exporter, producing nearly seven times as much gas as Norway, the largest European producer, and far more than was produced in the Netherlands, UK and Germany.

As we have seen, China and India decided to go the other way, benefitting from the availability of abundant Russian oil and gas supplies that were no longer bought by Western countries. In May 2014, shortly after the annexation of Crimea, China and Russia signed a thirty-year gas deal in which Russian state-owned gas provider Gazprom would start to sell gas via a pipeline from Siberia into northern China. In March 2021, China also sealed a twenty-five-year economic partnership with Iran in which China would buy Iranian oil and gas while also investing to improve its production facilities. China has remained hugely reliant on importing fossil fuels from Russia and the Middle East, and the security of its energy supplies is also high among Beijing's priorities.

Anti-Western countries like Iran can find more than enough demand for their oil and other fossil fuels in the non-Western world. Other emerging economies that are not anti-Western also keep their options open. India's major trading partners include oil exporters like Russia, Saudi Arabia and the UAE, which incentivises India to balance positive relations with all of these parts of the world as it also remains close to Western countries. Given India's rising energy needs, it can never afford to be drawn fully into one geopolitical camp.

All of this is a far cry from the world of the 1990s when India was a minnow in the world economy; when China's rise was still embryonic; when Russia lacked geopolitical confidence due to the recent collapse of the USSR; and when the US military led a victorious coalition of Arab and Western armies to evict the Iraqi troops who were occupying Kuwaiti oil fields. Throughout the 1990s and early 2000s, the US and UK air forces policed Iraq, flying regular missions from airbases located in Saudi Arabia, before toppling Saddam Hussein in 2003. Twenty years later, the geopolitical dynamics surrounding fossil fuel supply and demand are almost unrecognisable. This naturally suggests that, in twenty more years' time, when the world moves beyond its peak usage of fossil fuels and into a different era, the geopolitics of the energy trade will have metamorphosed once again.

For Western countries, it has made sense to trade in fossil fuels among trusted friends. As US and Canada oil production has increased, North America has improved its energy self-sufficiency, making the Western Hemisphere less dependent on fossil fuels imported from the Eastern Hemisphere, where supply will circulate through Asia instead. European countries will rely on increasing amounts of liquefied natural gas (LNG), which is a relatively low-carbon fossil fuel, and they may look to LNG reserves in several African countries for their supplies.[21] The advent of the less Western-dominated world overlaps with what is expected to be the waning years of peak fossil fuel demand – but this depends on the energy transition meaningfully progressing.

17

Easterly Winds

> Notes with concern that . . . the current levels of climate finance, technology development and transfer, and capacity-building for adaptation remain insufficient to respond to worsening climate change impacts in developing country Parties, especially those that are particularly vulnerable to the adverse effects of climate change.
>
> COP28's closing statement[1]

GIVEN THAT IT is such a major oil producer and exporter, the UAE's hosting of the COP28 summit was greeted with cynicism. Despite this, the annual COP summits are one of the few global gatherings where real effort is made to hear from different parts of the world, from national leaders and monarchs to financiers and civil society groups. At a time of worsening geopolitical rivalries and wars, the COP summits' calls for working in unity stand out positively, even if there are different perspectives on what needs to be done in the energy transition, how urgently to act and how to fund it.

The energy transition involves lessening our reliance on carbon-emitting fossil fuels. It is an ongoing project that affects virtually all nations and commercial activities to some extent. It also offers a unique window into how the world is changing. As with any human endeavour there are self-interests at play, but there are also common-sense incentives for taking action. Populations with the cleanest air and water will likely be more productive and prosperous, avoiding mass chronic illnesses that could saddle heavily polluted countries, resulting in huge health care bills and higher mortality rates.

Crucially, the energy transition has opened up new avenues for exercising moral authority in global leadership. Let's start with the very general perceptions held about the West when it comes to climate change and the energy transition. On the one hand the Western countries are seen as ranking high among the main historical greenhouse gas emitters. On the other hand, they may also be seen as walking wallets who need to help finance costly energy transitions elsewhere. And they are certainly not seen as unified among themselves. The EU has been more consistently committed to the energy transition but the US has been wildly inconsistent. Due to the swing of the US's political pendulum, its participation in the Paris climate change treaty has been stop–start.

President Obama's administration signed up to the climate change treaty agreed in Paris in 2015. There had been previous climate change summits, starting in Rio in 1992, but Paris 2015 was the first ever legally binding international agreement to reduce carbon emissions, with the overall goal being to limit the rise in global average temperatures to two degrees Celsius above pre-industrial levels, and preferably to one and a half degrees. The Paris agreement came into force on 4 November 2016 but just four days later, Trump was elected president. Once he entered the White House, he withdrew the US from the Paris deal, declaring it to have disadvantaged America's economic prospects 'to the exclusive benefit of other countries', with Trump singling out China, which had been given a grace period to increase its greenhouse emissions, while India would receive large amounts of foreign aid to guarantee its participation.[2]

Even after Trump made this announcement, it took the US four years to complete the UN's formal processes to officially exit the Paris climate deal. No sooner had that happened than Joe Biden made it one of his very first steps as president to have the US re-enter the deal in 2021. The US government tried to downplay the whole episode: 'Now, as momentous as our joining the Agreement was in 2016 – and as momentous as our rejoining is today – what we do in the coming weeks, months, and years is even more important.'[3] But the damage was done. As an advertisement for American global leadership on climate change, it was an unclear one. The US looked ridiculous in the eyes of its allies and the rest of the world for this flip-flopping incoherence.

China lapped this up – it could step into the limelight as the grown-up world power by sticking with the Paris deal. The BRICS countries wasted no opportunity to advertise their own commitment to the Paris deal in the face of Trump's withdrawal. During China's presidency of the G20 held in 2016 in its city of Hangzhou, the BRICS leaders reaffirmed their commitment to the Paris deal. The BRICS 'call upon all countries to fully implement the Paris Agreement', they said again in 2018 at their own summit.[4] From its self-interested perspective, China's government was killing several birds with one stone: responding to its needs to reduce pollution; improving its energy security given its reliance on importing fossil fuels; all the while displaying its credentials as a responsible global power.

To many outside eyes, the odiousness of China's one-party police state renders the possibility of it becoming a benevolent global leader too incongruous to compute. How could a country that operates a tech-enabled surveillance state, that limits free speech, and has persisted with its annexationist policies in Tibet and Xinjiang, be a moral global leader in any capacity? If China was to ever invade Taiwan, any of its claims to global benevolence would shatter, even if China tried to pass off any escalation over Taiwan as a domestic matter. Those who consider China's rise in its current form as a bad thing for humanity argue the harsher characteristics of China's style of rule disqualify it from being a responsible global leader in any capacity; moreover, they argue that anything China is doing to purportedly help humankind is simply a ruse to further its own rise.

And yet, in the decades to come, so long as China avoids starting or wading into a war where it is clearly the aggressor, whether in Taiwan or elsewhere, it is poised to be a lynchpin in the renewable energy transition. No one knows yet whether China can meaningfully cut its carbon emissions, but we already know that China is the world's largest manufacturer and exporter of products and technologies for the energy transition. Combined with also being the world's largest polluter, this places China in the odd position of being crucial to the problem and an enabler of the purported solutions.

What about the other emerging and developing countries? There is a moral yield awaiting those countries with a credible enough platform to seize it by speaking on behalf of and meeting the Global South countries' needs during the energy transition while helping facilitate and fund it.

Many Global South countries were highly exposed to climate change's negative effects, with small island nations being some of the most vulnerable of all to rising sea levels and other natural disasters. At COP27, held in Sharm El-Sheikh, Egypt, a historic agreement was made for creating a 'loss and damage fund', without quite specifying how it would be financed and what could be claimed, in which poorer countries would be financially assisted in responding to climate change-induced disasters. At COP28 held in Dubai, the focus shifted to finding the financing for this loss and damage fund, and for the technologies required for the energy transition to take place in developing countries. Every year at the COP, things edge forward. There is no easy solution, and pledges of funding are very different to seeing new renewable energy technologies manifest on the ground.

* * *

The energy transition has opened new forms of moral and material influence. No matter your personal stance on the science-based calculation around embarking on the energy transition, it is clear that future energy mixes will differ from historical ones, due to the finite nature of fossil fuels and security of supply issues alone. Those advocating urgency in the energy transition are clear: to achieve the internationally agreed goal of controlling the rise in average global temperatures, greenhouse gas emissions need to peak as soon as possible before rapidly declining and approaching net zero in the second half of the century.

There will be winners and losers in the energy transition. Platitudes aside, 'The demand for raw materials to build our clean energy infrastructure is as geopolitical as the age of oil. Countries that are able to become a part of these new clean energy supply chains will benefit,' wrote Henry Sanderson, whose journalism has focused on commodities and mining.[5] Attempts to move away from fossil fuels will increase demands for a mixture of nuclear power, renewable energy and battery-stored electricity. Batteries in turn depend on labour-intensive mining. Cobalt and nickel are required for lithium batteries; copper for the cabling in electric-powered infrastructure – in fact, no single material item will be as critical as the copper. Smil, the energy scholar, has estimated that 'decarbonisation will be highly mineral-intensive because the generation of zero-carbon electricity needs vastly more natural resources than fossil-fuel-based options.'[6] We are replacing one set of extractive practices for another.

A handful of countries are experiencing windfalls of demand for the vital mineral needed for greater electrification. Indonesia is the world's single biggest source of nickel and provides a large share of the world's supply. Nickel is a key mineral for the renewable energy battery industry but also for use in wind farms and other renewable energy technologies. Indonesia has been determined to take advantage of this by becoming, for instance, a crucial part of the electric vehicle supply chain. 'Indonesia produced 771,999 tonnes of nickel in 2020, twice that of the Philippines and around a third of global output. This was set to rise to 2.5 million tonnes of nickel by 2030, due to Chinese investment,' wrote Sanderson. By comparison, 'Europe produced only 14 per cent of the world's nickel, eight per cent of its cobalt and one per cent of its lithium and graphite.'[7] The extent of Chinese investment in Indonesia's nickel mining shows these savvy countries responding confidently to the surging demands for vital commodities.

China is the largest manufacturer of renewable energy and clean air technologies. The biggest share of solar and wind capacity is being built in China as its nuclear power and hydropower sectors are expanded. The percentage of China's electricity that is generated by fossil fuels and by coal in particular has been falling, albeit slowly and from a high level. China expects to peak in its carbon emissions by 2030 and aims to reach carbon neutrality in 2060. The huge advantage China has in the renewable energy era is still in its manufacturing sector. Electric vehicle manufacturing is being ramped up. Most strikingly, around 80% of the world's solar panels are manufactured in China.[8] China is the world's largest producer of aluminium, copper and steel, which are essential to electrification, to cables and to building wind turbines.

Where will Western countries fit into the equation? The Westless aspects of the energy transition are stark, as the academic Helen Thompson placed in historical context: 'If Britain was the power that climbed to dominance during the age of coal and the US the power that ascended during the age of oil and coal, the spectre haunting Washington is that without a decisive American strategic turn to renewables and electrification, the new energy age that depends on metals and minerals will belong to China'.[9] Hence the US's introduction of tax incentives to fund climate change technologies, announced by Biden in 2022 as part of the 'Inflation Reduction Act' legislation.

Even as Western countries reduce their dependency on China-centred supply chains, emerging and developing countries will likely continue to rely on China to a greater extent to equip themselves for their energy transition needs. As Daniel Yergin observed, 'Energy transition means different things to different nations, especially in the developing world. A billion people lack access to electricity; three billion do not have access to clean cooking fuels. Instead they burn wood or charcoal or crop waste or cow dung indoors, impairing their health.'[10] The overlap between the energy transition and poverty alleviation more generally is very evident for some communities. China has its own example of lifting people out of poverty in large numbers; it also has centrality in energy transition supply chains and may be better attuned to the needs of Global South countries.

The onus is now on the Western countries to lead with a compelling offer to the developing world to assist in their energy transitions. The advent of another Trump or Trump-like presidency in which the Paris climate treaty is abandoned once more would scupper the US's role in this, leaving the EU struggling to pick up the slack in the West's contribution to financing and supplying the technologies that are required for the shift away from fossil fuels.

Despite the consensus-building tone of the COP summits, the energy transition is not immune to the things that characterise all worldwide endeavours of such scale

– profiteering, rival claims to take the credit and selfishly securing the most advantageous deal that meets a country's needs. One way in which the West can demonstrate its global leadership credentials and its continued relevance to emerging and developing countries will centre around its role in the energy transition. Its nations having industrialised before everybody else's, emitting copious amounts of greenhouse gases in the process, the West could now lead by example by decarbonising more quickly than the others. To do so would offer a new example of Western leadership.

***

A race is underway that will provide its winners with a major moral and material yield, leading to commanding more global influence. The extent that Western countries successfully manage their rapid reductions in carbon emissions in the coming decades will impact their moral authority as stewards of the planet. The window for the Western countries and their closest allies like Japan and South Korea to race ahead is clear. Their window is also a function of China, India, Indonesia and other fast-developing economies still peaking in their carbon emissions at a time when the already industrialised Western countries can start to clean up their act. Consider China's and India's spiking carbon emissions: in 2006, China overtook the USA as producing the most. Around 2021, India was emitting about the same as the EU27 (although given their huge populations, the per-capita graph displaying carbon emission relative to population size is less unflattering to China's and India's negative impact on the environment through fossil fuel usage).[11]

To meaningfully reduce fossil fuel usage, everyday industrial processes, from making plastics to cement, will need to be overhauled, and there is a great deal of suspicion in some quarters that the task is too complex to be achieved by 2050.[12] Fossil fuels will continue to be used albeit in different quantities as part of a diversifying energy mix that includes less emphasis on coal and oil, and more emphasis on natural gas (the 'cleanest' fossil fuel compared to the other major contenders, albeit one that is less energy dense than oil and has specific complications in its transportation and storage). Nuclear energy and renewables will provide increasing contributions to the energy mix as fossil fuel dependencies recede. Looking across the world, there is a contrast in how urgency is portrayed when it comes to reducing fossil fuel usage. Different countries are running different races.

There is a lesson for the West: the climate debate will have to change from an adult-to-child tone towards a more adult-to-adult tone if the Western countries want to have credibility in engaging with the Global South countries, which have radically different motives and needs in the energy transition.

With a greater share of the growth in energy demand coming from the Global South, countries with little direct culpability in the historical build-up of greenhouse gases are at the forefront of climate change debates. These dynamics have placed the Western countries in tricky positions, even if they get their own houses in order by making progress in the energy transition. Whereas the conversations around net zero have been led by voices in the West, the responsibilities for implementation also sit outside the West. The West may well struggle to serve as a beacon to the world in leading the way on the energy transition, because its motivations and starting points are so distinct.

Aside from the US simply abandoning the energy transition wholesale as a matter of 'America First', the next worst thing the Western countries could do is to scold emerging and developing countries about their progress. As the energy transition focuses minds on raising the funds to invest in affordable wind, solar, battery and other non-fossil fuel power sources, huge amounts of money will be required to meet the target agreed at Paris in 2015 to keep average temperature rises to 1.5 degrees. The tone in which Western countries engage with others, and the evidence of their own actions, will constitute part of their global credibility and contribute to their influence in other parts of the world.

18

Friendly Shores

LIKE MANY OF US, I had never given much thought at all to container ships and had taken for granted that a hefty share of what was exported and imported around the world transited the seas and oceans. But the views leading up to the Malacca Strait have become more routine to me: container ships and other massive transporters are bobbing up and down on the water almost as far as the eye can see, suspended in the waters around the world's second busiest seaport in Singapore.

During the pandemic, their crews were often stuck aboard, not allowed to come ashore for fear of disease outbreaks on board. Even as international trade returned to normal after the pandemic, the fragile 'just in time' economy, in which things are shipped when they are needed and not stocked up in advance, was looked at afresh. The dependency of the Western world on these globe-spanning supply chains should also feature in any reflection on how it depends on the wider world.

There were maritime traders in Asia, Africa and the Middle East since ancient times, but it was not until the Europeans weaved the continents together across the oceans that globe-spanning patterns of trade began to be more routinely formed. Asian countries were important parts of these trading networks, with Spanish and Portuguese silver being used to buy Ming-era Chinese goods, and Ming pottery finding its way around the world. For these volumes of trade to dramatically increase, however, transportation technology had to move forward, which it has only done in its modern forms within living memory.

Around the time of World War Two, the huge diesel engines required for powering large ships became more common, allowing for rapidly increased volumes of trade as new and larger transportation vessels became more routine. It was even later that supertankers and bulk carriers began shipping huge quantities of oil or vital minerals all over the world, as well as developing the technologies to transport bulk quantities of natural gas in liquefied form.[1] The globalisation of trade has been Western-led, in particular due to the maritime networks of trade and safe shipping routes encouraged by the US and guaranteed by its navy after World War Two, including routes between the rebuilt post-war economies of Western Europe and Japan, for instance. It has created the possibility of importing not only from immediate neighbours but also from much further afield. Since then, the Asian countries that have experienced rapid export-led economic growth, including China and India, have benefitted massively. Is the Western world's privileged role at the centre of globalisation set to erode further?

Compared to its earlier incarnations, globalisation is being rewired. A more free-flowing version of globalisation took root after the Cold War in which lower costs was the driving logic of commercial exchange, and in which the distinction between the developed West and the developing rest of the world was starker. Things move on, however. Latterly, the pandemic, plus wars and strategic rivalries between states, have made many countries look afresh at the long supply chains they depend on as carrying serious vulnerabilities. 'There is ample reason to believe that globalisation may be changing in nature rather than in retreat,' observed one study on the matter.[2]

This leads us to the panoply of terms that have emerged to challenge existing assumptions around globalisation. The idea has arisen in the West that there are growing risks associated with trade dependencies for vital goods that rely on long, often opaque supply chains, especially if they pass through or originate from countries considered as rivals and challengers.

These terms started with 'decoupling', meaning cutting off supply chains entirely. When this proved less than practical, since so much of global manufacturing relied on China that the US struggled to cut it out of supply chains, the terminology changed to 'de-risking', meaning trying to limit exposure to politically unreliable factors in the supply chain. And there was 'friend-shoring' (importing vital components or finished goods only from friendly countries), 'near-shoring' (moving business activities or manufacturing nearer to where these outputs were to end up) or 'on-shoring' (bringing it all home rather than sourcing from abroad).

The global impact of supply chain disruption caused by Russia's invasion of Ukraine was a singular wake-up call, involving rising food prices as Ukrainian and Russian grain ceased being exported in the same amounts, especially to countries in Asia, the Middle East and Africa that relied on it. There was also massive disruption to the energy industry through the price caps and sanctions on Russian oil and gas being enforced by the West and its close allies. Coming right after the Covid-19 pandemic, this was further reason for multinational companies to build up the 'geopolitical resilience' of their operations to greater extents than before.

Security of supply has always been a concern in a globalised economy that heavily relies on shipping to move goods. It is worth recapping how relatively recently the World Trade Organization (WTO) was created, in 1995, to carry on the work of its predecessor body the General Agreement on Trades and Tariffs (GATT) in removing the barriers of protectionism. 'American and European companies were setting up supply chains that gather components from different parts of the world, assembled them in still other parts, and then packed the finished goods into containers and shipped them across oceans to customers anywhere in the world.'[3] These arrangements came about in a world in which the Western countries called the shots and in which the G7 economies were collectively responsible for a dominant percentage of global economic activity.

The breakdown of that world changes some of the patterns of international trade. A succinct indicator appeared in a UK government review of its national security and foreign policies called the Integrated Review: 'The global economic and trade order is changing' and 'we can expect further pressures as the net zero transition drives a major restructuring of the global economy'. The solution for the UK was clear: to work with like-minded countries and strengthen mutual solidarity.

Stick with your friends as the world changes. Stay closer to trusted friends rather than relying on countries you could fall out with.

***

Decoupling, it turns out, is essentially a myth. There is no way to cut out of global supply chains the countries that have become its vital nodes and hubs. For the West, the main aim has been to decouple supply chains from Russia and China. But to see how hard this might be, just take a look at the world's busiest ports, a vital part of the network in world trade given that shipping still moves the lion's share of goods:

> In terms of [container] shipping, China is becoming a major, if not dominant force. China is the second largest ship owning country behind Greece (although if Hong Kong is included then Greece loses its lead). China has obtained a 48 per cent share in the global shipbuilding industry by deadweight tonnes, and 97 per cent of the world's containers are made in the PRC. China's major port operator, COSCO, is now the second largest port operator in the world . . . Seven of the largest ten container ports by volume are now in China – Singapore, Busan and Rotterdam being the exceptions.[4]

According to Lloyd's List, one of the world's oldest shipping news services, the world's busiest ports 2016–2020 were: Shanghai; Singapore; Ningbo-Zhoushan; Shenzhen; Guangzhou; Qingdao; Busan; Tianjin; Hong Kong; Rotterdam; Jebel (in

Dubai); Klang (in Malaysia); Antwerp; Xiamen; Tanjung Pelepas (Malaysia); Kao-hsiung (Taiwan); Los Angeles; Hamburg; Long Beach California; Ho Chi Minh City.[5] In other words, even as Western companies in particular have expanded their production outside of China, a huge share of shipping trade is passing through Chinese ports and in Asia more generally. Cutting China out of global supply chains is virtually impossible.[6] As the historian John Darwin puts into context, 'Now it is the trans-Pacific traffic from Asia to North America that dwarfs all the rest – carrying nearly double what is sent from Asia to northern Europe, and almost ten times what crosses from North America to Europe, once the busiest of seaborne highways.'[7]

Despite all of this, the US Navy still has the larger global role in policing and keeping safe the 'free and open oceans' for trade. And of the largest container shipping companies, a large number are in fact European, even if the complexities of the shipping industry mean that crews and vessels may be sourced from different parts of the world. It was interesting to discover that, of all the transport ships bobbing along the Singapore coast and all over the world, an astonishing 25% of crews were made up of Filipinos, for instance.

Decoupling your economy from China makes for a nice anti-China statement, but it is effectively unachievable, which it is why it was rebranded as 'de-risking', because cutting Chinese production and materials fully out of complex supply chains is impossible. When the US reduced its trade with China, its alternative trading partners, such as Mexico, were in turn importing many of their inputs from China and selling them back to the US as manufactured products 'made in Mexico' but at least in part sourced from elsewhere. Wall Street struggles to abandon lucrative business opportunities that await in China, even as the US national security community and hawkish politicians try to isolate China and implore their allies to do the same. The EU sits somewhat on the fence over all of this, while much of South East Asia in China's direct periphery continues its trade. And as we have recapped earlier, even after waging its brutal war in Ukraine, many non-Western countries did not abandon Russia as a trade partner, while even the West and its closest allies found it tricky to completely expunge Russian crude oil and natural gas from all of its sources of energy supply. The world is too interconnected to prise itself apart fully, no matter how seemingly bitter the disputes have been so far.

Despite these difficulties, Western countries are increasingly committed to trading with those they more closely identify with. This will change our assumptions about global trade, making it less free-flowing and according more with geopolitical preferences. Globalisation of trade is at a turning point, according to a study by the Bank for International Settlements into how supply chains have changed in recent years. This 'does not mean the creation of Western-only regional trade networks. Instead, end users are sourcing basic and immediate goods from places such as China via intermediaries in countries like Vietnam,' meaning that 'what is emerging is not so much reshoring as reshuffling – a rising level of complexity that has expanded the distance in supply chains (layers between raw materials and end users).'[8] In line with a world of rising non-Western countries, the West is at the start of a long process of re-evaluating how best to secure its trading needs.

* * *

The West still rules the waves for now and retains the means for policing worldwide maritime supply chains. The idea of being an 'offshore balancer' is the strategic terminology for having deployable navies that can sit offshore and threaten to project force into any continent. The combined fleets of the West and its close allies can muster more warships than any challenger. China has been trying to rival this, and maybe it can succeed in levelling the naval balances in Asia at least. But there is another sensible approach for the West's challengers: to bypass Western naval dominance by going overland instead.

The scholar Wang Gungwu wrote that since 'the Chinese know their history' they will recall that 'the overland Belt across the Eurasian landmass to reach markets in Europe has not been attractive since the end of the Mongol empire' and investing in these routes may not pay for itself. 'China's south, however, is a different story. It is now central to future economic development, and keeping the waters secure for China's maritime linkages has never been so important. For the first time in history, the south is an existential problem for its national interests.'[9]

Hence China's Belt and Road Initiative (BRI), which has helped to deepen China's relationships with emerging economies and developing countries around the world. The BRI has developed with a mixture of overland and maritime routes. It kicked off in 2013 and was a signature of Xi

Jinping's approach to China's foreign engagements, bringing its investment, development and foreign policies together in ways that maximised China's strengths. According to one study, 'At its outset, the BRI was partly designed to address the problem of economic development in Western China. Far from the affluent ports of China's east coast on the East and South China seas, Western China was (and, to a lesser extent, remains) poorly connected to international trade routes.'[10] The US has led the Western charge in attempting to persuade other countries not to join the BRI and most European countries have either not joined or, in the case of Italy, have withdrawn, while Japan, India and South Korea have also not joined. But 150 of the 193 UN member states *have* signed up to the BRI (although the precise number fluctuates).

The West has been slow to compete with the BRI in launching its own infrastructure investment programmes that extend into the non-Western world. The EU has not offered anything to compete. The G7 launched its awkwardly named 'Build Back Better World' in 2021, abbreviated as B3W and later renamed PGII.[11] And then in 2022 came the 'Indo-Pacific Economic Framework', which was intended for the US to lead a coalition of countries in Asia and Australia for various economic development projects. But the BRI had a decade-long head start. And whereas a differently inclined future US government might dump any of these initiatives, the Chinese leadership seems likely to be committed to the BRI concept, framework, and to its annual summits.

Could the West be shut out? Tomorrow's trading clubs will reflect the reality of non-Western countries dealing profitably with each other. As Kevin Rudd warns, 'Over the last 20 years, Beijing's economic relationship with much of the developing world has become more important to many of them than their relationship with the US – a fact that policy makers in the US have missed or dismissed.'[12] China has signed big agreements with ASEAN for free trade, further integrating China into the economies of South East Asia. It is possible that China one day tries to build a trading club purposely to shut any hostile Western economies out. Friend-shoring in its own ways.[13]

One cannot preclude the advent of new non-Western trading blocs, or blocs in which Western participation is limited to a few European countries alone and therefore diluted by other influences. Hence the policies driven by Western countries to create specific partnerships around vital products, the clearest example of this being over semiconductors, such as more closely integrating the production in semiconductors in the US, Japan, South Korea and Taiwan (the latter two are responsible for much of the world's advanced semiconductor forging via Taiwan's TSMC and Korea's Samsung).[14] Is this the way the world is going – trading in the most vital goods to your economy by sticking closer to your friends than to those you are more ambivalent or even hostile towards? The logics of profit and efficiency alone are not sufficient guides to the supply chains of the coming era.

* * *

'Singapore-on-Thames' – of all the curiosities to emerge during the Brexit debate in Britain ahead of the vote in 2016, this phrase, used by certain advocates of leaving the European Union, was one of the oddest. They argued that the City of London, Britain's financial nerve centre, could outcompete the EU by emulating the lightly taxed, low regulation, pro-business model that is used so successfully by Singapore. It was a silly comparison made by some Brexiteers since it heeded nothing of the fundamental differences between London and Singapore; the latter being a tiny city-state with its own unique attributes and challenges.

With the longer arc of history in mind, it was striking that pro-Brexit British nationalists had invoked the path of a former British colony as being their inspiration, albeit with a sketchy understanding of how relevant Singapore was as an example. But oh, how history turns in a few generations, whereby the descendants of the old imperial master were dreaming of emulating vital aspects of a former colony. The UK regards Singapore highly, and in 2023 entered into a Strategic Partnership to bolster digital trade. It is a long time since East India Company officers Stamford Raffles and William Farquhar decided in 1819 to turn Singapore into a port city to eclipse Malacca.

Once Singapore left the British Empire, a few years passed before it also split from the larger Malay Confederation in 1965. Singapore was forced to think ingeniously as to how to thrive independently or else vanish into obscurity. You can drive from one side to the other in less than an hour. The path chosen by Singapore was to become a way station for global trade and an attractive hub for international businesses and global finance. Without offering something uniquely attractive to outsiders – Western, Asian and increasingly Chinese – Singapore would have remained little more than a stopover for ships passing the nearby Malacca Strait.

Singapore and London offer a rather interesting juxtaposition between the old world of the West and the newer world of rising Asia. Singapore's gleaming skyscrapers and sky-high greenery looks like some people's image of the future. With plants and creepers growing and hanging off the middle of high-rise buildings, parts of it resemble a jungle planet from an old science fiction film. If there were awards for mid-air gardening, Singapore's urban planners would surely qualify, with trees jutting out from skyscrapers.

Many Singaporeans are Anglophiles and some of the brightest studied at British and American universities. Singapore has a generally positive relationship with its British Empire legacy, memories bolstered by the terrifying comparison between British mercantilist imperial rule and the short, sharp violent shock of Japanese rule between 1942 and 1945. Following its independence, Singapore looked to the US for its security. The sight and sound of Singapore's American-supplied F-15 and F-16 jets overflying its bustling urban conurbation is an everyday experience. But at the same time, Singapore is heavily exposed by proximity to China's regional rise. Its population is majority ethnically Chinese, often the descendants of settlers from China's coastal provinces. This is not to suggest anything is awry about their different national loyalties. Being bilingual is not necessarily being bicultural. Singaporeans often bristle with indignation if assumed to hold Chinese views, since they are their own nation.

Singapore is a fascinating petri dish example of the difficulties of skilfully balancing the realities of the shifting world order. Its modern rise to wealth and influence unfolded as the embers of the British Empire still glowed, and as the American Century reached its apex. But when you look both east and west, and as the global balance of wealth, power and influence adjusts, you can be tugged between worlds. Not so much a frontline but as a bellwether of a changing region.

19

New Frontiers

> This project will last for 100 generations. From this day on, the courage and perseverance of mankind will be etched among the stars. This long voyage of hope through despair will last 2,500 years across the cosmos.
>
> Outro voiceover from the Chinese movie *The Wandering Earth* (2019)

THERE IS A stereotype comparing shorter Western political attention spans with some of the perspectives in the non-Western world that are supposedly better attuned to playing the long game. This stereotype, like many, needs treating with scepticism but not dismissing outright. Countries that enjoy the fruits of liberal democracy also by definition find their political decision-making is driven by four- or five-year prime ministerial or presidential terms of office. Which are in turn increasingly driven by the minute-to-minute social media calculations that modern politicians in Western countries make when managing their reputations and in their receipt of information.

Forget about the impatience of consumer habits – any part of the world exposed to capitalist consumption and with disposable incomes to fuel it will likely succumb. When it comes to rulership, carrying forward a truly generational project requires some very particular traits. Stable one-party states, whether odiously repressive or more benign, embody notions of generational continuity in their political systems. Liberal democracies look elsewhere for symbols of continuity, which is one reason why countries like Britain and the Netherlands retain their ceremonial monarchies and why republics like France and the US venerate the ideologies of state that passing political leaders are supposed to steward and hand over to the next incumbent.

The closing script to the Chinese science fiction film *The Wandering Earth* takes the notion of long-term thinking to its absurdist extreme. Of course, no society plans ahead for a hundred generations and the world will change beyond recognition in even a tenth of this time. It was around 250 years ago that Europe's leading nations had decisively broken from the pack of the other sophisticated empires and kingdoms of the world, expanding the Western realm at the expense of others, and building on the prior partial capture of the Americas that began around 500 years ago.

One of the things distinguishing modern phases of history has been the quickening pace of change in technological innovations, giving a decisive advantage to early adopters. History is littered with examples of past technological revolutions but they had tended to arrive with a slower frequency. One reason for this change is obvious: advanced technological changes beget yet more rapid advancements, moving from the industrial manufacturing era to that of the information revolution. Take for instance container shipping, as discussed in the previous chapter. It was one thing to build bigger ships in the 1950s featuring containerisation, and yet another for computing technology in the 1980s to revolutionise the speed at which calculations could be made about fuel and load-bearing, further refining the efficiency of the global shipping industry. Modern advances can have huge cumulative effects.

The speed of change makes even our recent innovations and breakthroughs sound quaint less than a generation later. Nor are our time-honoured paraphernalia safe. Even writing a letter or taking notes with paper and pen already feels old-fashioned for the habitually smartphone-wielding populace. Teaching at a university in the richer parts of the world today will be greeted by rows of students hidden behind laptops and tablets, the humble paper notebook being seen ever less frequently. So goes the unstoppable march of progress.

Among the Western world's commonly cited claims for being able to stay ahead of the global pack is that its societies are uniquely attuned to fostering innovation. This claim is based not only on Western legacies of historical innovation but also on the socio-cultural fostering of individuality and tolerance of eccentricity when it is the personal trait that is needed to innovate; and guardrails in intellectual property law to properly reward true innovators. Ask almost any staunch defender of the West's ongoing potential to inspire and lead the world in some if not all areas, and they will articulate these traits in their own ways.

These claims have a degree of truth to them, to which we must also add in national wealth, and how global power structures have for so long been angled towards boosting Western successes in ways that other regions have not enjoyed. These structural factors have elevated Western innovations to greater heights than the modern accomplishments of other places. Even something as second nature as the Nobel Prize, named after the nineteenth-century Swedish chemist Alfred Nobel, affords a Eurocentric Western stamp of approval to worldwide accomplishments. Even if the recipients of Nobel Prizes have in more recent decades started to globally diversify, there have been 413 Nobel laureates from the US; 137 from the UK; 115 from Germany; 75 from France; and 34 from Sweden, to take the top five countries of nationality for laureates. Moreover, most Nobel laureates are men, no matter where they come from. Surely, they are thoroughly deserving for their merits, but laureates from elsewhere have barely featured at all. This is one example of why it can be fairly easy to succumb to the notion that modern human progress has largely resulted from brain power and ingenuity being expended across the West and mainly by men.

There are still many new frontiers to explore. In the future, Western men may not be at the forefront so exclusively as they have been, given all of the ways in which the world is changing. With one eye on the impressive modern history of Western global influence, let us bring our study of Westlessness to a close by considering a highly likely coming phenomenon: that innovations from the West will be very quickly adopted by other nations, closing the technological gaps between them. And that sometimes these other parts of the world will be the ones that rocket ahead.

* * *

For a relatively recent invention, at least in the grand scheme of history, the World Wide Web must rank among the most influential on an everyday basis for the greatest number of people. The formation of the internet coincided with the apex of optimism in the Western liberal global project. The longer-term trends suggest the internet will now evolve differently around the world. The West, where the innovations behind the internet took place, has inevitably ceded its ability to control how the internet evolves as it has been adapted elsewhere.

One of the most instantly tangible ways we register being in a new country is switching on our phones, waiting for a local signal, and seeing which of our apps work. The early internet was Western and heavily American-led. Later iterations will be less so. China has become the clear global leader in 5G systems and infrastructure, having invested an estimated $180 billion since 2014 to fulfil a state-led plan to become the global 5G leader.[1] As writer James Griffiths summarises: 'We are at a pivotal moment in internet history. There are currently two major versions: the libertarian "information wants to be free" fantasy which enabled the growth of tech monopolies that abuse our data, control our expression and endanger our privacy; the hyper controlled Chinese model, where the state acts as the ultimate arbiter of what can and should be said, for our own good and its perpetual power.' When you put it like that, neither vision of the internet sounds appealing, but that is precisely why its future is so open to contending interpretations.[2]

Russia has even tried to build its own sovereign internet, separate from the World Wide Web, to better control information flows into the country. These efforts have given rise to the term 'Splinternet' to explain bifurcations in how the internet will function, and the desire for authoritarian states to limit inward information flows while retaining the power to effectively turn off the internet for its citizens in whole or in part, especially to dissolve fomenting protests.

An EU-published report about the Splinternet, 'A short history of the unification of the Internet', reminds us how very Western-world its early days were. What became the established standard for computer networking – the World Wide Web – was invented by Robert Cailliau and Tim Berners-Lee while working at CERN, which is the European Organization for Nuclear Research. The World Wide Web Consortium was established in 1994, leading to the web's core languages becoming HTML. Thereafter, the US firm Microsoft achieved a huge share of the consumer market for accessing the Web with its Internet Explorer. Services provided by Google, Apple and many others diversified the ways in which the Web was commonly accessed. But it is reasonable to say that the early ubiquity of the Web was driven by innovations taking place in the West. The geopolitical dimensions of what happens next to the Web are fascinating. As the US Brookings think tank considered, 'The internet, as it exists today, is an artefact of a time in which global cooperation seemed reasonable, even inevitable', whereas in the future we are likelier to witness 'internet fragmentation'.[3]

As different kinds of internet censorship rise around the world, often reflecting different national governmental priorities enacted by private intermediaries, a more fragmented internet in a less Western-centric world seems likely. Turning on your phone when arriving in a foreign country and finding some apps working and others either redundant or simply deactivated and blocked will be one of the basic ways of gauging the prevailing levels of solidarity across the parts of the world you have travelled between.

* * *

The archetypal new frontier remains outer space. Dreams of exploration, from Christopher Columbus to Yuri Gagarin to Neil Armstrong, seem to have been personified by white men of European heritage of different sorts. Such was the era in which space exploration took off, deep in the Cold War. The present and future of space exploration is less centred around the traditional leaders, the US and the USSR/Russia. Even science fiction has caught up, and despite not being much of a Trekkie, I could not fail to notice the series' latter-day scriptwriters making sure to include the USS *Zheng He*. The idea that this fictional ship would be named after a Chinese admiral is interesting, but the formulation still feels odd – 'USS', denoting United Space Ship, still sounds as if it stands for 'United States Ship', the real-world naval use of USS. Relinquishing control in fictional imaginations, let alone in real life, of a well-established sense of past ownership of space exploration by the US above all other nations will be an interesting and consequential spectacle to observe.

As mentioned earlier, in July 2023, the Chandrayaan-3 moon rover made India only the fourth country to achieve this feat after the US, USSR and China. Four years before, China landed a space probe on the 'dark side' of the moon enabling the Yutu-2 rover to be the first to ever explore this region. Already, a growing share of active satellites orbiting Earth are Chinese, even if the majority of them remain American. Western space programmes have changed a great deal from the glory days of NASA to the privately funded ventures of SpaceX and are now paid for by business tycoons such as the founder of the Amazon web service, Jeff Bezos. European space programmes are based on individual European nations collaborating through the EU.

A RAND think tank study on 'Space, 2050' posited a vivid picture of where things might be headed with 'mining colonies on the moon and tourist resorts floating in Earth's orbit' as 'people play sports in space, generate power in space, even grow expensive, trendy coffee beans in space'.[4] As the costs of space travel are expected to drop in the future, some of this may happen. Dreams of routine space flights and further commercial and military uses of space will become realities during the Westless era, raising crucial questions of retaining as much comity as possible between the regions of the world while on terra firma but also while weightless in space.

* * *

Do you recall Concorde? Soaring high in the sky, this supersonic airliner could fly to the edge of space. Its invention showed how advanced Britain and France still were during the Cold War when engineers from these countries collaborated to design the aircraft. Even after their nations' post-war and post-imperial slumps, and while the US and USSR were racing into space, Britain and France could still forge ahead in inspiring ways. An aviation icon of the twentieth century, Concorde was briefly a contender for the future of passenger air travel. Its distinctive airframe remains a dart-shaped symbol of the modernisation of its day.

It can be instructive to revisit the cutting-edge innovations of yesteryear because that very cutting edge can suddenly be blunted. From Concorde's maiden flight in 1969, its airline career came to a horrific end due to a disaster in 2000 when Air France Flight 4590, from Paris to New York, crashed shortly after take-off, the only fatal accident in the airliner's history. Air France and British Airways stopped flights in 2003 after thirty years of service, and the idea of smaller and faster passenger planes lost out in commercial viability to the slower and larger commercial passenger aircraft we are most accustomed to.

When considering its old routings, Concorde linked three iconic cities – London, Paris and New York – offering a nice reminder of when different corners of the West unquestionably captured imaginations as the cities of modernity. Far beyond the passing of the British and French dream of Concorde, and its loss in last century's aviation competition to America's Boeing and its equally iconic airliners like the 747 jumbo jet, lies a deeper theme. To where in the world do we now look for the ideas and innovations of the future?

There is no questioning the standing of London, Paris and New York in influencing the whole world and animating so many imaginations inside and outside of the West. London was forging ahead in culture and in commerce, speeding up after the Industrial Revolution. Paris was a beacon of art and of the Enlightenment, followed by the political revolution of republicanism that influenced constitutions the world over including in the US and contributing to revolution in France's colony of Haiti. New York was a product of Dutch and English colonisation of North America, with the Hudson River named after an English explorer employed by the Dutch East India Company who sailed the river in 1609. The city was an icon of the New World's vitality, famous for finance and for popularising jazz music and for so much more, including Ellis Island, the arrival point for countless émigrés to the US. All three cities have modern reputations as melting pots for many cultures who intermingle in dynamic settings that still captivate for their uniqueness.

Point me to the world cities that can compete with this triumvirate for their financial, cultural and historical influences. Like Concorde, flying high in the sky above the Atlantic, the West remains an idea floating above the grandeur of its parts, achieving unprecedented altitude in the twentieth and early twenty-first centuries. But nothing and nowhere can remain the way of the future in perpetuity. One day, the future becomes the past. One day, other cities elsewhere in the world will earn this hyperbole, too.

The Path Ahead

HOW DO YOU weigh up the hopes, anticipations and uncertainties surrounding the journey into the new epoch when its precise shape will only reveal itself with the passage of time? One way to deal with all of this is through denial.

'There's no place like home,' uttered Dorothy in *The Wizard of Oz* when she longed to return to the world she knew back in Kansas. Snapping our heels and wanting to reset the global balance to how it used to be will get us nowhere. The Technicolor Westless world is becoming reality for more of us with every passing moment. This need not be a bad thing, and it will certainly offer a very different path through life for those who tread in our wake. They may even look back at the overly Western-dominated world and see in it more than a hint of monochrome.

History does not move backwards. It is becoming more difficult to imagine how balances of influence in the world could ever trend back to the ways we remember from past decades. Just consider the wording used by the US intelligence community when longingly presenting its best-case future world scenario. This would involve 'a renaissance of democracies' to be 'led by the US and its allies' in which 'rapid technological advancements fostered by public-private partnerships in the US and other democratic societies are transforming the global economy, raising incomes, and improving the quality of life for millions around the globe.'[1] And thus, the Western model glistens more brightly all over the globe with the US at the vanguard, leading the way for others to follow. Yet, things seem set to transpire differently.

Having surveyed many disparate trends, nine takeaways are drawn out to bring these themes together. This uncharted path need not be a fear-inducing one that risks Armageddon. Instead, it may spell an enriching evolution for our species in its many branches and tribes. No matter what happens, we are trending in a less Western direction and here is how to prepare for what is ahead.

Where Westlessness strikes . . .

Of the trend lines examined across Parts One, Two, Three and Four, some already fizz and crackle with the energy of change. First, there are the demographics of a declining share of the world populace for the Western countries. The shifting weight of numbers will start to tell in areas of life that we cannot foresee yet. It is not as if the West will dwindle numerically to such an extent that it becomes niche – far from it, and notions of the West as an 'endangered species' remain the stuff of populist nonsense. What the West produces, whether in entertainment or in education, will reflect greater influences from elsewhere, at the very least to increase its dual appeal and hence widen marketability and profitability. There may also be changing tastes inside Western countries, not only through the diversification of their own populations, but also because Westerners themselves may become ever more interested in understanding and rationalising where they now fit into the wider world.

In terms of political systems, there is no putting the genie back into the bottle as to the impacts of social media and artificial intelligence. Western liberal democracies and those cast in their mould carry considerable vulnerabilities. In politics as well as in other things, defending the integrity of its own systems from external influences will take up a greater share of Western governmental undertakings. Hence the current obsession for finding 'like-minded countries' around the world, with places like Japan and South Korea the present-day perennials in making this list for the US and UK.

India's independence of spirit continues to frustrate Western dreamers who would love to enlarge their tent further to include more fully the world's largest democracy. But it is no longer the West's tent to enlarge. Nor is world opinion the West's to decisively sway through its own moralising. In a number of ways, the West is moving from its previous expansionist phases to a more defensive phase of consolidating its standing in the world. A change that is underpinned by the shifting share of global wealth and the differing growth prospects of the emerging economies.

These are intermingling trend lines. Materially and ideationally, they weave into each other in complex ways. It is their *cumulative* effects on the standing of the West that is the crucial matter to observe. But it is not all doom and gloom for the West, far from it. Western countries, speaking individually or collectively through whatever structures they rely on in the future, will still be correct on many things, and will still win and persuade others in many arguments and will benefit from the residues of their dominance. This is a time of change; it is not the 'End Times' for the West. Which leads us to . . .

. . . Where Western influence holds strong

For now, Western influence holds in enough crucial areas of the world that some people might still be wondering what the fuss is about. There are many areas in which more typically Western ways of operating and thinking are advantageous to those who choose them. They are so entrenched, due in part to historical first-mover advantages, that their shelf lives seem healthy.

The most glaringly obvious is the extraordinary spread of the big four European-origin languages through colonialism, settlement and globalisation, namely English, Spanish, French and Portuguese. Between them, a significant share of humanity is conversant. Even as diatribes are voiced against the dastardly deeds of Westerners, some of these diatribes are formed in a European tongue. There will be a wicked irony in this for the West's staunchest defenders, naturally. No non-European language yet seems close to competing with English as the global lingua franca. Sophisticated translation apps will likely embed this. Not freezing it in time but bridging it so effectively that the effort required to master non-European-origin languages need not always be expended by some Westerners, even as the demography and the economic power of the West wanes relative to its past highs.

The West is still ahead in global intellectual leadership, having created a network of leading universities in which English is increasingly used, even in many non-Anglophone Western institutions. In educating elites and middle classes from around the world, these Western advantages seem enduring and guided by their own momentum. When it comes to hard power, the US excels in the might of its military as magnified through the NATO alliance; and in the might of its currency with supporting roles played by the European countries' and Japan's still considerable financial heft. The West's precise alliance and partnership configurations might change, but the US still commands the most potent military alliance and the West and its allies still control the lion's share of the global money supply.

The catch-up by others will take time. One cannot look with anything but healthy scepticism at its putative rivals; much will have to change for the BRICS+ or the SCO or any other non-Western club to develop the kind of challenge potential that would really threaten the West. Even if the symbolic threshold of building bigger non-Western groupings has now been crossed, they exist in parallel to the West, they do not yet eclipse it.

There is no room for Western complacency, however. We can see how the West's attributes of power are becoming decidedly *unbalanced* as some wane and others hold. What are the implications of the US retaining military and currency power but sitting atop partnerships like the G7 that represent a declining slice of global economic power? And while the

Western countries command declining levels of moral credibility in parts of the Global South?

One of the biggest variables is whether the US still chooses to lead the West in a world that considers it with less regard, or whether it retreats across the waters into its own hemisphere of opportunity. Even if the US remains powerful and prosperous in its own right as the world changes, it cannot carry the West on its shoulders alone. The question of whether the EU can develop a greater standing in the world beyond its impressive regulatory powers is becoming more acute. Between them, the UK will one day likely have to return to its bridging role between Washington and Brussels, if the different parts of the West are to hold together more coherently in a fast-changing world.

Towards the 2030s

We are still reacting to the onset of the Westless world. The next few years are a time of great peril in world affairs as the US–China rivalry reaches a new and difficult phase, and as everyone gets used to the diffusion of power from the West while still clearly remembering when the West was unquestionably dominant. In the second half of the 2020s and beyond, the number of oncoming crises could propel some of the trend lines of change forward faster than the speed at which they are currently travelling. Not least in the stewardship of the West itself, and if future political leaderships in Washington DC prove to be uncommitted to managing both America's and the West's global roles, then the slide could come faster than otherwise. The anticipation around another Trump or Trump-like presidency is an obvious point.

We can expect the European countries to be in the midst of their demographic changes and their energy transitions, while having to work harder to generate influence in parts of the world that have started to approach European levels of prosperity among their middle classes. To the extent a transatlantic West survives with its coherency at least broadly intact into the 2030s, the concessions that Western countries start to make to other places in terms of trade or other forms of cultural exchange will become more telling. In certain specific things that are yet to arise, such as in the response to a particular crisis or in the advancements produced by a particular technological innovation, we cannot rule out others rallying behind Western leadership again, although this is looking less likely.

The 2030s will be the decade of crystallisation of the Westless world. The US–China rivalry will remain a predominant factor but there will be a wider blossoming of other parts of the non-Western world, and a lessening sense of there being a singular US or Chinese camp. What we are looking towards is the maturation of the Westless world, in the sense that it becomes more of a second-nature reality than a novelty to become accustomed to. There are some markers along the way that, even without knowing precisely what is in store, we can be sure will carry significance.

The centenarians

The 2040s will be the decade in which we will see the Westless world normalised. Not because the West gives up the ghost but because more levelling out between the world's different regions has occurred. Humanity must hope for a steadier evolution and not a series of violent revolutions to reach the point, likely two decades from now, when rebalancing stabilises into the new normal. Acclimatisation takes time. No matter the issues of most acute attention in this decade, the sense of an overly concentrated amount of global power and influence sitting in Western hands will have lessened considerably.

Near the close of the decade, two important centenaries will be marked. In 2047, it will be one hundred years since India's independence from Britain. In 2049, it will be one hundred years since the Chinese Communist Party took power after its victory in China's civil war. These are essential symbolic moments at which point these nations will take stock of success. This will also be the centenary year of Indonesia gaining independence from the Dutch. By this decade, Russia's weak demographics and its over-reliance on fossil fuels will have become more of an anchor weighing them down. This will reduce its power substantially in relation to neighbouring China, which is projected to retain its stature as the world's number two or to become the number one economy in terms of nominal GDP. The European-based inhabitants of Russia will find their country isolated by rich Asian powers and may become more reconciled with the West as a consequence of greater cultural alienation in Asia.

These independence centenaries arrive later in other parts of the world (2060 in Nigeria, for instance, 2063 in Kenya, and so on). What's in a number? Well, the hundred-year mark is only a symbolic moment in the passage of time after the formal end of colonialism and nothing more. But it also indicates the shorter amount of time that many African countries have had to advance along such indicators as workforce education, further expansion of their middle classes and GDP growth. For these countries, their independence centenaries will be moments at which to take stock of their progress, and to reflect with pride on their own journeys.

These are speculative time frames and too much can happen to predict anything other than the clearest trend: that Global South countries will rely more than ever on each other to get ahead, even as they carry on their relations with the West.

Recasting Western leadership

Where are the Western countries in all of this? Following its phases of colonial empire and globalisation, this is the third act of the West in the modern world. What's next? Comeback? Consolidation? Dissolution? The idea of the West has always been evolving.

In the more distant past, these evolutions were determined by the geography of Europe, by race and by religion. The idea of the West has already changed a great deal including during its modern history. Now, the West survives by broadening its tent and becoming less Western in the old-fashioned meaning of that term, which denoted European heritages. Western countries will continue to attract outsiders to their shores while partnering closely with 'like-minded countries'. The idea of the 'geopolitical West' will gain more strength even as its constituent parts are ever-changing. The US is changing further in its linguistic and ideological composition; Europe's demographic health relies more than ever on immigration from outside the continent; and Japan's growth potential as a powerful pillar of the world economy seems limited by its own ageing population.

Melting it down and refashioning the West is less likely than an evolution. Ideas of Westerners just needing self-confidence – marching into the room like you own it and everyone will follow – will not be good enough anymore, whether in business or politics or on an individual basis. Westerners may have to work harder to assume leadership positions in more global endeavours as time passes, most comfortably sharing the stage with non-Westerners from these 'like-minded countries', and eventually having to routinely share the stage with those from political systems and cultures that remain foreign in both senses of the word.

At the moment, parts of the West do not really know what to do in a world where others do not always agree with them and can choose to go their own ways. Eventually, this just becomes the norm, leading to forms of Western leadership that rely less on being the aspirational model that others want to follow, and more on having to offer something tangibly worthwhile to corral others. The 'à la carte West', in which its own mix-and-match partnerships see it assuming equal roles with some non-Western partners, is coming. The next phase of the West in the world will be a true test of its diplomacy: when you don't have most of the money and most of the power anymore, but want to be respected and still have much to give.

Avoiding Armageddon

All of this depends on one very BIG thing. No one wants a civilisation-altering event, whether climate- or pandemic-induced or caused by warfare and nuclear weapons. There are dangers aplenty on this path, not least in the possibility of a version of World War Three breaking out as the US and its allies on one side and China, Russia, Iran and North Korea on the other become embroiled in wars over principles or over territory. Even these geopolitical alignments cannot be expected to hold firm over the course of successive decades.

Achieving diversity in the world, seeing different forms of power diffuse from the West, and avoiding war along the way remain paramount concerns for all of humanity. There is a clear contrast between the 1990s and 2000s, and the emerging world of the 2020s and 2030s.

Whereas previously the US military and its closest Western allies pursued the promotion and imposition of democracy abroad, including through military means, today, the mission is about forging greater solidarity between the existing democracies and close allies in order to shut them off from Chinese and Russian influence. Which leaves a host of countries, like Türkiye and Saudi Arabia, somewhat in the middle, able to play both sides. India, a democracy with no interest in preaching its system of government abroad, also falls into this category. If wars are to happen (and history shows that they tend to), the most optimistic scenario is that they remain localised, even if they have a wider 'West vs Others' dimension to them.

Arms spending around the world is currently on a steep rise as countries accustom themselves to a more uncertain world. One of the biggest risks is of more countries acquiring nuclear weapons. Currently, aside from the Iranian nuclear programme, Saudi Arabia, Japan and South Korea are countries that are said to be ready to move towards developing their own nuclear weapons. It is expected that these countries would only try for their own nukes if their sense of protection by the US wanes. We cannot de-invent the knowledge to build nuclear weapons, even if in an ideal world we could restore momentum to arms-control efforts that have fallen by the wayside of geopolitical rivalry in the 2020s. Doing so will be an important part of future-proofing the Westless era against the very worst our nightmares could imagine.

No rest for the West

With the risks of war in mind, it is worth remembering that there is no way to predict whose side specific countries might be on in the more distant future. Who, honestly, can predict the geopolitical alignments of India or Indonesia or South Africa or Saudi Arabia several decades from now? The greater fluidity of arrangements between countries means that there are mix-and-match partnerships between Western and other countries and regions on a pick and mix of issues. The West itself might even be influenced or changed by the different countries it seeks closer partnerships with.

The fate of the BRICS, let alone the BRICS+, with all of its additional members, will be one determinant – but even if the BRICS slogan is replaced by something else or by another arrangement entirely, the era of powerful non-Western clubs of countries is here to stay. There is nothing to preclude other non-Western alignments and clubs from forming in certain regions. This is one of the ways non-Western countries will seek to protect themselves against one of the West's most powerful tools to date – excommunication.

To have been expelled by the West, whether from a set of global financial arrangements or from the polite company of international diplomacy, will become a less significant feature. Any expulsion has less impact if there is a real set of alternatives to turn to. The West as the rule-maker and as the rule-enforcer – cherished responsibilities for those who have contributed to them – will begin to recede.

Bragging rights

Pride is a strange commodity, poisonous if imbibed in too large quantities but also essential in the form of the self-respect and self-confidence that is required to scale the lofty heights of success. There is an underlying nightmare that the West never quite says out loud but fears: of significant parts of the rest of the world building effective and powerful institutions excluding the West, and organising themselves without consulting the West.

Being ignored is an insult all of its own. It is clear that the Westfull era has allowed the most influential Western heads to be held up higher than most. In some quarters, Westerners may in fact start sulking that their bragging rights are diminishing. One solution is to remain only in the company of others who laud you for your historical accomplishments and never speak as if they have achieved more than you have. Flattery will still get you everywhere in life. Conversely, getting used to learning from others will be a novel and habit-forming experience for some parts of the West. There is nothing especially sinister at play here: only the habits of mind that form from the feeling that others in the world venerate you, and of these habits of mind shifting into uncharted eras. Managing residual Western-world pride will become an interesting feature of the new world and is potentially one of its sources of instability.

The art of balance

Imagine the metaphor of dealing sartorially with the Westfull world: packing Western-style suits for the occasions that require it while relaxing into national dress in other circumstances. To the extent that Western-style norms have become global ones, people will still manage these parallel worlds. Striking the right balance for some people around the world currently involves paying adequate tribute to the Western-derived ways of comporting oneself and presenting one's actions, if for no other reason than to be able to interact with the Western countries and to benefit when doing so.

In the future, we will have to look in many more directions than towards the West, learning the art of balance – including for Westerners, who will experience the novelty of more habitually looking at others' systems and achievements with awe and appreciation once reserved for their own accomplishments.

This will not suddenly happen overnight but will come into focus as the century matures. The youngest among us will see the full story play out beyond 2100; at which point the balance between the regions will be completely transformed. The idea of the Western countries being the shepherds who guide others will be consigned to a quaint but important era studied in the history books, not practised in everyday life. Further into the future, that any of our ancestors were ever the shepherds or the sheep will vanish further from view. And not necessarily because we have equality within our countries, but because we have greater equity between our regions.

Acknowledgements

Being peripatetic with intent affords an abundance of experiences. I have enjoyed working in several organisations over the years and I thank colleagues along the way who stimulated my thinking. That said, this book in no way reflects the policies or stances of any organisation I have worked for or been affiliated with, past and present.

The conceptualisation of this book resides in lived experiences and in my non-Western family heritage. Thanks to the Munich Security Conference (MSC) for coining the 'Westlessness' term and injecting it into the public debate as a spur for wider discussion. In no way is this book affiliated with or representative of the MSC, its perspectives or that of its research staff. I am only the latest author among several who have used the 'Westlessness' term as a springboard for their own reflections in their published work and I doubt I will be the last.

During the path to writing this book I have benefitted from the wisdom and kindness of peers, colleagues and eminent figures in the field of international affairs, broadly wrought. Thanks to Lam Peng-er, Rohan Mukherjee, Olli Suorsa, Yougesh Khatri, Raffaello Pantucci, Jonathan Grant, Michael Rainsborough, Abhijnan Rej, Samuel Kasumu, Bronwen Maddox, Olivia O'Sullivan, Clare Menozzi, Gokul Sahni, Tim Huxley, Greg Austin and Nick Joseph.

Thanks also to William and Kara and all our friends in Singapore. Needless to say, I bear sole responsibility for everything within.

Mid-way through writing this book I suffered the greatest of heartbreaks. Out of nowhere, I had to say goodbye to my dear mother. She had only recently returned from East Africa, her birthplace and her home in spirit. As I dropped everything to be with her, exchanging our loving, parting words and laying her to rest, I was overwhelmed. Such is the permanence of death, the moment eternity fails, that what was once enjoyed in abundance slips away in an instant. It is to her memory I dedicate this book.

Thanks are due to my cousins, aunts and uncles for their support in this harrowing period. To Shastri Ji, Mr R. A. Patil, Councillor Manjula Sood and Ashish at Moksh Indian Funeral Services. To Melanie and Dave for taking CousCous back into their home, a decade after my mother and I collected him in Cambridgeshire. To the kindness of neighbours: Patrick and Jordan went above and beyond. To Kate Moore for her help. To Jon B., Nick R. and Toni M. for the warmth of their friendship in the coldest of times. This book simply would not have been completed without those who rallied to help.

On a happier note it has been a pleasure working with Rupert Lancaster and the Hodder team; with Darryl Samaraweera at Artellus; and with Yash Verma at Cutting Chai films. It would be remiss not to mention Mr Chew Joo Chiat's namesake locality, starting at The House of Braised Duck. Thanks to Tita Mime for everything, including the adobo. And last but most of all, my love and admiration to Anna, the real superhero of the show, for allowing us to stand tall in the face of adversity, while scaling her own heights with true elegance. And to Asmi, simply for being herself.

Notes

What is Westlessness?

1. 'Westlessness' is not common parlance. It was coined by the Munich Security Conference (MSC) in 2020 to spur wider discussion about Western unity in the face of numerous global challenges. See the 'Munich Security Report 2020: Westlessness' (authors Tobias Bunde, Randolf Carr, Sophie Eisentraut, Christoph Erber, Julia Hammelehle, Laura Hartmann, Juliane Kabus, Franziska Stärk and Julian Voje). The term also appeared in a number of subsequent academic papers outside the MSC, including Alexandra Ludewig, 'Westlessness? Challenges for the EU's Soft Power Approach', Australian and New Zealand Journal of European Studies (13:1, 2021). She pointed out, 'Neither the Oxford nor the Macquarie dictionaries have thus far included the term which was coined in 2020 in the lead-up to the annual MSC'.
2. 'Essay on America and future colonial policy' (RA GEO/ADD/32/2010) Royal Archives. Reproduced by the Georgian Papers Programme, https://georgianpapers.com/2017/01/23/america-is-lost/
3. Andrew Emmerson, president of the Telecommunications Heritage Group, in a letter to the *Guardian* newspaper: 'How were telephone dialling codes allocated to countries – eg 32 for Belgium, 33 for France, 44 for UK?', undated. https://www.theguardian.com/notesandqueries/query/0,5753,-2211,00.html
4. Stephen Walt, 'The myth of American exceptionalism', *Foreign Policy* (2011). https://foreignpolicy.com/2011/10/11/the-myth-of-american-exceptionalism/
5. Kishore Mahbubani, *Has China Won?* (New York: Public Affairs, 2020).
6. Putin speech to the Eastern Economic Forum, 7 September 2022.
7. Daniel Yergin, *The New Map: Energy, Climate and the Clash of Nations* (New York: Penguin Books, 2021), p. 56. 'Russia was a major beneficiary of the commodity super cycle in the BRIC era and the strong demand from emerging market countries that defined it. More than anything, that meant China and its economic growth.'
8. Jaishankar speaking at Munich Security Conference 2022. https://www.youtube.com/watch?v=HMPq4GQbMw4
9. Jaishankar speaking at Bratislava Forum June 2022. https://www.youtube.com/watch?v=DEiQe5Hkzrk
10. The *Economist*, 'Saudi Aramco makes an eye-popping $160bn in profit', 16 March 2023.

11. According to football's governing body, 'More than half the world watched record -breaking 2018 World Cup', 21 December 2018. https://www.fifa.com/tournaments/mens/worldcup/2018russia/media-releases/more-than-half-the-world-watched-record-breaking-2018-world-cup
12. The *Washington Post*, '(UPDATED) The toll of human casualties in Qatar', 27 May 2015; The *Guardian*, 'Revealed: 6,500 migrant workers have died in Qatar since World Cup awarded', 23 February 2021.
13. Janen Ganesh, 'Qatar World Cup Critics are unprepared for the rest of this century', *Financial Times*, 22 November 2022. https://www.ft.com/content/257d918e-029b-4c4a-b3d1-83ad5fcf60b2
14. European Commission, 'Just and sustainable economy: Commission lays down rules for companies to respect human rights and environment in global value chains', 23 February 2022. https://ec.europa.eu/commission/presscorner/detail/en/ip_22_1145
15. Jawed Naqvi, 'Hypocrisy's penalty corner', *Dawn*, 22 November 2022. https://www.dawn.com/news/1722359/hypocrisys-penalty-corner
16. *BBC News*, 'Iran football manager Queiroz confronts BBC's Shaimaa Khalil', https://www.bbc.com/news/av/world-middle-east-63750753
17. Amitav Ghosh, *Flood of Fire* (New York: Farrar, Strauss and Giroux, 2015), p. 220.

Chapter 1

1. Naoise Mac Sweeney, *The West: A New History of an Old Idea* (London: Penguin, 2023), p. 2. See also David Gress, *From Plato to NATO: The Idea of the West and its Opponents* (New York: Free Press, 1998), p. 16: 'My title, therefore, is ironic. The standard history began with the Greeks and ended with the political West as organised for mutual security in the Atlantic Alliance, in NATO.' But 'this history was not so much wrong as superficial . . . The West was not a single story but several stories.'
2. Mac Sweeney, *The West*, pp. 174, 195, 240. She argues this is post-hoc nonsense. Firstly, Hellenic influences diffused across Asia as well as Europe; secondly, the 'Greco-Roman' contraction was misleading since distinct Hellenic and Roman influences fell in and out of favour at different times in later European societies; thirdly, there was a protracted act of reinvention during the age of European empires to backcast this heritage as a uniquely civilised inheritance that justified defeating and in some cases enslaving non-white peoples; fourthly, white settlers in the USA used this heritage to explain why they shouldn't be 'enslaved' by the British Empire's unfair taxation but in turn could enslave people of African and Native American heritages, since they were culturally inferior.
3. Immanuel Wallerstein's 'world systems theory' saw Western Europe's advantages arising from labour availability, large urban populations, merchants, joint stock companies and government policies that allowed for long-distance trade and reinvesting the profits back home. Modern examples include Niall Ferguson,

Civilisation: The West and the Rest (London: Allen Lane, 2011); Ian Morris, *Why the West Rules . . . For Now* (London: Profile Books, 2011); and Jared Diamond, *Guns, Germs and Steel* (New York: Norton, 1999). Diamond argued that geography, climate, coastlines and other factors explain why the Europeans lived in a place that made them more likely to develop technologies to conquer the world.

4. Hugh Trevor-Roper, *The Rise of Christian Europe* (London: Thames and Hudson, 1965).
5. Samuel Huntington, *The Clash of Civilizations* (London: Simon & Schuster, 1996), pp. 46–47.
6. Roger Osborne, *Civilization: A New History of the Western World* (London: Vintage Books, 2007) p. 156. During this time, 'the Crusades entwined the religious identity of the western Europeans with their racial background. In the twelfth century Europeans and Muslims began to write about "the Christian people" and "the Christian race." The Crusader armies were a polyglot of nationalities and languages.'
7. Marco Polo, *Travels in the Land of Kubilai Khan* (London: Penguin Great Ideas, 2005), p. 1.
8. Wang Gungwu, *China Reconnects: Joining a Deep-rooted Past to a New World Order* (World Scientific, 2019), p. 117.
9. Fernando Cervantes, *Conquistadores: A New History* (Penguin Random House UK, 2021), pp. 5–6.
10. John Darwin, *Unlocking the World* (London, Penguin: 2020), p. 6.
11. Nicholas Ostler, *Empires of the Word* (London: Harper Perennial, 2006) pp. 335, 339: 'No previous empire had been gained or maintained through the control of oceanic seaways. Now for the first time a subject territory could be a continent away from its government, the link through projection of power by a navy.'
12. Fernando Cervantes, *Conquistadores*, pp. xv–xvi.
13. Jason Sharman and Andrew Phillips, *Outsourcing Empire: How Company-States Made the Modern World* (Princeton University, 2020).
14. Sharman and Phillips (2020), pp. 40–44.
15. Osborne, *Civilization*, p. 269: 'Whatever the courage and determination of the early coastal settlers, European settlement of North America was not a benign mixture of adventure and community-building. The three factors that blighted every colonial adventure – the treatment of the native population, the impact of disputes between Europeans, and slavery – were all evident in the colonisation and continuing history of North America.'
16. The *New York Times Magazine*, '1916 Project'. www.nytimes.com/interactive/2019/08/14/magazine/1619-america-slavery.html
17. Howard French, *Born in Blackness: Africa, Africans, and the Making of the Modern World, 1471 to the Second World War* (New York: Liveright, 2021). Osborne, *Civilization*, pp. 273–280.
18. Sharman and Phillips, *Outsourcing Empire*, p. 62. Europeans were 'far from alone in embarking on large-scale projects of imperial expansion in the early modern period. In size of territories conquered, they were overshadowed by the Ottomans, Mughals and Manchus. Rather than size, it was the transoceanic character of European expansion that made it distinctive . . . With the exception of Chinese

15th century forays into the Indian Ocean, neither Indian nor Chinese rulers saw value in investing resources to develop blue water naval capabilities.'

19. Dominic Lieven, *Empire: The Russian Empire and its Rivals* (Yale: Nota Bene, 2002).
20. Darwin, *Unlocking the World*, pp. 56, 82.
21. Darwin, *Unlocking the World*, p. 348.
22. Parliament of New South Wales, '1788 to 1810: Early European Settlement'.
23. Ronald Hyam, *Britain's Imperial Century, 1815–1914* (Hampshire: Barnes & Noble Books, 1976), pp. 128–133.
24. Darwin, *Unlocking the World*, p. 76.
25. Darwin, *Unlocking the World*, p. 125.
26. Xiaobing Tang, *Global Space and the Nationalist Discourse of Modernity: The Historical Thinking of Liang Qichao* (California: Stanford University Press, 1996), pp. 18, 26.
27. *National Geographic*, https://www.nationalgeographic.co.uk/travel/2022/09/benin-bronzes-return-to-nigeria
28. Dierk Walter, translated from German by Peter Lewis, *Colonial Violence: European Empires and the Use of Force* (London: Hurst & Company, 2017), p. 136.
29. William II, 'Hun Speech', 27 July 1900. https://germanhistorydocs.ghi-dc.org/sub_document.cfm?document_id=755&language=english
30. Liu Mingfu *The China Dream: Great Power Thinking & Strategic Posture in the Post-American Era* (CN Times Books, 2015): 'The Chinese Empire never used these methods of exporting problems abroad, instead preferring to internalise all problems' rather than using colonialism 'for easing internal conflicts by storing international conflicts'. Pertinent when you think of the defeated young Germans who went off to fight for imperial France in Indo-China in the 1950s, for example.
31. Rabindranath Tagore, *Nationalism* (Penguin Great Ideas, 2010), pp. 4, 54, pp. 72–74.
32. Pankaj Mishra, *From the Ruins of Empire: The Revolt Against the West and the Remaking of Asia* (London: Allen Lane, 2012), p. 21.
33. Kenneth Pomeranz, *The Great Divergence: China, Europe, and the Making of the Modern World* (New Jersey, Princeton University Press, 2000), pp. 3–5. Acknowledges the 'vital role of internally driven European growth but emphasises how similar those processes were to processes at work elsewhere, especially in east Asia, until almost 1800'. The great divergence in the nineteenth century occurred 'in a context shaped by Europe's privileged access to overseas resources'.
34. Marshall G. S. Hodgson, *Rethinking World History: Essays on Europe, Islam and World History* (Cambridge: Cambridge University Press, 1993), p. 6.

Chapter 2

1. Bill Emmott, *The Fate of the West,* (London: Profile Books, 2017) p. 1.
2. 'Westernisation" as defined here: https://www.britannica.com/topic/Westernization
3. Samuel Huntington, 1996 *Foreign Affairs* article entitled 'The West Unique, Not Universal'.
4. Benjamin Barber's term 'McWorld' criticised global corporate culture as creating cultural homogenisation in the name of profit and consumption (1995) in 'Jihad vs McWorld', *The Atlantic,* March 1992. www.theatlantic.com/magazine/archive/1992/03/jihad-vs-mcworld/303882/
5. Edward Keane, *Beyond the Anarchical Society: Grotius, Colonialism and Order in World Politics* (Cambridge: Cambridge University Press, 2002), pp. 97–100. 'The fundamental principle of the Westphalian system was that each state should recognise the territorial sovereignty of the others' but 'beyond Europe, international order was dedicated to a quite different purpose: the promotion of *civilization.* Simply put, Europeans and Americans believed that they knew how other governments should be organised, and actively worked to restructure societies that they regarded as uncivilised.'
6. Vijay Prashad, *Darker Nations; The People's History of the Third World* (New York: The New Press, 2007), p. 5. Jawaharlal Nehru, *The Discovery of India* (1946 /New Delhi: Hindi Sahita Sadan, 2009), p. 98.
7. Jane Burbank and Frederick Cooper, 'Empires after 1919: old, new, transformed'. *International Affairs* 95: 1 (2019) pp. 81–100. The 'League of Nations and the Mandates Commission opened up a new stage in an endeavour that had been under way since the Congress of Vienna of 1815: the definition of an imperial club, with rules for competition among empires and norms for their interactions with subordinated peoples.'
8. Margaret MacMillan and Patrick Quinton-Brown, 'The uses of history in international society: from the Paris peace conference to the present', *International Affairs* 95: 1 (2019) pp. 181–200.
9. Benedict Anderson, *Imagined Communities* (London: Verso, 1983), p. 63.
10. Agency must be accorded to the local champions of independence. Oliver Stuenkel, *Post-Western World: How Emerging Powers are Remaking Global Order,* (Cambridge; Polity Press, 2016), p. 64: 'many of the rules and norms that are today thought to be Western-inspired, such as national sovereignty and self-determination, were in fact the products of negotiations between Western and non-Western actors and are not Western impositions.'
11. I have previously written about how, as the Western powers ended their direct political control around the world, their legacy continued to be felt. Samir Puri, *The Great Imperial Hangover* (London: Atlantic Books, 2020).
12. Wang Gungwu, *China Reconnects: Joining a Deep-rooted Past to a New World Order* (World Scientific, 2019), p. 103.
13. Tom Holland, *Dominion: The Making of the Western Mind* (London: Little, Brown, 2019), p. 505.
14. Deepak Lal, 'Does Modernization Require Westernization?', *The Independent Review,* Summer 2000, Vol. 5, No. 1, pp. 5–24, p. 10.

15. Ben Ryan, *How The West Was Lost: The Decline of a Myth and the Search for New Stories* (London: Hurst & Company, 2019), pp. 6–7 and p. 211.
16. Emmott, *The Fate of the West.* Also, Alastair Bonnett, *The Idea of the West: Culture, Politics and History* (Palgrave Macmillan, 2004).
17. Andrew Roberts, *A History of the English-Speaking Peoples since 1900* (London: Weidenfeld & Nicolson, 2006) Introduction.
18. Hyam, *Britain's Imperial Century, 1815–1914*, p. 53.
19. Stephen Wertheim, *Tomorrow the World* (Cambridge, Mass.: Harvard University Press, 2020), pp. 1–3.
20. Albert K. Weinberg, *Manifest Destiny* (Baltimore: The John Hopkins Press, 1935). American empire-building evolved to favour tactics like 'intervention, acquisition of extensive treaty rights, and the pretension to a sphere of influence'.
21. Daniel Immerwahr, *How to Hide an Empire* (London: Bodley Head, 2019): 'In exchange for its privileged position within the world economy, Japan surrendered a great deal of autonomy.' For instance, 'Okinawans had little interest in helping the US fight in Vietnam, but they desperately needed the money' and 'In the face of protests, the US returned Okinawa to Japan in 1971. But they kept its bases.'
22. Stephen Wertheim, *Tomorrow the World*, pp. 176–177.
23. Ben Ryan, *How The West Was Lost*, pp. 81–82.
24. Timothy Garton Ash, *Facts are Subversive* (London: Atlantic Books, 2009) pp. 126–132.
25. Anu Bradford, *The Brussels Effect: How the European Union Rules the World*, (Oxford; Oxford University Press, 2020), p. xiv.
26. Joseph Stiglitz, *Globalization and Its Discontents* (W. W. Norton and Company, 2002).
27. Amartya Sen, *The American Prospect*, 1 January 2002: https://prospect.org/features/judge-globalism/

Chapter 3

1. Oswald Spengler (1880–1936), *The Decline of the West, Volume I: Form and Actuality* (1918) p. 74.
2. Niall Ferguson, *Civilisation*, p. 258. He adds that 'The first time Western civilisation crashed, as Gibbon tells the story, it was a very slow burn.' (292). 'The financial crisis that began in the summer of 2007 should therefore be understood as an accelerator of an already well-established trend of relative Western decline' (p. 308).
3. Ian Morris, *Why the West Rules – For Now . . .* (Profile, 2010) p. 11.
4. A newer entry to this canon, *Why Empires Fall: Rome, America and the Future of the West*, by John Rapley and Peter Heather (Allen Lane, 2023), articulates similar concerns.

5. Spengler, *The Decline of the West* (1918), p. 13 and pp. 16–18. Furthermore: 'It is self-evident that for the Cultures of the West the existence of Athens, Florence or Paris is more important than that of Loyang or Pataliputra. But is it permissible to found a scheme of world-history on estimates of such a sort? If so, then the Chinese historian is quite entitled to frame a world-history in which the Crusades, the Renaissance, Caesar and Frederick the Great are passed over in silence as insignificant.'
6. Sir John Glubb, *The Fate of Empires* http://people.uncw.edu/kozloffm/glubb.pdf
7. Ray Dalio, *The Principles for Dealing with the Changing World Order* (New York: Simon & Schuster, 2021).
8. Emmott: 'Our current ailments can, and should, be blamed on the long aftermath of what in 2008 was the greatest financial calamity that Western countries had seen since the 1930s'. It was a fry cry from better times: 'in the US and Europe from roughly 1993 until 2007 was what is known as "the great moderation": a period of low inflation and steady economic growth that led politicians and pundits to believe even that the economic cycle might have been conquered.'
9. Kevin Rudd, *Avoidable War: The Dangers of a Catastrophic Conflict Between the US and Xi Jinping's China* (New York; Public Affairs, 2022).
10. Jean-David Levitte, 'With the end of four centuries of Western dominance, what will the world order be in the 21st century?', 7 January 2019. https://www.brookings.edu/on-the-record/with-the-end-of-four-centuries-of-western-dominance-what-will-the-world-order-be-in-the-21st-century/
11. 'In Conversation with Rory Stewart', Chatham House, 6 October 2023. https://www.youtube.com/watch?v=ttcWJqNAksA
12. Pankaj Mishra, *From the Ruins of Empire*, pp. 7–8.
13. Samir Amin, *Eurocentrism: Modernity, Religion, and Democracy: A Critique of Eurocentrism and Culturalism* (New York: Monthly Review Press, 1989), p. 183.
14. Amin, p. 151.
15. Martin Jacques, *When China Rules the World* (London: Penguin, 2012), p. 17.
16. Linda Jakobson, 'Reflections From China on Xi Jinping's 'Asia for Asians'', *Asian Politics & Policy* (Volume 8, Issue 1 – 2016). http://chinamatters.org.au/wp-content/uploads/2016/03/Jakobson-2016-Asian_Politics__Policy-1.pdf
17. Liu Mingfu, *The China Dream*, concedes that 'if we list America as an imperialist power and compare it to other imperialist powers, through Chinese eyes, American imperialism is a benign variety of imperialism – a reasonable imperialism, and the imperialism least resented by China's people', with much to inspire China's rise.
18. Chandran Nair's *Dismantling Global White Privilege: Equity for a Post-Western World* (Berrett-Koehler Publishers, 2022).
19. Kevin Rudd, *Avoidable War.*
20. Theodore H. Von Laue, 'The World Revolution of Westernisation', *The History Teacher*, Vol. 20, No. 2 (Feb., 1987), pp. 263–279

Chapter 4

1. Yotam Ottolenghi, *Flavour* (Ebury Press, 2020).
2. 'The Macaroni Journal', 15 October 1929, pp. 32 and 34. https://ilovepasta.org/wp-content/uploads/macaroni/1929%2010%20OCTOBER%20-%20The%20New%20Macaroni%20Journal.pdf See also Kantha Shelke, *Pasta and Noodles: A Global History,* (London: Reaction Books, 2016).
3. Silvano Serventi and Francoise Sabban, *Pasta: The Story of a Universal Food,* (New York: Columbia University Press, 2002), p. xiii, pp. 7–8. 'I earnestly want to lend credence to Marco Polo's mission to Venice in 1296 as an emissary of pasta from a culinarily advanced China, importing that future staple to the peninsula' but a 'fable it is, alas'.
4. 13 June 2023, https://www.chathamhouse.org/events/all/members-event/strategies-more-resilient-world
5. Government of South Africa, 'BRICS Newsletter Issue 1, 22 August 2023', https://brics2023.gov.za/brics-newsletter-issue-1-22-august/
6. Paul Mashatile, speaking publicly at the National University of Singapore, 12 December 2023. Furthermore, as David Monyae from Johannesburg University explained: 'BRICS is not anti-Western. It does not want to smash the system. It wants to renegotiate the system. For instance, it is not anti the US dollar; it wants to increase the number of currencies in which the BRICS countries can trade.' Comments in Quincy Institute webinar, 21 August 2023 entitled 'BRICS and the Global South's Assertion', https://quincyinst.org/events/brics-and-the-global-souths-assertion/
7. Stanley Brandes, 'The Day of the Dead, Halloween, and the Quest for Mexican National Identity', *The Journal of American Folklore,* Vol. 111, No. 442 (Autumn, 1998), pp. 359–380. *National Geographic* feature.
8. Octavio Paz, *The Labyrinth of Solitude* (1961), pp. 10, 57–58.
9. Francis Fukuyama, *Liberalism and its Discontents* (New York: Farrar, Strauss and Giroux, 2022).
10. Mahbubani, *Has China Won?*

Chapter 5

1. The *Economist,* 'Is China's power about to peak?', 11 May 2023.
2. Hal Brands and Michael Beckley, *Danger Zone: The Coming Conflict with China* (W.W. Norton & Company, 2022).
3. *Bloomberg News,* '"China Faces Decades-Long Growth 'Plateau'," Says EU Chamber Head', 23 May 2023. https://www.bloomberg.com/news/articles/2023-05-23/china-faces-decades-long-growth-plateau-says-eu-chamber-head#xj4y7vzkg
4. Xinhua: '"Socialism with Chinese characteristics enters new era": Xi', 18 October 2017. http://www.xinhuanet.com/english/2017-10/18/c_136688475.htm
5. George Yeo delivering the Goh Keng Swee lecture, 'China in a Multipolar World',

15 December 2023, at the National University of Singapore, https://www.youtube.com/watch?v=DNbYXaE1FxM

6. John Naisbitt, *Megatrends* (New York: Warner Books, 1982), p. 2.
7. John Naisbitt and Doris Naisbitt, *Mastering Megatrends* Asian Edition (Singapore: World Scientific Publishing, 2017), p. viii and p. 4.
8. Ibid., p. 76.

Chapter 6

1. John Wilmoth, 'Demography Department Brown Bag', Berkley Population Sciences,23September2015.https://www.youtube.com/watch?v=6JoOjMhUmaM
2. UN Department of Economic and Social Affairs, Policy Brief 153: 'India overtakes China as the world's most populous country'. And Policy Brief 140: 'A World of 8 Billion'.
3. UN Department of Economic and Social Affairs, 'World Population to Reach 8 billion on 15 November 2022'.
4. Thomas Piketty, *Capital in the Twenty-First Century* (Cambridge Mass.: Belknap Press, 2017), p. 104.
5. Wilmoth, 'Demography Department Brown Bag', op. cit.
6. UN Population Division, 'World Population Prospects 2022: Summary of Results', UN Department of Economic and Social Affairs (New York: UN, 2022), pp. i and 5.
7. The UN demography data has been visualised here: 'Population by World Region: Historic estimates with future projections based on the UN medium-fertility scenario', https://ourworldindata.org/grapher/population-regions-with-projections. The UN historical demography data was further reproduced in Piketty, *Capital in the Twenty-First Century*, Chapter Two, 'Growth: Illusions and Realities'.
8. Gregg Lee Carter, *Population and Society*, (Cambridge: Polity Press, 2016).
9. Massimo Livi Bacci, *A Concise History of World Population Sixth Edition* (John Whiley & Sons, 2017).
10. Carter, *Population and Society:* 'In the 17th and 18th centuries, the Dutch East India Company sent one million Europeans (many of them emigrants from German states) to Asia, especially to Indonesia'; while 'In the 18th and early 19th centuries, two-thirds of Irish, English, Scotch, French, and German immigrants to North America paid their way through indentureship' and 'after Brazil abolished slavery in 1888, demand for replacement workers motivated over a million and a half Italians alone to emigrate there'.
11. Bacci, *A Concise History of World Population.*
12. Hyam, *Britain's Imperial Century, 1815–1914*, pp. 24–25.
13. John Darwin, *Unlocking the World*, p. 103. citing William Woodruff's 1966 book, *Impact of Western Man.*
14. Bacci, 'Imagining that emigrants had remained in Italy and, as a group, had grown at the same rate of the Italian population in Italy (a fairly restrictive

hypothesis), that would in 1981 have numbered 14 million, about 25% of the national population at that time.'

15. Parag Khanna, *Move* (New York: Simon & Schuster, 2021), Gideon Rachman, *Easternisation: War and Peace in the Asian Century* (London; The Bodley Head, 2016), called it 'demographic imperialism', explaining that 'in 1900 European countries represented about 25% of the world population and Europe was still sending settlers all over the world. By 2015, the 500 million people in the 28 EU nations accounted for 7% of world population.'
16. Carter, *Population and Society.*
17. Al Jazeera, 'Japan's birth rate drops to fresh record low', 2 June 2023.
18. John Wilmoth on GCTV with Bill Miller, 11 September 2019. youtube.com/watch?v=7aEPkwZ4wc4. 'The demographic transition, this process of change [involving] first the longer life, then the smaller families, causing this period of population growth in between, this is happening all over the world. But it's taking place at different times in different parts of the world. In some parts of the world this transition has happened and growth rates are very low or even negative. In some parts of the world, we really are in that high growth phase, like sub-Saharan Africa.'
19. Clare Menozzi, a Population Affairs Officer in the United Nations Population Division in New York, explained to me how this works.
20. John Wilmoth on GCTV with Bill Miller, 11 September 2019.
21. Piketty, *Capital in the Twenty-First Century.*
22. Interview with Claire Menozzi, UN Population Division.
23. Wang Feng, Yong Cai and Baochang Gu, 'Population, Policy, and Politics: How Will History Judge China's One-Child Policy?' *Population and Development Review*, 2012, Vol. 38, Population and Public Policy: Essays in Honor of Paul Demeny (2012), pp. 115–129.
24. Nancy E. Riley, *Population in China* (Cambridge: Polity Press, 2017).
25. Carter, *Population and Society.*
26. Top 20 most populous countries now and in 2050. UN Population Division, 'World Population Prospects 2022'.
27. Mauro Guillen, *2030: How Today's Biggest Trends Will Collide and Reshape the Future of Everything* (St. Martin's Publishing Group, 2020).

Chapter 7

1. British Council, 'Languages for the Future: The foreign languages the United Kingdom needs to become a truly global nation', 2017. https://www.britishcouncil.org/sites/default/files/languages_for_the_future_2017.pdf
2. Rosemary Salomone, *The Rise of English: Global Politics and the Power of Language* (Oxford ; Oxford University Press, 2022), p. 5.
3. British Council, op. cit. The report identified not just the most widely spoken languages in the world, but 'Languages needed for cultural, educational,

diplomatic and security purposes' and 'for economic purposes', based on the 'Top ten emerging markets in order of expected growth to 2020, together with their official languages.'

4. Macaulay's 'Minute on Education', 2 February 1835, in which he ceded only this: 'It will hardly be disputed, I suppose, that the department of literature in which the Eastern writers stand highest is poetry. And I certainly never met with any orientalist who ventured to maintain that the Arabic and Sanscrit poetry could be compared to that of the great European nations.' http://home.iitk.ac.in/~hcverma/Article/Macaulay-Minutes.pdf
5. The US Census Bureau, 'What languages do we speak in the United States? Nearly 68 million people spoke a language other than English at home in 2019', 6 December 2022. https://www.census.gov/library/stories/2022/12/languages-we-speak-in-united-states.html
6. Pew Research Center, 'Latinos' Views of and Experiences With the Spanish Language', 20 September 2023. https://www.pewresearch.org/race-ethnicity/2023/09/20/latinos-views-of-and-experiences-with-the-spanish-language/
7. Nicholas Ostler, *The Last Lingua Franca: English Until the Return of Babel* (New York: Walker Publishing Company, 2010), p. xv. 'The decline of English, when it begins, will not seem of great moment' because International English is mainly used as 'a language of convenience. When it ceases to be convenient – however widespread it has been – it will be dropped, without ceremony' and 'People will just not get around to learning it, not see the point, be glad to escape a compulsory subject at school. Only those who have a more intimate relation to it, its native speakers, may feel a sense of loss . . . But the world as a whole will shrug and go on transacting its business in whatever language, or combination of languages, next seems useful.'
8. Moreover, only English and French are the working languages of the UN Secretariat (where the Secretary General sits). https://www.un.org/en/our-work/official-languages#:~:text=There%20are%20six%20official%20languages,%2C%20French%2C%20Russian%20and%20Spanish
9. Top 20: https://www.ethnologue.com/insights/ethnologue200/
10. Cindy Blanco, '2022 Duolingo Language Report', 6 December 2022. https://blog.duolingo.com/2022-duolingo-language-report/
11. Aanu Adeoye and Idris Mukhtar, *CNN*, 'China's influence in Africa grows as more young people learn to speak Mandarin', 10 April 2019. https://edition.cnn.com/travel/article/mandarin-language-courses-africa-intl/index.html
12. Ostler, *Empires of the Word*, pp. 24 and 381.
13. Ostler, *Empires of the Word*, p. 395: 'the growth of Portuguese to its present state . . . owes almost everything to the economic development, and consequent population growth, of Brazil over the past 300 years, and very little to its spread from Portugal as a language for colonial administration.'
14. Ostler, *Empires of the Word*, p. 400. Also, John McWhorter, *Power of Babel: A Natural History of Language* (Arrow Books, 2011).
15. British Council, 'Languages for the Future'.
16. Aside from France, French is either the only or joint official language in Benin, Burkina Faso, Burundi, Cameroon, Central African Republic, Chad, Comoros,

Congo, Côte d'Ivoire, Djibouti, Gabon, Guinea, Mali, Niger, Rwanda, Senegal, Seychelles, Togo and Vanuatu. And the Canadian region of Quebec and in Geneva in Switzerland too.

17. 'France's sway in the region is waning. In January [2023], hundreds demonstrated in Ouagadougou, Burkina Faso's capital, against French involvement in the region. This follows the withdrawal of French soldiers from Mali in 2022 ... Similarly ... the ECOWAS is in the process of establishing a new common currency in the region, to break away from the French-controlled CFA franc currency.' https://www.global-weekly.com/post/la-fran%C3%A7afrique-n-est-plus-the-impact-of-france-s-diminishing-role-in-sub-saharan-africa
18. Frantz Fanon, *Black Skin, White Masks* (New York: Grove Press, 2008), p. 2.
19. Ostler, *Empires of the Word*, pp. 454. 'Any hearts and minds that may have been won through 50 years of (relatively) peaceful colonialism were definitively lost in the terminal rampages of the Japanese army through East & South-East Asia ... Japan ended 1945 confined to the islands it controlled in 1868, even losing the outlying Kurils and Ryukyus.'
20. British Council, 'Languages for the Future': 'It has official status (sometimes as one of two languages, e.g. in Morocco, Somalia and Israel) in 25 countries: Algeria, Bahrain, Chad, Comoros, Djibouti, Egypt, Eritrea, Iraq, Israel, Jordan, Kuwait, Lebanon, Libya, Mauritania, Morocco, Oman, Palestine, Qatar, Saudi Arabia, Somalia, Sudan, Syria, Tunisia, United Arab Emirates and Yemen ... Modern colloquial Arabic differs from one region to another ... Arabic script is also used in languages such as Farsi, Urdu and Pashto.'
21. Ostler, *Empires of the Word*, p. 530–533.
22. McWhorter, *Power of Babel*: 'pidgins have always formed throughout the world when people needed to use a language on a regular basis without having the motivation to acquire it fully' while '*creoles* are definitely distinct "languages" from the ones from which they take their words'. Notably, the slave trade and its aftermath under a different name in the 1800s gave birth to several dozen creoles and 'Most creoles formed a century or more ago' from older versions of European languages. Hence 'most semi creoles are, like most creoles, spoken by brown-skinned people. Yet ... there is nothing inherently "Third World" about the process. Afrikaans of South Africa, for instance, is a semi creole ... when it arose after the Dutch colonisation of the Cape of Good Hope in 1652, it was called "Cape Dutch".'
23. 'EF English Proficiency Index 2022': https://www.ef.com/assetscdn/WIBIwq6RdJvcD9bc8RMd/cefcom-epi-site/reports/2022/ef-epi-2022-english.pdf
24. Ostler, *Empires of the Word*, p. 13.
25. Nick Hillman, 'Over one-quarter of the world's countries are headed by someone educated in the UK and another quarter are headed by someone educated in the US – HEPI'S 2023 SOFT-POWER INDEX', 22 August 2023. https://www.hepi.ac.uk/2023/08/22/over-one-quarter-of-the-worlds-countries-are-headed-by-someone-educated-in-the-uk-and-another-quarter-are-headed-by-someone-educated-in-the-us-hepi-2023-soft-power-index/
26. https://www.topuniversities.com/university-rankings/world-university-rankings/2024?&page=6 The remaining eighty-four are in the West: forty-nine universities

in the Anglosphere (mainly the USA and UK with strong showings for Canada and Australia); and thirty-five elsewhere in Europe (Belgium, France, Germany, Netherlands, Sweden and Switzerland).

27. Times Higher Education World Rankings 2024.
28. Nigeria's 'National Universities Commission ... said only one per cent of Nigerian population form the total enrollment of students in the 164 universities across the country'. Azeezat Adedigba, *Premium Times*, 4 July 2018.
29. The British Council, 'The Future of International Tertiary Education to 2037', November 2022, p. 14. https://www.britishcouncil.org/sites/default/files/the_future_of_international_tertiary_education_to_2037.pdf
30. 'Fudan-Latin America University Consortium (FLAUC)': https://fddi.fudan.edu.cn/fddien/wudanwwatinwwmericawwniversitywwonsortiumwwwwwwww/list.htm

Chapter 8

1. Quoted in Richard Maltby 'Introduction: "The Americanisation of the World"' in Melvyn Stokes and Richard Maltby, *Hollywood Abroad: Audiences and Cultural Exchange* (Bloomsbury, 2019).
2. D. Bondy Valdovinos Kaye, Jing Zeng, Patrik Wikstrom, *TikTok: Culture and Creativity in Short Video* (Cambridge: Polity Press, 2022).
3. https://www.washingtonpost.com/news/worldviews/wp/2015/10/26/mark-zuckerberg-gave-a-20-minute-speech-in-mandarin-to-chinese-students/
4. Chris Stokel-Walker, *TikTok Boom: China's Dynamite App and the Superpower Race for Social Media* (Surrey: Canbury Press, 2021), pp. 28–29.
5. For the original argument see Joseph Nye, 'Soft Power', *Foreign Policy*, (Autumn 1990), pp. 153-171. Nye considered 'cultural attraction, ideology, and international institutions' as components of soft power, which could add to the 'co-optive power' of 'getting others to want what you want'. For the rejoinder, see Eric Li, 'The Rise and Fall of Soft Power', *Foreign Policy*, 20 August 2018. https://foreignpolicy.com/2018/08/20/the-rise-and-fall-of-soft-power/
6. For a compact account of Nintendo's rise, see Jeff Ryan, *Super Mario: How Nintendo Conquered America* (Penguin Publishing Group, 2011).
7. Ezra F. Vogel, *Japan as Number One* (Harvard University Press,1979).
8. The *Economist*, 'Super Mario Diplomacy', 21 March 2023. For revenue numbers see: https://mobilegamer.biz/2022s-top-grossing-mobile-games-honor-of-kings-pubg-mobile-genshin-impact-and-more/
9. Milken 2023 Asia Summit. 'Gamechangers: Exploring the Gaming and Entertainment Revolution across Asia', 13 September 2023. Moderator Gary Liu; panellist Deborah Mei. https://milkeninstitute.org/panel/14822/gamechangers-exploring-gaming-and-entertainment-revolution-across-asia
10. www.statista.com/forecasts/308454/gaming-revenue-countries
11. Newzoo Global Games Market Report 2022, p. 48.
12. Newzoo Global Games Market Report 2022. The so-called 'mobile-first growth

markets' encompass the Middle East and Africa, worth $6.8 billion in 2022, and Latin America, worth $8.4 billion.

13. Maltby, 'Introduction' in *Hollywood Abroad.*
14. Melis Behlil, *Hollywood Is Everywhere: Global Directors in the Blockbuster Era* (Amsterdam University Press, 2016) pp. 18–21, pp. 30–33, p. 39. Émigrés have always come to Hollywood. Moreover, 'although the terms "Hollywood" and "American film industry" are still used interchangeably today, Hollywood was largely de-Americanized after the mid-1970s on multiple levels,' since 'while Los Angeles remains the industrial core for production, on-location shooting has increasingly spread'.
15. The *Economist*, 'India's film industry: Growing up', 10 August 2000, and the *Economist*, 'India's film industry: Bollywood Rising', 7 February 2008.
16. Behlil, *Hollywood Is Everywhere*, p. 47–48. 'In addition to the prevalence of runaway productions, with technological developments, production outsourcing has also become particularly common in animation. US animation is frequently outsourced to India, and Japanese studios outsource parts of their work to the Philippines and South Korea.
17. The *Economist*, 'Hollywood's Chinese conundrums', 27 August 2020; 'Chinese Cinema: No direction', 27 April 2006.
18. The *Economist*, 'Hollywood and China. Un-American activities', 27 August 2020; 'Hollywood and China. Red carpet', 27 August 2020; 'Lost in Shangywood', 15 October 2015; 'The International Film Industry. Avatar 2: Made in China?' 24 August 2012. As reported in 2020: 'In the past 15 years China's box-office takings have risen 35-fold, to $9.7 billion. That is not far off America's $11.1 billion . . . America's blockbusters increasingly rely on Chinese audiences to recoup their vast production budgets.' A movie industry report explained 'the growing popularity of Chinese, Japanese, South Korean, and Indian movies & music [plus] The rising popularity of music & videos from other developing countries such as India, the Philippines, Vietnam, and Australia is further estimated to support the market growth in the region.'
19. https://deadline.com/gallery/red-sea-international-film-festival-2022-red-carpet-gallery/closing-night-gala-awards-the-red-sea-international-film-festival-8/ The *Economist*, 'Saudi Arabia is getting into film production. Saudiwood is betting big on Arab audiences', 18 November 2022.
20. www.pwc.com/gx/en/industries/tmt/media/outlook/outlook-perspectives.html PWC 'Perspectives from the Global Entertainment & Media Outlook 2022–2026: Fault lines and fractures: Innovation and growth in a new competitive landscape'.
21. Ibid.
22. www.ifpi.org/wp-content/uploads/2023/03/Global_Music_Report_2023_State_of_the_Industry.pdf
23. www.dni.gov/files/documents/Global%20Trends_Mapping%20the%20Global%20Future%202020%20Project.pdf

Chapter 9

1. Viet Thanh Nguyen, *The Sympathizer*, p. 148.
2. eBook *'Non-Western Identity'*, https://link.springer.com/book/10.1007/978-3-030-77242-0
3. Partha Chatterjee, *The Nation and Its Fragments* (Princeton University Press, 1993).
4. Amartya Sen, *Identity and Violence*, pp. 4–5, p. 114.
5. Ben Ryan, *How The West Was Lost*: 'one of the central underpinning beliefs of the West has been that its values are not particular but universal', contributing 'to the idea that the West can, and should, expand to other places . . .'
6. George Yeo TV interview for *South China Sea Morning Post*, 'Talking Post'. https://www.youtube.com/watch?v=pEQ-a6sgjvc
7. Wang Gungwu, https://www.thinkchina.sg/wang-gungwu-what-does-it-mean-be-ethnically-chinese-singapore
8. And this tweet: https://twitter.com/jessiepeterson/status/1313700078280945664?ref_src=twsrc%255Etfw%257Ctwcamp%255Etweetembed%257Ctwterm%255E1313700078280945664%257Ctwgr%255E23a14d7b8e3fbc0c2aa4d685043be7ee00a139f8%257Ctwcon%255Es1_&ref_url=https://coconuts.co/jakarta/lifestyle/eddie-van-halens-indonesian-roots-inspire-asian-pride-as-tributes-pour-in/.
9. Viet Thanh Nguyen, *The Sympathizer*, p. 258.

Chapter 10

1. On Singapore, M.L.R. Smith reflected, its 'political system may not be very democratic, but it was at least honest. The authorities made little secret of their disdain for aspects of Western democracy, and their lack of tolerance for political dissent. Combined with a record of competent government [they] could sustain their claim to rule. Competence and honesty present themselves as potentially attractive alternatives to the hypocrisy of twisted idealism.' https://www.cieo.org.uk/reviews/the-quiet-americans/.
2. https://www.europarl.europa.eu/about-parliament/en/democracy-and-human-rights/global-democracy
3. https://www.youtube.com/watch?v=jw6pFnHBgKA
4. https://freedomhouse.org/report/freedom-world/2023/marking-50-years
5. Larry Diamond, *The Spirit of Democracy: The Struggle to Build Free Societies Throughout the World* (Holt Paperbacks, 2008), p. 22.
6. https://www.journalofdemocracy.org/wp-content/uploads/2015/01/Diamond-26-1_0.pdf
7. Kanti Bajpai, *International Affairs*, Summer 2023. 'Several states in Asia qualify as liberal democracies, above all Japan and Korea today, and except for China and Vietnam, they are all elected democracies to varying degrees. But no Asian state

wants political liberalism with its various features – institutional checks and balances, enforcement of justiciable individual human rights and guarantees of an independent media – to be the dominant long-term norm in the international system, one that is used in an exclusionary or otherwise punitive way . . . To varying degrees Asian states are sceptical of the insistence that liberal democratic governance must be the aspirational standard of international order . . . Modi and Widodo certainly supported electoral democracy, they avoided the term *liberal.*'

8. Teresa M. Bejan, *Mere Civility* (Harvard University Press, 2017), p. 21.
9. Siva Vaidhyanathan, *Anti-Social Media: How Facebook Disconnects Us and Undermines Democracy* (New York: OUP, 2018) pp. 5–7.
10. Francis Fukuyama, 'Making the internet safe for democracy', *Journal of Democracy* (Volume 32, Number 2, April 2021) and Fukuyama in *Liberalism and its Discontents.*
11. https://www.pewresearch.org/short-reads/2023/01/25/many-countries-in-europe-get-a-new-government-at-least-every-two-years/ 'To find out, Pew Research Center consulted ParlGov – a clearinghouse for cross-national political information – and calculated the median length of government in the 22 parliamentary member states of the European Union, as well as the UK, from the end of World War II through the end of 2022.'
12. Ray Dalio, *The Principles for Dealing with the Changing World Order.*
13. John Keane, *The New Despotism* (Harvard University Press, 2020), pp. 99–103, 212.
14. Fareed Zakaria, 'Turkey points to a global trend: Free and unfair elections', 19 May 2023. https://www.washingtonpost.com/opinions/2023/05/19/erdogan-turkey-autocrats-manipulation-elections/
15. The *Economist,* 'Global democratic backsliding seems real, even if it is hard to measure', 15 September 2023. It uses a composite index based on its own Economist Intelligence Unit data, juxtaposed with Freedom House, V-Dem and other indexes to track the decline in liberal democracy globally.
16. David Gress, *From Plato to NATO,* pp. 1 and 213.
17. Lembong interview, The *Economist,* 'What will Indonesia look like after Jokowi leaves?', 9 September 2023.

Chapter 11

1. UK Department for International Trade *Global Trade Outlook* (September 2021), pp. 7, 9 and 26. Based on the IMF World Economic Outlook April 2021 and DIT calculations.
2. John Darwin, *Unlocking the World,* p. 358.
3. Thomas Piketty, *Capital in the Twenty-First Century,* Chapter One, 'Income and Output'.
4. Gary Gerstle, *Rise and Fall of the Neoliberal Order,* (Oxford University Press, 2022) pp. 10–11.

5. Oliver Stuenkel, *Post-Western World*, p. 201. He wrote that 'from a historical perspective, the end of Western dominance is little more than the end of an aberration that saw an extreme concentration of wealth and power . . . [Hence] it is normal that this unusual – and, one may add, unnatural – concentration of power would end eventually.'
6. 'One of the two main methods of conversion uses market exchange rates – the rate prevailing in the foreign exchange market (using either the rate at the end of the period or an average over the period). The other approach uses the purchasing power parity (PPP) exchange rate – the rate at which the currency of one country would have to be converted into that of another country to buy the same amount of goods and services in each country . . . developing countries get a much higher weight in aggregations that use PPP exchange rates than they do using market exchange rates.' https://www.imf.org/en/Publications/fandd/issues/Series/Back-to-Basics/Purchasing-Power-Parity-PPP
7. Figures rounded to the nearest percentage point by the author. The full data set is from the International Monetary Fund, 'World Economic Outlook 2023' https://www.imf.org/external/datamapper/
8. The *Economist*, 'From strength to strength: America's economic outperformance is a marvel to behold', 13 April 2023.
9. Lord Jim O'Neill, 'Building Better Global Economic BRICs', Goldman Sachs Report, November 2001. https://www.goldmansachs.com/intelligence/archive/building-better.html and for the original report; https://www.gspublishing.com/content/research/en/reports/2004/01/27/fcaffb70-04fc-11da-8624-b16d0c0183a5.pdf
10. Daniel Yergin, *The New Map*: 'When GDP is measured by exchange rates, the US economy is still larger than China's. By the other measure of GDP – purchasing power parity – China is already the largest economy in the world. By that measure, it overtook the US in 2014 . . .'
11. https://www.imf.org/external/datamapper/PPPSH@WEO/OEMDC/ADVEC/WEOWORLD
12. Daniel Yergin, *The New Map*, p. 56.
13. I thank Gokul Sahni for explaining these dynamics to me.
14. UK Department for International Trade *Global Trade Outlook* (September 2021), p. 7.
15. Lord Jim O'Neill, 'Does an expanded BRICS mean anything? The influence of BRICS will depend on its effectiveness, not on its composition or size', Chatham House, 27 August 2023. https://www.chathamhouse.org/2023/08/does-expanded-brics-mean-anything?utm_source=linkedin.com&utm_medium=organic-social&utm_campaign=brics&utm_content=g20
16. Biden National Security Advisor Jake Sullivan comment, 2023.
17. UK DIT report (2021), p. 9. The measurement used is nominal GDP.
18. The *Economist*, 'Can the West win over the rest of the world?' 16 May 2023. 'In purchasing-power parity terms, the BRICS grouping, of Brazil, Russia, India, China and South Africa, has surpassed the G7's share.' James Kynge, 'China hopes expanded Brics will turn world upside down', *Financial Times*, 25 August 2023.
19. https://www.stimson.org/2023/assumption-testing-multipolarity-is-more-dangerous-than-bipolarity-for-the-united-states/ Emma Ashford, 'A multipolar

system doesn't require three powers of equal size; it just requires that significant power is concentrated in more than two states . . . It's a common misconception that multipolarity must involve many states of roughly equal capabilities (i.e., that it must be balanced). But in fact, multipolar systems are often unbalanced, with two or three big powers and several middle powers all jockeying for position.'

20. Goldman Sachs Economics Research Paper, 'Global Economics Paper The Path to 2075 – Slower Global Growth, But Convergence Remains Intact', 6 December 2022.
21. Petros C. Mavroidis and André Sapir, *China and WTO* (Princeton University Press, 2021): 'Never before had the WTO or GATT admitted a member so big and with an economic system so different from the liberal market economy system upon which they were predicated . . . US cannot handle China the way it handled Japan in the past, when it also threatened US economic hegemony. The other lesson is that China and the WTO cannot sit idle about the gap between the Chinese economic system and the WTO system.'
22. Brands and Beckley, *Danger Zone.*
23. Keyu Jin, *The New China Playbook* (Penguin, 2023).
24. Piketty, *Capital in the Twenty-First Century.* Chapter One, 'Income and Output'.

Chapter 12

1. https://www.straitstimes.com/singapore/speech-by-us-defence-secretary-distorted-facts-china-embassy-in-singapore?close=true To show its even-handedness, Singapore's *Straits Times* newspaper covered Austin's lecture and then a day later also printed the Chinese embassy response.
2. US Undersecretary of Defense Colin Kahl, speaking on the record at Chatham House in London, 7 July 2023.
3. https://www.pmo.gov.sg/Newsroom/PM-Lee-Hsien-Loong-Closing-Dialogue-at-the-Asia-Future-Summit-2023
4. Paul Kennedy, *The Rise and Fall of the Great Powers: Economic Change and Military Conflict from 1500 to 2000* (New York: Random House, 1989), p. xxiii.
5. International Institute for Strategic Studies, *Military Balance* (Routledge, 2023).
6. SIPRI, 'Trends in World Military Expenditure, 2022'. sipri.org/sites/default/files/2023-04/2304_fs_milex_2022.pdf
7. SIPRI, 'Appendix 5A. Military expenditure data, 2000-2009' from the *SIPRI Yearbook 2010.* https://www.sipri.org/yearbook/2010/05/appendix5A and the *Economist,* 'America is less dominant in defence spending than you might think', 12 March 2023. With the biggest defence spending increases taking place in Ukraine, Russia, China, Saudi Arabia and India, Western governments by contrast were loath to also increase defence budgets sharply.
8. 'Final Report on the Congressional Commission on the Strategic Posture of the US', October 2023, p. vii. https://armedservices.house.gov/sites/republicans.armedservices.house.gov/files/Strategic-Posture-Committee-Report-Final.pdf

9. 'China's 2023 defense budget to rise by 7.2%, remaining single-digit for 8th year', 6 March 2023. http://english.scio.gov.cn/chinavoices/2023-03/06/content_85146919.htm
10. Liu Mingfu, *The China Dream.*
11. Samir Puri, 'Interventions in Armed Conflicts: Waning Western Dominance' in *Armed Conflict Survey 2021*, International Institute for Strategic Studies, (Routledge, 2021).
12. Elbridge Colby, *Strategy of Denial: American Defence in an Age of Great Power Conflict* (New Haven and London: Yale University Press, 2021).
13. https://www.fmprc.gov.cn/mfa_eng/wjbxw/202302/t20230221_11028348.html In 2022, China's government announced its 'Global Security Initiative', its first ever framework for China's approach to global security. As well as endorsing the UN Charter, UN peacekeeping forces and regional bodies like the African Union, China's Global Security Initiative wanted to 'leverage the roles of the Shanghai Cooperation Organization' and 'BRICS cooperation'. In other words, to minimise or shut out any security initiatives run exclusively or dominated by the USA or the West.
14. RAND Corporation, *China's Global Basing Ambitions.* A larger list of other possible hosts were judged as being lower either in feasibility or desirability to China: Morocco, Equatorial Guinea, Gabon, Angola, Tanzania, Kenya, Yemen, Oman, Saudi Arabia, Bahrain, Lebanon, Uzbekistan, Tajikistan, Kyrgyzstan, Laos, Thailand, Sri Lanka and Indonesia.
15. Tony Blair, 'remarks to Congress made on Thursday, July 17, 2003', https://www.cbsnews.com/news/full-text-of-blairs-speech/ and Blair, 'Speaking before the Chicago Economic Club, April 22, 1999', https://archive.globalpolicy.org/empire/humanint/1999/0422blair.htm

Chapter 13

1. Janet Yellen interviewed by Fareed Zakaria, CNN, https://www.youtube.com/watch?v=bwgHwzhfoXo
2. Lula speech to the New Development Bank in Shanghai, quoted in *Financial Times*, 13 April 2023. https://www.ft.com/content/669260a5-82a5-4e7a-9bbf-4f41c54a6143
3. www.telegraph.co.uk/news/1399693/A-history-of-sterling.html
4. Craig Karmin in the *Biography of the Dollar* (New York: Crown Publishing, 2008); Darshini David, *The Almighty Dollar* (London: Elliott and Thompson Limited, 2018).
5. https://www.imf.org/en/Blogs/Articles/2021/05/05/blog-us-dollar-share-of-global-foreign-exchange-reserves-drops-to-25-year-low
6. Alan Wheatley (ed.), *The Power of Currencies and Currencies of Power* (Routledge, 2013).
7. https://www.forex.com/en-us/news-and-analysis/the-top-10-most-traded-currencies/

8. http://en.kremlin.ru/events/president/news/70748
9. https://www.cnbc.com/2009/03/27/brazil-president-blames-white-people-for-crisis.html
10. 'Speech by President Luiz Inácio Lula da Silva during the Summit for a New Global Financial Pact, in France', 23 June 2023. https://www.gov.br/planalto/en/follow-the-government/speeches/speech-by-president-luiz-inacio-lula-da-silva-during-the-summit-for-a-new-global-financial-pact-in-france
11. https://www.bis.org/statistics/rpfx22_fx.pdf 'The BIS Triennial Central Bank Survey is the most comprehensive source of information on the size and structure of global over-the-counter (OTC) markets in foreign exchange (FX) and interest rate derivatives. The Survey aims to increase the transparency of OTC markets, helping central banks and market participants monitor global financial markets, and to inform discussions on reforms to OTC markets. Activity in FX markets has been surveyed every three years since 1986, and in OTC interest rate derivatives markets since 1995.' See also International Settlements Triennial Survey (2019).
12. US Department of the Treasury. 'Major Foreign Holders of Treasury Securities', https://ticdata.treasury.gov/Publish/mfh.txt
13. https://www.longfinance.net/media/documents/GFCI_33_Report_2023.03.23_v1.1.pdf Its areas of competitiveness are explained on p. 9.
14. https://lkyspp.nus.edu.sg/docs/default-source/case-studies/entry-1516-singapores_transformation_into_a_global_financial_hub.pdf?sfvrsn=a8c9960b_2; Lee Kuan Yew, *From Third World to First* (HarperCollins, 2000), pp. 71-82.
15. http://www.brics.utoronto.ca/docs/150709-ufa-declaration_en.html 'We will also continue to work to intensify our financial and economic cooperation, including within the New Development Bank and the BRICS Contingent Reserve Arrangement to build upon our synergies. We welcome and support the creation of a platform of joint discussion for trade cooperation amongst BRICS countries . . . We reaffirm the important role played by the BRICS Interbank Cooperation Mechanism in expanding the BRICS countries financial and investment cooperation.'
16. Gideon Rachman, *Easternisation.*
17. www.aiib.org/en/news-events/annual-report/2021/_common/pdf/2021_AIIBAnnualReport_web-reduced.pdf NDB strategy: 'Est. in 2015, the New Development Bank (NDB) is a multilateral development bank established by BRICS with the purpose of mobilising resources for infrastructure and sustainable development projects in emerging markets and developing countries.' Page 17 of the strategy explains that 'Local currency financing continues to be a key component of NDB's value proposition. In the 2022–2026 strategy cycle . . . NDB targets to provide 30% of its total financing commitments over the five-year strategy period in national currencies of member countries.'
18. Zongyuan Zoe Liu and Mihaela Papa, *Can BRICS De-dollarize the Global Financial System*, Cambridge University Press, 2022. See also *IISS Strategic Comment* Vol, 29 No. 14, July 2023, 'The state of de-dollarisation in the Gulf region'. https://www.iiss.org/en/publications/strategic-comments/2023/the-state-of-de-dollarisation-in-the-gulf-region/

Chapter 14

1. https://www.reuters.com/article/us-usa-iraq-albright-idUSN2220804120070223
2. https://www.reuters.com/world/europe/ukraine-helped-west-find-itself-again-zelenskiy-says-2022-12-28/
3. Tim Murithi, 'Order of Oppression', *Foreign Affairs*, May/June 2023.
4. Ben Shapiro on the USA; Konstanin Kisin on the UK; Hersh Ali on the Netherlands.
5. According to a study published by Harvard University, 'Moral power is the degree to which an actor, by virtue of his or her perceived moral stature, is able to persuade others to adopt a particular belief or take a particular course of action. We see moral power as a function of whether one is perceived to be morally well intentioned, morally capable, and whether one has moral standing to speak to an issue . . . all three are needed for an actor to have moral power.' https://scholar.harvard.edu/files/cwinship/files/moral_power--final_1.pdf
6. The *Economist*, 'How to survive a superpower split'. However, 'The West thinks it is watching a sequel of the Cold War; the rest of the world sees an entirely new film.' When it comes to projecting moral power, the analogy of Cold War doesn't work anymore. The UK Integrated Review refresh explained, 'Today's international system cannot simply be reduced to "democracy versus autocracy", or divided into binary, Cold War-style blocs. As IR2021 identified, an expanding group of "middle-ground powers" are of growing importance.'
7. https://www.bennettinstitute.cam.ac.uk/publications/a-world-divided/
8. I thank Dr Rohan Mukherjee for sharing his articulation of this argument at the RSIS seminar, 'The Ukraine War and International Order in a Time of Global Power Shifts', 4 August 2023. Building on his published work, *Ascending Order: Rising Powers and the Politics of Status in International Institutions* (Cambridge University Press, 2022). The interpretation is my own.
9. https://ecfr.eu/publication/united-west-divided-from-the-rest-global-public-opinion-one-year-into-russias-war-on-ukraine/ 'The most popular view in Russia and China is to expect a more even distribution of global power among multiple countries – namely, for multipolarity to emerge . . . In an increasingly fragmented and polarised world, countries such as India and Türkiye appear attracted to free--floating sovereigntism – where every conflict between superpowers becomes an opportunity to assert one's relevance and capacity to take sovereign decisions.'
10. Henry Foy, 'Rush by west to back Israel erodes developing countries' support for Ukraine', The *Financial Times*, 18 October 2023.
11. International Court of Justice, 'The Republic of South Africa institutes proceedings against the State', 29 December 2023. https://www.icj-cij.org/sites/default/files/case-related/192/192-20231229-pre-01-00-en.pdf and *Al Jazeera*, 'Which countries back South Africa's genocide case against Israel at the ICJ?', 9 January 2024.

Chapter 15

1. Ghali's foreword to Vijay Prashad, *The Poorer Nations: A Possible History of the Global South* (Verso books, 2012).
2. Sukarno quoted in Amitav Acharya and See Seng Tan, *Bandung Revisited: The Legacy of the 1955 Asian-African Conference for International Order* (Singapore: National University of Singapore Press, 2008).
3. Quoted in Margaret MacMillan and Patrick Quinton-Brown, 'The uses of history in international society: from the Paris peace conference to the present', *International Affairs* 95: 1 (2019) pp. 181–200.
4. Amitav Acharya, 'Hong Siew Ching Speaker Series by Professor Amitav Acharya on Race, World Order and the "Power Within" Nations' lecture to NUS, 7 September 2023.
5. https://history.state.gov/milestones/1953-1960/bandung-conf
6. Kissinger quoted in Seymour Hersh, *The Price of Power* (New York: Summit Books, 1983), p. 263.
7. Vijay Prashad, *The Poorer Nations: A Possible History of the Global South* 'The geopolitical battlefield for the rest of this decade is going to become increasingly partisan, with the danger of global divisions occurring unless the West can find ways to accommodate both China, Russia and the now Western ambivalent new global order that is currently coalescing.'
8. I thank Raffaello Pantucci for articulating this point eruditely for me to interpret. https://amp-scmp-com.cdn.ampproject.org/c/s/amp.scmp.com/comment/opinion/article/3232557/expanded-brics-key-message-west-not-only-show-town See also Sarang Shidore in *Foreign Affairs*. 'The Return of the Global South. Realism, Not Moralism, Drives a New Critique of Western Power' https://www.foreignaffairs.com/world/return-global-south-critique-western-power : 'It exists not as a coherent, organized grouping so much as a geopolitical fact,' writes Sarang Shidore, and its members are still 'driven by national interests rather than the idealism of southern solidarity'.
9. Sarang Shidore. Comments in Quincy Institute webinar, 21 August 2023 entitled 'BRICS and the Global South's Assertion', https://quincyinst.org/events/brics-and-the-global-souths-assertion/
10. Stuenkel, *Post-Western World*, p. 56.
11. 'Full text: Remarks by Li Xi at Summit of the Group of 77 and China', 16 September 2023. https://www.mfa.gov.cn/eng/zxxx_662805/202309/t20230916_11144052.html
12. *China Today*, full text of 'Proposal of the People's Republic of China on the Reform and Development of Global Governance', 14 September 2023. chinatoday.com.cn/ctenglish/2018/zdtj/202309/t20230914_800342206.html; 'Global Security Initiative Concept Paper', 21 February 2023 https://www.fmprc.gov.cn/mfa_eng/wjbxw/202302/t20230221_11028348.html 'Progress Report on the Global Development Initiative 2023', https://www.cikd.org/ms/file/getimage/1671666077130727426
13. https://carnegieendowment.org/2023/08/15/term-global-south-is-surging.-it-should-be-retired-pub-90376

Chapter 16

1. The *Guardian*, 'Alok Sharma "deeply frustrated" by India and China over coal', 14 November 2021. https://www.theguardian.com/environment/2021/nov/14/alok-sharma-deeply-frustrated-by-india-and-china-over-coal
2. https://www.indiatoday.in/magazine/interview/story/20211129-ldquo-rich-countries-failed-to-keep-their-promise-on-finance-rdquo-1878371-2021-11-19 'Climate finance isn't charity,' Yadav told AP on the sidelines of the conference. 'This is an obligation, responsibility, duty and a vow.' See also Yadav translated from Hindi: https://www.youtube.com/watch?v=BprsgNpoX30
3. Ibid.
4. https://www.straitstimes.com/asia/se-asia/jakarta-rushes-to-improve-air-quality-as-residents-mask-up-in-world-s-most-polluted-city.
5. https://unfccc.int/sites/default/files/resource/INDONESIA_cop26cmp16cma3_HLS_EN.pdf
6. Vaclav Smil, *Energy and Civilisation* (MIT Press, 2017), p. 17.
7. The *Economist*, 'Stabilising the climate', 27 October 2021.
8. https://world101.cfr.org/cfr_glossary/336 and https://www.carbonbrief.org/revealed-how-colonial-rule-radically-shifts-historical-responsibility-for-climate-change/
9. Vaclav Smil, *Making the Modern World: Material and Dematerialization.*
10. International Energy Agency, 'Oil 2023: Analysis and Forecast to 2028'. https://iea.blob.core.windows.net/assets/6ff5beb7-a9f9-489f-9d71-fd221b88c66e/Oil2023.pdf
11. Ibid., p. 12.
12. Daniel Yergin, *The Quest: Energy, Security and the Remaking of the Modern World* (Penguin Books, 2011).
13. Daniel Yergin, *The New Map: Energy, Climate and the Clash of Nations* (New York: Penguin Books, 2021) and Helen Thompson, *Disorder: Hard Times in the 21st Century* (Oxford University Press, 2022).
14. https://iea.blob.core.windows.net/assets/6ff5beb7-a9f9-489f-9d71-fd221b88c66e/Oil2023.pdf
15. Vaclav Smil, *Making the Modern World: Materials and Dematerialization,* 'Raw material inputs into the global economy, and hence the eventual worldwide output of finished products have soared in absolute terms during the first two decades of the 21st century, mostly thanks to China's continued economic rise, with substantial new demand coming also from India, Indonesia and Brazil.'
16. In 2022, the USA's top sources of oil importing were: Canada (52%); Mexico (10%); Saudi Arabia (7%); Iraq (4%); Colombia (3%). https://www.eia.gov/energyexplained/oil-and-petroleum-products/imports-and-exports.php
17. Daniel Yergin, *The New Map*. See also Meghan O'Sullivan, *Windfall: How the New Energy Abundance Upends Global Politics and Strengthens America's Power* (New York: Simon & Schuster, 2017). 'American president after president has declared the need to pursue energy independence.'
18. https://www.eia.gov/energyexplained/us-energy-facts/imports-and-exports.php
19. Daniel Yergin, *The New Map*.

20. https://iea.blob.core.windows.net/assets/6ff5beb7-a9f9-489f-9d71-fd221b88c66e/Oil2023.pdf
21. Yergin; *The Economist* 'Why Africa is poised to become a big player in energy markets' 18 July 2023. 'Africa may be the answer to Europe's immediate gas problem and its longer-term carbon one. It has 13% of global gas reserves, only a touch less than the Middle East, and 7% of the world's oil as well as vast green-energy potential.'

Chapter 17

1. https://unfccc.int/sites/default/files/resource/cma2023_L17_adv.pdf
2. 'President Donald Trump On Paris Climate Accord Withdrawal', *New York Times*, https://www.youtube.com/watch?v=deTcuNgKN-E
3. https://www.state.gov/the-united-states-officially-rejoins-the-paris-agreement/#:~:text=On%20January%2020%2C%20on%20his,unprecedented%20framework%20for%20global%20action.
4. https://brics2023.gov.za/wp-content/uploads/2023/07/BRICS-Leaders-meeting_2016-1.pdf https://brics2023.gov.za/wp-content/uploads/2023/07/Informal-Meeting-of-BRICS-Leaders_2017-1.pdf https://sdg.iisd.org/news/brics-declaration-calls-for-full-implementation-of-paris-agreement-and-2030-agenda/
5. Henry Sanderson, *Volt Rush: The Winners and Losers in the Race to Go Green* (Oneworld Publications, 2022).
6. Vaclav Smil, *Making the Modern World: Materials and Dematerialization,* p. 210. Moreover, 'batteries for electric cars are not strictly renewable in the same way but they could count if the electricity by which they are recharged happens to be the product of wind or sunlight.' Daniel Yergin, *The Quest*, 'The prospects for electric power in the 21st century can be summarised in a single word: growth. Electricity consumption, both worldwide and in the US, has doubled since 1980. It is expected on a global basis to double again by 2035.'
7. Henry Sanderson, *Volt Rush.*
8. James Dinneen, 'Can China turn the world green?', *New Scientist*, 7 October 2023, pp. 12–14.
9. Helen Thompson, *Disorder.*
10. Daniel Yergin, *The New Map.*
11. EC's 'JRC Science for policy report' called 'Co2 emission of all world countries', https://edgar.jrc.ec.europa.eu/report_2022?vis=gdp#emissions_table
12. Vaclav Smil, *Making the Modern World: Materials and Dematerialization*: Regarding the energy transition being completed by 2050. 'I have concluded that these are unrealistically ambitious goals because the proponents of rapid transformation do not sufficiently appreciate the scale and the complexity of the global task. This transition requires not just . . . much more extensive electrification of final energy uses (be it in transportation, industries, services, or households) but also fundamental shifts in the ways we produce and use non-carbon

fuels as well as replacing carbon fuels that now dominate many basic industries (steelmaking, production of cement, and synthesis of ammonia and plastics) . . . In sum, it is a transformation of an entire system of energy use, not just a replacement of some constituent parts.'

Chapter 18

1. Vaclav Smil, *Prime Movers of Globalisation: The History and Impact of Diesel Engines and Gas Turbines* (MIT Press, 2010). It was in the 1950s that the three major categories of long-distance ocean shipping grew rapidly: wet bulk carriers for products like oil; dry bulk carriers and container ships.
2. Centre for Strategic Futures, 'Foresight 2021', Singapore Government, 23 December 2021. https://www.csf.gov.sg/media-centre/publications/foresight-series/
3. Daniel Yergin, *The Quest.*
4. Sam Olsen and Stuart Paterson, 'Geopolitics and trade past, present and future' in Tim Hartnoll and Stephanie Zarach, *Feeder Fever: The importance of container shipping thought the eyes of a father and son* (Singapore: published privately), p. 198.
5. Source, Lloyd's List ranked by throughput volume. Sourced from Almanac.
6. 'China's dominance in world trade makes cutting it out of global supply chains impossible, one of the world's largest container shipping groups has said.' *Financial Times* 23 April 2023.
7. John Darwin, *Unlocking the World,* p. 358.
8. Gillian Tett, https://www.ft.com/content/98766d3f-65ad-41c0-84cc-9b6e2757a17c sourced from https://www.bis.org/publ/bisbull78.pdf
9. Wang Gungwu, *China Reconnects.*
10. IISS, 'Belt and Road Initiative' Strategic Dossier (London: Routledge, 2022).
11. Leslie Vinjamuri, 'Why multilateralism still matters. The right way to win over the Global South', *Foreign Affairs* 2 October 2023.
12. Kevin Rudd, *Avoidable War.*
13. Colby: 'An aspiring hegemon like China would have three reasons to pursue an economic bloc approach privileging its own economy and prejudicing the American one: economics, geopolitics, and status . . . a trading or regulatory bloc anchored in Asia that they can control or substantially influence preferable to exposure in a competitive global market they do not control.' [Modern Co-Prosperity Sphere] '. . . a discriminatory regional system is for status . . . ensuring that China does not establish hegemony over Asia must be the US's cardinal aim.'
14. Brands Beckley: 'exercising convening power, not coercive hegemony. The US doesn't have to be the leader of even a member of every anti-China coalition. The overarching goal of a free-world economic bloc is to achieve collective resilience through diversity, preventing Chinese dominance by fostering an array of alternative products and supply chains.'

Chapter 19

1. Kevin Rudd, *Avoidable War.*
2. James Griffiths, *The Great Firewall of China* (London: Zed Books, 2019), p. 376.
3. https://www.brookings.edu/articles/the-consequences-of-a-fragmenting-less-global-internet/
4. RAND Europe, 'Future Uses of Space Out to 2050: Emerging threats and opportunities for the UK National Space Strategy' (California: RAND, 2022). https://www.rand.org/pubs/research_reports/RRA609-1.html

The Path Ahead

1. US Government, National Intelligence Council. 'Global Trends 2040: A More Contested World'.

Sources

Acharya, Amitav and See Seng Tan, *Bandung Revisited: The Legacy of the 1955 Asian-African Conference for International Order* (Singapore: National University of Singapore Press, 2008)

Amin, Samir, *Eurocentrism: Modernity, Religion, and Democracy: A Critique of Eurocentrism and Culturalism* (New York: Monthly Review Press, 1989)

Anderson, Benedict, *Imagined Communities* (London: Verso, 1983)

Bacci, Massimo Livi, *A Concise History of World Population Sixth Edition* (John Whiley & Sons, 2017)

Bajpai, Kanti, 'Asian conceptions of international order: what Asia wants', *International Affairs* (99:4, 2023)

Behlil, Melis, *Hollywood Is Everywhere: Global Directors in the Blockbuster Era* (Amsterdam University Press, 2016)

Bejan, Teresa M., *Mere Civility* (Harvard University Press, 2017)

Brandes, Stanley, 'The Day of the Dead, Halloween, and the Quest for Mexican National Identity', *The Journal of American Folklore*, (111:442, 1998)

Brands, Hal and Michael Beckley, *Danger Zone: The Coming Conflict with China* (W. W. Norton & Company, 2022)

British Council, 'Languages for the Future: The foreign languages the United Kingdom needs to become a truly global nation', 2017

Black, James, Linda Slapakova and Kevin Martin, *Future Uses of Space Out to 2050: Emerging threats and opportunities for the UK National Space Strategy* (California: RAND, 2022)

Blanco, Cindy, '2022 Duolingo Language Report', 6 December 2022

Bradford, Anu, *The Brussels Effect: How the European Union Rules the World*, (Oxford: Oxford University Press, 2020)

Bunde, Tobias, Randolf Carr, Sophie Eisentraut, Christoph Erber, Julia Hammelehle, Laura Hartmann, Juliane Kabus, Franziska Stärk and Julian Voje. 'Munich Security Report 2020: Westlessness'

Burbank, Jane and Frederick Cooper, 'Empires after 1919: old, new, transformed'. *International Affairs* (95: 1, 2019)

Cervantes, Fernando, *Conquistadores: A New History* (Penguin Random House UK, 2021)

Chatterjee, Partha, *The Nation and Its Fragments* (Princeton University Press, 1993)

Colby, Elbridge A., *The Strategy of Denial: American Defense in an Age of Great Power Conflict* (New Haven and London: Yale University Press, 2021)

Dalio, Ray, *The Principles for Dealing with the Changing World Order* (New York: Simon & Schuster, 2021)

Darwin, John, *Unlocking the World* (London: Penguin, 2020)

David, Darshini, *The Almighty Dollar* (London: Elliott and Thompson Limited, 2018)

Department for International Trade, 'Global Trade Outlook', 2021

Diamond, Larry, *The Spirit of Democracy: The Struggle to Build Free Societies Throughout the World* (Holt Paperbacks, 2008)

Emmott, Bill, *The Fate of the West*, (London: Profile Books, 2017)

Fanon, Frantz, *Black Skin, White Masks* (New York: Grove Press, 2008)

Ferguson, Niall, *Civilisation: The West and the Rest* (London: Allen Lane, 2011)

French, Howard, *Born in Blackness: Africa, Africans, and the Making of the Modern World, 1471 to the Second World War* (New York: Liveright, 2021)

Fukuyama, Francis, *Liberalism and its Discontents* (New York: Farrar, Strauss and Giroux, 2022)

Garafola, Cristina L., Stephen Watts and Kristin J. Leuschner, *China's Global Basing Ambitions: Defense Implications for the Unites States* (California: RAND Corporation, 2022)

Garton Ash, Timothy, *Facts are Subversive* (London: Atlantic Books, 2009)

Gerstle, Gary, *Rise and Fall of the Neoliberal Order* (Oxford University Press, 2022)

Ghosh, Amitav, *Flood of Fire* (New York: Farrar, Strauss and Giroux, 2015)

Gillen, Mauro, *2030: How Today's Biggest Trends Will Collide and Reshape the Future of Everything* (St. Martin's Publishing Group, 2020)

Goldman Sachs Economics Research Paper, 'The Path to 2075 – Slower Global Growth, But Convergence Remains Intact', 2022

Gress, David, *From Plato to NATO: The Idea of the West and its Opponents* (New York: Free Press, 1998)

Griffiths, James, *The Great Firewall of China* (London: Zed Books, 2019)

Hartnoll, Tim and Stephanie Zarach, *Feeder Fever: The importance of container shipping through the eyes of a father and son* (Singapore: published independently)

Hersh, Seymour, *The Price of Power* (New York: Summit Books, 1983)

Hodgson, Marshall G. S., *Rethinking World History: Essays on Europe, Islam and World History* (Cambridge: Cambridge University Press, 1993)

Holland, Tom, *Dominion: The Making of the Western Mind* (London: Little, Brown, 2019)

Huntington, Samuel P., 'The West Unique, Not Universal', *Foreign Affairs* (75:6, 1996)

Huntington, Samuel P., *The Clash of Civilizations* (London: Simon & Schuster, 1996)

Hyam, Ronald, *Britain's Imperial Century, 1815–1914* (Hampshire: Barnes & Noble Books, 1976)

Immerwahr, Daniel, *How to Hide an Empire* (London: Bodley Head, 2019)

International Energy Agency, 'Oil 2023: Analysis and Forecast to 2028'

International Institute for Strategic Studies, 'Belt and Road Initiative' Strategic Dossier (London: Routledge, 2022)

International Institute for Strategic Studies, *Military Balance* (London: Routledge, 2023)

Jacques, Martin, *When China Rules the World* (London: Penguin, 2012)

Jakobson, Linda, 'Reflections From China on Xi Jinping's "Asia for Asians"', *Asian Politics & Policy* (8:1, 2016)
Jin, Keyu, *The New China Playbook* (Penguin, 2023)
Karmin, Craig, *Biography of the Dollar: How the Mighty Buck Conquered the World and Why it's Under Siege* (New York: Crown Publishing, 2008)
Kaye, D. Bondy Valdovinos, Jing Zeng, Patrik Wikstrom, *TikTok: Culture and Creativity in Short Video* (Cambridge: Polity Press, 2022)
Keane, John, *The New Despotism* (Harvard University Press, 2020)
Keane, Edward, *Beyond the Anarchical Society: Grotius, Colonialism and Order in World Politics* (Cambridge: Cambridge University Press, 2002)
Kennedy, Paul, *The Rise and Fall of the Great Powers: Economic Change and Military Conflict from 1500 to 2000* (New York: Random House, 1989)
Khanna, Parag, *Move* (New York: Simon & Schuster, 2021)
Lal, Deepak, 'Does Modernization Require Westernization?', *The Independent Review*, (5:1, 2000)
Lee Carter, Gregg, *Population and Society*, (Cambridge: Polity Press, 2016)
Lieven, Dominic, *Empire: The Russian Empire and its Rivals* (Yale: Nota Bene, 2002)
Liu, Mingfu *Chinese Dream: Great Power Thinking & Strategic Posture in the Post-American Era* (CN Times Books, 2015)
Liu, Zongyuan Zoe and Mihaela Papa, 'Can BRICS De-dollarize the Global Financial System', Cambridge University Press, 2022
Ludewig, Alexandra, 'Westlessness? Challenges for the EU's Soft Power Approach', *Australian and New Zealand Journal of European Studies* (13:1, 2021)
Mac Sweeney, Naoise, *The West: A New History of an Old Idea* (London: Penguin, 2023)
MacMillan, Margaret and Patrick Quinton-Brown, 'The uses of history in international society: from the Paris peace conference to the present', *International Affairs* (95: 1, 2019)
Mahbubani, Kishore, *Has China Won?* (New York: Public Affairs, 2020)
Mavroidis, Petros C. and André Sapir, *China and WTO* (Princeton University Press, 2021)
McWhorter, John, *Power of Babel* (New York: Harper Perennial, 2003)
Mishra, Pankaj, *From the Ruins of Empire: The Revolt Against the West and the Remaking of Asia* (London: Allen Lane, 2012)
Morris, Ian, *Why the West Rules . . . For Now* (London: Profile Books, 2011)
Mukherjee, Rohan, *Ascending Order: Rising Powers and the Politics of Status in International Institutions* (Cambridge University Press, 2022)
Murithi, Tim, 'Order of Oppression: Africa's Quest for a New International System', *Foreign Affairs*, May/June 2023
Nair, Chandran, *Dismantling Global White Privilege: Equity for a Post-Western World* (Berrett-Koehler Publishers, 2022)
Naisbitt, John, *Megatrends* (New York: Warner Books, 1982)
Naisbitt, John and Doris Naisbitt, *Mastering Megatrends* Asian Edition (Singapore: World Scientific Publishing, 2017)
Nehru, Jawaharlal, *The Discovery of India* (1946/New Delhi: Hindi Sahita Sadan, 2009)
Nguyen, Viet Thanh, *The Sympathizer* (New York: Grove Press, 2015)

Newzoo 'Global Games Market Report 2022'
Ostler, Nicholas, *Empires of the Word* (London: Harper Perennial, 2006)
Osborne, Roger, *Civilization: A New History of the Western World* (London: Vintage Books, 2007)
O'Sullivan, Meghan, *Windfall: How the New Energy Abundance Upends Global Politics and Strengthens America's Power* (New York: Simon & Schuster, 2017)
Piketty, Thomas, *Capital in the Twenty-First Century* (Cambridge, Mass.: Belknap Press, 2017)
Polo, Marco, *Travels in the Land of Kubilai Khan* (London: Penguin Great Ideas, 2005)
Pomeranz, Kenneth, *The Great Divergence: China, Europe, and the Making of the Modern World* (New Jersey, Princeton University Press, 2000)
Prashad, Vijay, *The Poorer Nations: A Possible History of the Global South* (Verso Books, 2012)
Prashad, Vijay, *Darker Nations: The People's History of the Third World* (New York: The New Press, 2007)
PricewaterhouseCoopers, 'Perspectives from the Global Entertainment & Media Outlook 2022–2026'
Puri, Samir, *The Great Imperial Hangover* (London: Atlantic Books, 2020)
Puri, Samir, 'Interventions in Armed Conflicts: Waning Western Dominance' in *Armed Conflict Survey 2021*, International Institute for Strategic Studies, (London: Routledge, 2021)
Puri, Samir, *Russia's Road to War with Ukraine* (London: Biteback, 2022)
Rachman, Gideon, *Easternisation: War and Peace in the Asian Century* (London; The Bodley Head, 2016)
Rapley, John and Peter Heather, *Why Empires Fall: Rome, America and the Future of the West* (Allen Lane, 2023)
Riley, Nancy E. *Population in China* (Cambridge: Polity Press, 2017)
Roberts, Adam, *A History of the English-Speaking Peoples since 1900* (London: Weidenfeld & Nicolson, 2006)
Rudd, Kevin, *Avoidable War: The Dangers of a Catastrophic Conflict Between the US and Xi Jinping's China* (New York; Public Affairs, 2022)
Ryan, Ben, *How The West Was Lost: The Decline of a Myth and the Search for New Stories* (London: Hurst & Company, 2019)
Ryan, Jeff, *Super Mario: How Nintendo Conquered America* (Penguin Publishing Group, 2011)
Tagore, Rabindranath, *Nationalism* (Penguin Great Ideas, 2010)
Trevor-Roper, Hugh, *The Rise of Christian Europe* (London: Thames and Hudson, 1965)
Salomone, Rosemary, *The Rise of English: Global Politics and the Power of Language* (Oxford: Oxford University Press, 2022)
Sanderson, Henry, *Volt Rush: The Winners and Losers in the Race to Go Green* (Oneworld Publications, 2022)
Sen, Amartya, *Identity and Violence* (W. W. Norton & Co., 2006)
Serventi, Silvano and Francoise Sabban, *Pasta: The Story of a Universal Food*, (New York: Columbia University Press, 2002)
Sharman, Jason and Andrew Philips, *Outsourcing Empire: How Company-States Made the Modern World* (Princeton University, 2020)

Shidore, Sarang, 'The Return of the Global South. Realism, Not Moralism, Drives a New Critique of Western Power', *Foreign Affairs* (August 2023)
Smil, Vaclav, *Prime Movers of Globalisation: The History and Impact of Diesel Engines and Gas Turbines* (MIT Press, 2010)
Smil, Vaclav, *Making the Modern World: Materials and Dematerialisation* (John Wiley & Sons, 2014)
Smil, Vaclav, *Energy and Civilisation* (MIT Press, 2017)
Spengler, Oswald, *The Decline of the West, Volume I: Form and Actuality* (1918)
Stiglitz, Joseph, *Globalization and Its Discontents* (W. W. Norton and Company, 2002)
Stockholm International Peace Research Institute, 'Trends in World Military Expenditure, 2022'
Stokel-Walker, Chris, *TikTok Boom: China's Dynamite App and the Superpower Race for Social Media* (Surrey: Canbury Press, 2021)
Stokes, Melvyn and Richard Maltby, *Hollywood Abroad: Audiences and Cultural Exchange* (Bloomsbury, 2019)
Stuenkel, Oliver, *Post-Western World: How Emerging Powers are Remaking Global Order*, (Cambridge; Polity Press, 2016)
Tang, Xiaobing, *Global Space and the Nationalist Discourse of Modernity: The Historical Thinking of Liang Qichao* (California: Stanford University Press, 1996)
UN Population Division, 'World Population Prospects 2022: Summary of Results', UN Department of Economic and Social Affairs (New York: UN, 2022)
US Government, National Intelligence Council, 'Global Trends 2040: A More Contested World', 2021
US Government, 'Final Report on the Congressional Commission on the Strategic Posture of the US', 2023
Vogel, Ezra F., *Japan as Number One* (Harvard University Press, 1979)
Von Laue, Theodore H., 'The World Revolution of Westernisation', *The History Teacher* (20:2, 1987)
Walt, Stephen, 'The myth of American exceptionalism', *Foreign Policy* (2011)
Walter, Dierk, translated from German by Peter Lewis, *Colonial Violence: European Empires and the Use of Force* (London: Hurst & Company, 2017)
Wang, Feng, Yong Cai and Baochang Gu, 'Population, Policy, and Politics: How Will History Judge China's One-Child Policy?', *Population and Development Review* (Vol. 38, 2012)
Wang, Gungwu, *China Reconnects: Joining a Deep-rooted Past to a New World Order* (World Scientific, 2019)
Weinberg, Albert K., *Manifest Destiny* (Baltimore: The Johns Hopkins Press, 1935)
Wertheim, Stephen, *Tomorrow the World* (Cambridge, Mass.: Harvard University Press, 2020)
Wheatley, Alan (ed.), *The Power of Currencies and Currencies of Power* (London: Routledge, 2013)
Yergin, Daniel, *The Quest: Energy, Security and the Remaking of the Modern World* (Penguin Books, 2011)
Yergin, Daniel, *New Map: Energy, Climate and the Clash of Nations* (New York: Penguin Books, 2021)

Index